Your Book of Life

Accessing the Akashic Records

by

Gary Bonnell

Richman Rose Publishing
Atlanta, Georgia

First Edition - Second Printing

ISBN 1-879604-00-0

Library of Congress Catalog Card Number: 96-69504

Cover and interior illustrations by Gary Bonnell
Cover design and interior layout Kathleen Pringle

Printed in the United States of America by BookCrafters

Printed on recycled paper.
The publisher plants two trees for every tree used
in the manufacturing of its books.

Published by Richman Rose Publishing,
Post Office Box 7766,
Atlanta, Georgia 30357-0766

Also by Gary Bonnell

ASCENSION The Original Teachings of Christ Awareness

Acknowledgements

I would like to acknowledge the following individuals for their support during this three year project.

A profound thanks to the thousands of wonderful clients who have sought me out these many years. Your attendance at my workshops and your word-of-mouth about our private sessions allows me to express part of my Soul's purpose.

My deep heartfelt thanks to those who allowed me to quote your workshop experiences in this book and to those clients who have allowed me to use their case material in my writings and lectures. My life is richer knowing you.

To Kate Lord Brown. With your help and God's will I may one day become a writer. Thank you for your wisdom, friendship and support.

Diana Goure. Having the ability to focus on what is working, knowing that what doesn't work will take care of itself, is rare. I am thankful for your keen eyes.

Mylle Myllerup. Your early guidance was paramount in bringing the many pieces of notes together in a presentable package. You are a bright light.

A special thanks to the team at the Whole Life Expo offices in California, to Marie Georges of "Where Angles Play" in Ohio, to Claude and Lois Dunmire in Colorado and to Masumi Hori at Voice, Inc., my publisher and booking agent in Japan. The opportunities you create for the sharing of new thought concepts are wonderful.

Much appreciation to my dear friends and fellow seekers of the greater response to life. What a great game we have dreamed to play. May you always find yourself in the greatest of circumstances.

To my wife Kathleen
&
my daughters Jennifer and Heather

"Knowing does not make you immune."

Albert Einstein

Table of Contents:

Your Book of Life
Accessing the Akashic Records

Introduction

The existence of the Akashic Records with each individual's Book of Life astounds me. Our ability to access the information held within the Records is truly remarkable, and yet each one of us does this in every moment – accesses the data we placed within the Records prior to incarnating, and accesses the data placed there through our responses to life. Everyone accesses the Akasha unconsciously through intuitive feelings, sudden urges, vivid dreams, inspirations, spiritual insights or just plain gut feelings. Although unconscious access has its place, accessing the Records in this manner shows so little of what is actually stored there, while conscious access reveals so much. To consciously tap into this vast system, we must first understand how Human Consciousness interacts with the data in the Akasha.

There are two primary views of Creation that remain constant in the Records and appear to be experienced in the same manner through all known dimensional realities of time and space and Consciousness – the macro view with its "big picture" overview of Consciousness; and the micro attitude of Human Consciousness as it tries to figure out how it fits into the big picture. And if it does fit, how it will manage the details of that reality, since it has somehow forgotten who it was in the first place.

The Macro

This wonderful globe we call home, with its varied and vast systems of life, could be compared to the many dimensional realities within creation the way a few grains of sand compare to the beaches of our world. If each one of us could see, just for a moment, the immensity of reality and our unique place within it, all our fears would vanish leaving us with the sweetness of what it means to be fully conscious, Self-Realized Beings. We are grand adventurers and explorers, investigators of the firmament. We are hardly just the latest evolutionary point in a line descended from a far flung Creatural seed. We are who we have been from the very first moment – the senses of our Creator.

In this dimensional reality we are part of an enormous gathering of Souls. We have come to this world to witness each other's moments of awakening, and THE final moment of Realization for the Collective Mind. One of the most significant moments in our journey in this dimension is that moment when we fully realize that there are vast numbers of Beings manifested within this dimensional reality, and unseen parallel realities, that have our greatest interest at heart. And we theirs. It is when we awaken to this unlimited reality of communion, to the level of Love as Existence, that we truly begin our purpose here in this dimension – to Create everything anew with each passing moment.

The Micro

In the micro view, we experience ourselves apart from each other and Creator, wounded by our aloneness, devastated by the secrets we keep from each other; we therefore hunger for acceptance and knowledge. We seek to validate belief boundaries and ideas of reality established by our cultural lineage; we tend to sameness. We project control and blame out into the world; we deny responsibility and inflict guilt. Out of our imagined insanity we loop our Consciousness from genius to ignorance, from creativity to destruction and back again; we therefore believe in a need for balance. In desperation we cling to the hope that all will eventually turn out "good," and that those who work against the greater Collective Truth will be brought to some appropriate justice. The more we advance in technology, the less we have of ourselves. We are locked in ever widening circles of superstitions and half truths. The more we memorize the less we know.

The Earth is referred to in the Records by two different names: Urantia, place of Light, and Saros (Saras), place of sorrow. Out of our dissatisfaction with the endless Unity of Mastery/Mystery, we asked for Self knowledge, to know ourselves as individuated Consciousness. As the Judeo/Christian story goes, God banished us from the garden, dropping us into the neighborhood of the giving and taking, the disabling and enabling, the independent and co-dependent, the self-confident and self-conscious, the genuine and pretentious, and the philanthropic and the stingy. Here we became bundles of stress waiting to explode back into Unity, into Authenticity.

It is through our willingness to separate from the Whole, to fully live each misconception, that we contribute the most to ourselves and the Whole of Creation.

This is true paradox – Duality – Macro and Micro; Consciousness and energy. We, as the Conscious aspect of Creation, are the witness to the phenomenon of energy. Energy is best observed by Consciousness in a polarized dimension, polarized meaning a realm of opposites. This is why we search the firmament for dimensions that have duality as part of their makeup. When duality is present, we deepen our knowing of ourselves and Creation through our observations of the assemblage points of manifest matter.

Purpose

What is central to our purpose in this microcosm is to completely share the wonders created by the duality of this dimensional reality with each other, without bias or intentional distortion, each relating a unique view to the Collective Whole. The Akasha exists as the repository for this wholly shared view.

With the warehouse of the Akasha in place, we are at liberty to completely immerse ourselves in the journey, to fully examine the few grains of sand, to even forget who we are and the sharing that is central to our purpose. It is in our forgetfulness that our response to the physical realm becomes the most primal and therefore the most impressive. Here lies our greatest contribution – raw, genuine, unadulterated response.

As we become civilized and begin to care more about how others perceive our responses, our attitude toward Creation becomes contrived. It is here that we feel disconnected from our Source and invent external images of the Creator as a God who is angry with our performance as Human Beings. We then support these external images of God with dogmatic beliefs and superstitions.

The good news is we soon tire of this farce. Usually within six to seven thousand years.

As we awaken from our civilized hypnosis and remember our Self and our purpose for being here, our response changes from one of survival to one of awakened Witness. Before awakening we are at the mercy of the world and all its unknowable forces; after awakening we are in the world, not of the world. Before the realization of Self we feel the threat of death; after Self-Realization we feel the wonder of Life. One exists as war, the other as peace.

Our purpose here is to respond with all our being; to share, instead of judge. It is through non-judgment that we behave in the likeness of God Creator and fulfill our sole purpose. In this state of mind we are fully connected with our Source, and we are, once again, the Conscious Awareness of our Creator. As such, God knows itself as Creation.

Accessing the Akasha is one way we can remember the interconnectedness of all dimensional realities. As we remember our true nature we are no longer concerned with just a few grains of sand, but once again have all the beaches as our playground. Now our Witness is complete. Here we see the end of duality and the emergence of the indwelling Kingdom of God Creator expressing as Individuated Self.

The Akasha, this living library of all that is known, awaits our wakeful presence in the same manner a host would await invited guests. Once we arrive nothing is withheld from us as the pathway of our journey reveals itself in the Records. Here we realize each incarnation as a separate facet of a Unified Self and a connecting point of view to the simultaneous Whole. Once this connecting point of the Collective Mind is realized, the Inner Teacher begins to fully blend our doubt and understanding, our sorrow and joy, our self-centeredness and Selflessness into Unity. We come full circle. We are once again the mystic, the timeless observer in a glorious world filled with the continuous NOW. At long last we express as Unified Mind, creating as Ultimate-Cause, Selfless-Self.

The Akasha

An Overview of the Akashic Records and The Book of Life

Unfortunately, little historical information on the Akasha has survived from earlier cultures and civilizations. What we do know is all too often cloaked in stories of ritual magic and legends of wizards that seem much larger than life. As in all oral traditions many of these rather hard to believe myths have fascinating true stories at their beginnings. It would be difficult to fully understand what really happened back in the Garden of Eden if we only had the Book of Genesis as our guide, just as it would be difficult to explain the Aka-sa

(Akasha) with just one historical reference. To get the big picture we must explore forgotten books, or interview members of those secret societies still practising the art of looking into the Book of Life.

The Akasha, or Akashic Records as it is now known, derives from two words, Aka - space (also storage place or repository) and Sa - sky (also secret or hidden). These terms originate out of the ancient cultures of northern India and Tibet. This puts the earliest historical evidence of the Akasha in Tibet around 7500BCE[1]. It was known to the pre-Buddhist priests of the Himalayan religion that each Soul wrote every moment of it existence in a great book prior to its first incarnation. It was further known that these lesson plans could be viewed in their entirety if one was of the right mind. These early teachings were brought forth by the gyatso, or monks from the first days of mankind on Earth and formed many of the stories written in the Sanskrit sutras.

3500 years later, around 4000BCE, the Egyptians, Persians and Chaldeans in the Mideast demonstrated a profound awareness of both astrology and the Akasha. Plato used the Records to reach into the cultures that predated his own and gives the first accounting of the Atlantian culture. The Akasha indicates that Egypt was colonized by the inhabitants of Atlantis. In Egypt, as in Atlantis, those who could read the Records were called, Rehk-Get-Amon. These individuals held high social standing and are often shown on the wall murals of Egyptian tombs advising Pharaohs in the day-to-day activities of the common people. They also advised Pharohs on the practical meaning and interpretation of their dreams. One of Persia's most noted prophets and readers of the Akasha was Al Hakim. He told of the birth of Jesus and Mohammed. He was also a noted astrologer and taught his craft throughout the known world. There were so many noted fortune tellers in Chaldea that if by chance one should wander outside the city limits and was found to be Chaldean it was assumed that he read the stars or the Book of Life.

The ancient Greek oracles of Delphi, Dodona and Trophonius[2] used the hidden repository of the Akasha as a means of foretelling the futures of most of the known world's generals and rulers. These are just three of the many sites where temples were erected to the science of divination and the Akasha. The Delphic seer was perhaps the most famous of the oracles and was acknowledged throughout the known world as the eyes of the Gods.

The Chinese had many great prophets who used the Records. One of the most famous was Sujujin. His ability to read the karma of an individual was legendary. It was widely reported that all he needed was the first name of anyone to tell their complete life's history from beginning to end, before the end was known. Many ruling families used his talents to increase their positions. There was another, a gentleman by the name of Tajao, mentioned in Richard H. Allen's book, *The Annals of China*. Tajao's discoveries within the Records are dated from around 2608BCE and cover a wide variety of subjects that span over two thousand years. He was also a noted astrologer who understood the Soul of the zodiac.

The Hebrew prophets of the Old Testament had this knowledge. The nadi used the Akashic Records to predict the fates of many of the world's leaders of their time. They also foretold of the distant future of the Jews as a race consciousness. They were truly amazing when it came to understanding the symbolic language of the Akasha.

The life of a messiah, a savior, was foretold by the early Hebrew prophets. Many people at the time felt this messiah to be the great teacher/healer/prophet Jeshua Ben Joseph, or simply Jesus. Jesus often spoke with great authority from the Records. Most of his concepts of Unity can be found at the core of the Collective Human Mind. His most remembered use of the Records was the account of the life events of the Samaritan woman at the well (John 4: 7-26). Other documents concerning the life and teachings of Jesus are the Nag Hammadi[3] and Dead Sea Scrolls.[4] Although somewhat vague, there are references made in these scrolls to the study of the eternal records of humankind. Surprisingly, Catholic church documents (200CE) reveal early Christian Mystics with the knowledge to transport their Awareness to the Hall of Records. There are two documents, *Wings of Mithara* and *Sword of El*, taken from a small chapel in Wales in the early part of the first century that formed the basis for the meditative practices of these mystic church elders. In England and Wales, The Myrdwyns of the Druid culture (400-900CE) showed the ability to access the Akasha. Merlin (born around 415CE) is by far the best known of these Spiritual leaders. His predictions range some 1,200 years in all. *The Bardic Triads* compiled by Llewellyn Sion of Glamorgan symbolically tell of the system used by the Druids to enter the Records. The Roman historian Pompeius Trogus declared the Celts to excel in accuracy of details when reading from the Records and the stars. Maelmaedhog au Morgair used the Akashic Records when he gave his famous papal prophecies describing each pope from 1143CE to present time. Its accuracy has stood the test of time.

The work of Nostradamus (1503-1566CE) has to be the most exciting evidence of the existence of a Hall of Records. He not only told of individuals' futures, but he spoke of nations and their future activities in surprising detail. Nostradamus was Jewish by birth and Catholic by virtue of his parents choice to convert. I believe it was the influence of early Christian mysticism and an in-depth study of the Kabala that gave him the opportunity to find his way into the Records. His predictions cover some seven centuries and are so accurate that many individuals still use them to determine where and how they will live.

A complete study of the Akasha would also include the Americas. The Mayans explored the future with amazing accuracy. Their astronomical observations rival modern day scientific achievements in that field. Through the Akasha they even foretold of the coming unification of the Collective Mind in the year 2011CE. They determined that to be the end of time as they understood it, and the beginning of a people who lived outside the dimensions of time. Quetzalcoatl taught the ancient Americans astrology and use of the Records. Montezuma accessed the Records and saw a hand upon the seal of the Book of his people but misinterpreted the symbol to mean that the coming Spanish invasion was fortuitous. The descendants of the indigenous people of Mexico, and Central and South Americas might argue otherwise.

History is full of the accounts of individuals who have consciously used the Hall of Records. In recent times, individuals such as; Edgar Cayce, Alice Bailey, John Ford, William Lilly, Lilian Treemont, Manly P. Hall, Emanual Swedenborg, Mary Baker Eddy, John Smith, Rudolph Steiner, Dion Fortune and George Hunt Williamson, to name only a few, have all demonstrated the traditions of the Akasha. As a westerner I have mainly explored this subject from the western point of view; however, because the Akasha is of the Collective Mind, I'm sure there are many individuals in eastern societies who are aware of the

Akasha and are able to interpret the symbols.

The most widely known modern day proponent of the Akashic Records would have to be Edgar Cayce. There are few mystics in modern times who have given the Records such attention as Mr. Cayce. Cayce focused primarily on present life health issues originating from unresolved past life influences, or karma. His ability to help individuals bring about desired physical and emotional changes was truly remarkable. From the scope of his work it appears he had the entire Hall of Records at his disposal.

Another individual worth mentioning is George Hunt Williamson author of *"Secret Places of the Lion"* and *"Other Tongues, Other Flesh."* His clear interpretations of the Akashic Symbols take the reader on a wonderful journey into a past free of the usual vested point of view found in history books. In *"Secret Places of the Lion,"* Mr. Williamson gives astonishing details about the incarnation patterns of certain Souls as they fulfill their purpose in this realm.

The Origin of the Akasha

Through oral and written histories of ancient cultures we can piece together enough fragments of information to offer a colorful history of the Akasha. There is more. We have known for thousands of years the Akasha exists and is accessible, but how did it originate?

Any conversation on the subject of the Akasha must include an overview of how Consciousness is structured within the Conscious Physical Universe dimension at the assemblage point of manifest reality within Creation. The Akashic view of Creation has little to do with the points of reference offered by modern cultures. The Akashic view is a non-plural observation that relates to data in terms of micro and macro. It is more associated with the ancient mystical understanding of Creation than that of creationists or modern science. (Author's note: The following information reads like the first book of the Bible genealogy. This overview is taken directly from the Akasha and can be a little tedious. Be encouraged to wade through this version of how Consciousness originally assembled itself. It will be helpful once you are in the Records.)

There are twelve Universes known to the Akasha, each with twelve[5] originating Logos entities. A Logos, also referred to as YAH WEH El-Auh-Heem Christ Soul in the Records, is identified with God as the source of all activity and generation, and is also the power of reason residing in the Human Soul. The Sole Being, Mich-I-El-Ah, one of the original Twelve Logos of this Universe, created the matrix of energy fields that serve as the foundation for the Akashic Records.

When seen from outside the Conscious Physical Universe, the Etheric energy system of the Akasha encircles the Earth like a spider's web. This grid like web is comprised of particles of Etheric light gathered in ribbon like waves with 144,000 intersecting points, each connected to the other at precisely equal distances. These connecting bands of energy with their intersecting points are the circuit board, if you will, of the Akasha. These intersections known as Eau-Aum Ta-Rah are the vortex points of the Etheric body of the planet. The planetary Etheric body is a system of ley lines and vortices which could be described as the cosmic nervous system, or the Etheric brain of the Collective Mind expressing in the physical substance of the planet.

The most popular definition of Eau-Aum Ta-Rah is "Beginning Sound." In the Records, "Eau" means pure, unsoiled, or can even mean barren when relating to lower human functions. "Aum" is vibration or oscillation, thus — pure vibration. "Ta-Rah" read together means Beginning Source or Source Power. Thus you have – pure vibration from the Source. The Jewish Bible, used for four millennia, and the Christian New Testament, in place for nearly two thousand years, refers to the Eau-Aum Ta-Rah as "The Word", "*In the beginning was the Word, and the Word was with God and the word was God.*" (John 1: 1)

Each of these 144,000 points, which serve as points of manifest focus for the YAH WEH El-Auh-Heem Christ Souls[6], split into twelve equally fashioned, non-plural, intersecting points each in perfect communion with the next. The 1,728,000 Entities who concentrate themselves at these intersections are True individuated communal aspects of the original 144,000 Christ Souls. If observed with the human eye these enormous bundles of Light, each appearing larger than our sun, would seem to have three equally brilliant concentric centers, the second slightly smaller than the first, the third just a bit smaller than the second. This is why the interpretation of these symbols in the Records is Tir-El Sau, or something like Triad Sovereign Souls.[7] A shortened version might be, Trinity Souls.

Trinity & Over Souls

Each Trinity-Soul has twelve singular, Unified, Self-Realized entity projections expressing as polarized individuated male and female elements, six each, called Sai-Aus Sau-El, or Celestial Soul Consciousness. Here there are 20,736,000 expressions within the Akasha that serve the function of synapse connections within the Collective Mind. The Celestial level is genderless, so these entities are only referred to as male and female to suggest polarity. So, although extremely inadequate, our male and female concept is our only way to understand the dynamic relationship at work in the Sai-Aus Sau-El.

It is through the twelve male and twelve female polarized projections of the Celestial Soul Consciousness, called Ev-Ada Sau-El,[8] or simply Over-Souls, that the YAH WEH Christ Souls concentrated in the 144,000 originating Eau-Aum Ta-Rah gain entry into the Earth plane as Individuated Sovereign Witness. At this level we have 497,664,000 connecting points in the Akasha.

The Higher Self

The Higher Self, or Yam-Rah Teh as it is known in the Records, is an aspect of the Over-Soul, much the same way the mental body is a part of the triad entity called Human, which is made up of our mental, emotional and physical bodies. In a way, the Higher Self could be referred to as the mental body, or personality of the Over-Soul entity. It is here that the concept of separation, or original sin begins. Although the Higher Self is truly only an aspect of the Over-Soul, the Higher Self entity has twelve male and twelve female polarized projections that serve in Consciousness as Angelic entities, called Yam Nah-Teh. These Angelic entities exist as projections from within the Logos system but truly have all the abilities and knowing of their fifth and sixth dimensional[9] Angelic Being counterparts. The main distinction between the Angelic entities of the Higher Self, and the fifth and sixth-dimensional Angelic Beings is that the former are from the system of Human Consciousness and serve as Guardians to the Human experience. The fifth and sixth-dimensional Angelic Beings exist outside the Conscious Physical Universe and the Human Consciousness experience. They assist in the process of bringing Human Consciousness to completion. Their "reward" is to witness the rebirth of Human Consciousness into the levels of Super Conscious Reality that begin at the Trinity Soul level. In the beginning of creation these Angelic Beings helped to form the hierarchical structure of Consciousness within the Conscious Physical Universe, and now serve to inspire Human Consciousness to higher Spiritual levels. They have the ability to do this because they are outside the system and can observe the many different levels and communicate those observations and understandings to lower human forms. For those still counting, we now have 11,943,936,000 connecting points of view in the Akasha.

Each Angelic entity has as its Individuated Conscious Expression, twelve male and twelve female plural projections, referred to in the Records as Hau-Na Teh.[10] Even though these are duality forms they have the same symbol in the Records. "Soul Mentor" is the commonly used interpretation of this symbol. It is because of this that the New Age practitioners lovingly refer to this level of Human Consciousness as, "Spirit Guides." At this point, there are now 286,654,464,000 cells in the Akasha, and we have yet to manifest the first physical body!

Human Consciousness

Each of the Spiritual Guides has twelve male and twelve female projections called Ah-Ney Ea (males) and Ah-Na Ese (females). This is the first point in Creation where Human Consciousness manifests in the Conscious Physical Universe as the Human Soul. In our descending journey from Originating Christ Souls to the children of Hau-Na Teh, we have 6,879,707,136,000 connected cells within the Collective Mind. We thought it was crowded here on Earth as we approach the six billion mark.

Here is where the unfolding, the begetting and begatting of the Collective Mind of the Akasha comes to an end.

Center Stage

The physical Human experience sits at a great divide in Creation. We have the best seats in the house – center stage – the center of the Mobius. On one side we have the descending projections of Originating Christ Souls, YAH WEH El-Auh-Heem Christ Souls, we have been discussing. On the other we have the ascending nonhuman levels of Conscious Awareness generated by the Ah-Ney Ea and Ah-Na Ese as they manifest in physical human bodies. These Human projections are the life forms that inhabit the domains of unmanifested thought referred to as the Realms of Pan-Au (Pan) and Geh-Hen-Ah (Hell). The ascending entities of the lower Realms have as many levels of Conscious Awareness as do the descending aspects of Consciousness from YAH WEH El-Auh-Heem Christ Souls to manifested Male/Female Human entities.

For the most part, it is difficult for those who live in the Realms of Pan and Hell to see beyond the Human Conscious level, so they envision us, Manifest Human Consciousness, as their Creator. This isn't so hard to believe when you think of our inability to see beyond the Realms of Christ Awareness. It is because of our unwillingness to see further that we perceive the Elohim, Christ Conscious Awareness, as our Creator.

Now there are those in Pan who can see beyond Human Consciousness and have awakened from their Dream, just as there are those Humans who have seen beyond the Christ Conscious Awareness and glimpsed Nirvana. The Master teacher, Jeshua Ben Joseph, showed the way when he said, "*I and the Father are One*," (John 10: 30) and, "*These things I do, You will do and more*." (paraphrased from John 14: 12)

Pan Realm

The Pan Realm, with its entity expressions of Brownies, Fairies, Gnomes, Leprechauns, Trolls,[11] etc., acts more like a parallel Universe than an aspect of the Conscious Physical Universe. Those awakened or enlightened members of the Pan realm who understand their place in relationship to Human Consciousness are watching the experiences of Human Consciousness very closely, determining how it is they will accomplish their destinies once they have ascended to the Human Consciousness experience.

At this point it would be useful to clear up some tired myths about our neighbors below our position in Creation. While it is true that the "Little Ones" allow Humans to stumble and fall where they could willingly intercede, it is also true that if a Human endeavor interests them, or if a certain Human project will allow them to accomplish their goals once they ascend to Human Consciousness, they will rally a great effort to ensure its success. With the residents from Pan behind you it would be impossible to fail.

Unlike most Humans, entities within Pan are seldom confused about their role in Creation – to experience each moment as an assemblage of Consciousness and energy. Therefore, they have nothing to be right about or keep elite as a way of gaining power . Because of this, the cultures of those dimensions have no religions or universities. That is why the few who have spontaneously looked into these realities have declared them Godless, unrefined, mindless actualities. They, the Little Ones, are deeply connected to the Spirit of the Planet and know Her as their Mother Creator. Her moods and seasons guide their thoughts and deeds. She is their religion and school.

Many stories place these mostly indifferent observers at the source of much Human suffering . Victimhood is one Human expression that attracts much attention from our little friends. From their point of view the faster we grow tired of being victims, the faster we become Self-Realized; the faster we become Self-Realized, the faster we ascend off the wheel of birth and death. The faster we ascend, the faster they evolve out of their dimly lit realms and ascend to the experience of Light. Wherever they can help us with this, they will. It is important to note that their response is driven by desire and is therefore more automatic and subconscious than deliberate.

The "Little Ones" see us as Originating Source just as we see YAH WEH El-Auh-Heem Christ Souls as our Originating Source. They are greatly disenchanted with our foibles, just as we have become disillusioned with our images of God. The difference is, even though we are their Creator, they can directly witness our lack of understanding. We see all levels of Consciousness above us as perfect and complete and feel it inappropriate to question the performances of those from the 'upper ranks'. This is a very militaristic way of seeing Creation, but one that is ingrained in Humans.

(Author's note: as for the subject of Hell, I have little interest in exploring those realms. I understand they are wonderfully intoxicating and seductive in every way conceivable, offering many forms of pleasure. I also know that of the many Humans who venture in, few return.)

†Σ†

Footnotes:

[1] The very ancient teachings of Tibet are forever lost to the Western world now that China has complete control of the Tibetan culture. For example, in 1995 Chinese government officials set out to find the incarnation of the past Panchen Lama (second holiest figure in the Himalayan culture). This is customary and a part of a treaty between Tibet and China. When they had eliminated all but six candidates, the present Dalai Lama announced his choice from the six, which is also the custom. As a matter of fact, the Dalai Lama is the only one qualified to choose the Panchen Lama. This move outraged the Chinese officials who were looking to install a puppet Panchen Lama in the spiritual hierarchy. The Chinese government took the Dalai Lama's choice into their capital to be educated at their discretion and named their choice to be the true Panchen. Tibet now has two Panchen Lamas – one blessed by the Himalayan faith's god-king and one sanctioned by the atheist communist Chinese government. It will kill the Tibetan culture to have a pretender as second spiritual leader.

[2] In Greek mythology Gods sit on top of Mount Olympus observing the happenings of humans. They do this through an opening in their celestial floor. This describes the living mosaic in the floor of the Great Hall of Records in the Akasha.

[3] This is a wonderful work produced somewhere around the first century and explains in detail the mysteries of Jesus' teachings.

[4] Much is still unknown about the total contents of these scrolls. They have recently been released for study around the world. Until then they were only available to a few scholars. See additional reading list under Michael Baigent and Robert Eisenman for more info.

[5] Each of the twelve planets of our solar system has a Logos entity as a manifest

expression of its Soul. We are presently aware of only nine planets and some four hundred planetoids, and a great many asteroids. These asteroids were in fact a satellite planet called Maldec that exploded some 8,000 to 12,000 years ago. The dating is a little difficult because of how the Maldecians viewed the progression of time. The Akashic Records for the Urantia Star, our Sun, show that Maldec was the original planet to be inhabited 206,000,000 years ago by physical human forms. The second was Mars. Earth was colonized some 56 million years ago by Human Consciousness in etheric form, then later in physical form some 4.5 million years ago. If it were not for the fact that Mars was in such a close orbit to Maldec when it exploded we would still have space brothers and sisters to include in our family trees. The entire atmosphere of Mars was vaporized, along with most of the structures that served as cities for those who lived on the surface. There are a few remaining structures on the surface, but most are buried under surface debris. The face and the pyramids recently photographed by NASA on the surface of Mars are man-made.

[6] Also referred to in the Akasha as Christos-Sol-Seal – Christ Sun Soul. This is a designation as to: *point of origin* – <u>Chris</u>t Realm; *dimensional reality* – Matter Universe; *system* - Urantia Star we call <u>Sun</u>; *expressed manifest form* – <u>Soul</u>; .

[7] In the Records – Tir, equaling Triad; El, equaling Sovereign; Sau or Seal, equaling Soul.

[8] Ev symbolizes the feminine, negatively charged, electromagnetic conscious substance. Ada is the opposing field of electromagnetic substance, and is male or positively charged. Sau-El is the designation for the highest aspect of non-singular conscious originality. The negative and positive references here have nothing to do with the concept of good or bad.

[9] See page 92 for descriptions of the dimensional realities.

[10] The Hau-Nau Teh act as Inner Teachers and are found at all levels of Conscious manifestation, from the realms of Tir-El Sau, to the lower Astrals. Their sole mission is to help integrate experience into the Collective Mind as multi-dimensional intention.

[11] Read the Germanic, or northern European Fairy Tales. Also, many of the Irish stories of the Little People give an accurate accounting of the Leprechauns' attitudes toward Humans.

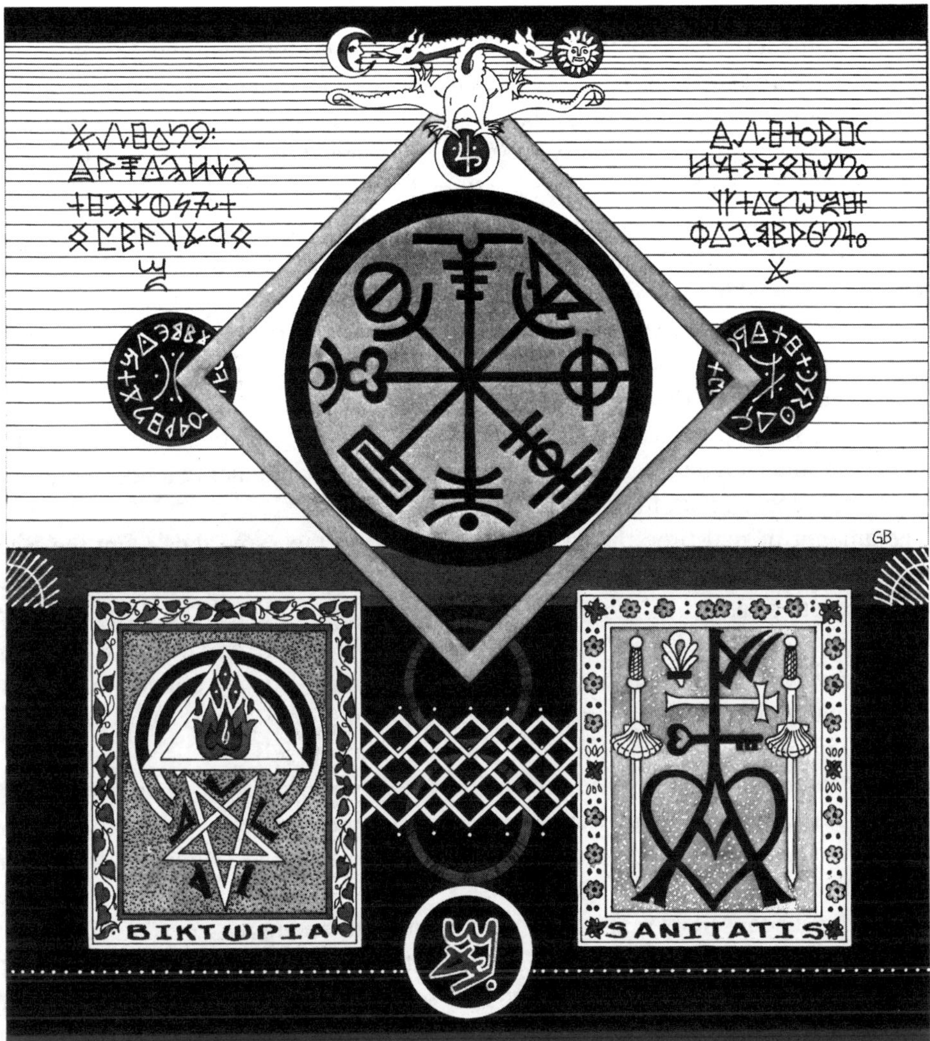

The System of the Akasha

The Collective Mind

Conscious entry into the Records is fairly simple and requires only a minimum of real effort on the part of the practitioner. What keeps most from gaining entry is their lack of knowledge of how the system works and the subconscious belief that we as common people are not allowed into this sacred vestige. Each one of us is a cell within the Collective Mind. By virtue of this fact we already have access to all that the Collective Consciousness is capable of exposing. Because interviews with the Akasha are of a Collective nature, the experience can seem immediately very big. The point is to not be put off by this. You are up to this conscious experience of the Records and it is natural to be overwhelmed by the magnitude of the information available. The following example will put this into perspective. Just ten years ago when you picked up the phone to make a call, a single copper wire carried your voice to the receiving phone. The answering phone also required a single copper wire – one wire carried your voice, the other carried the voice of party to whom you were speaking. Now when you make a call, one fiber optic filament the size of a human hair carries both your voices, and can also carry up to 85,000 two way conversations simultaneously as well! Our technologies are actually making it possible for us to fully understand the levels at which we are capable of communicating data.

If you were to study the main events of an individual's personal history by interviewing that individual and their relatives, and those who witnessed their journey, it would take quite a measure of time – days, if not weeks. This is due in part to the use of language as the medium of transferring the data. It is also due to the human need for assessing the information collected, and then putting that data in a logical, orderly manner that best represents the chronological progression of that individual's life.

The amount of real time that would elapse getting the same data from the Records would be about two minutes. Why? The system of the Akasha does not rely on the gathering of interpretive facts. In the Akasha there is only raw data. The data is given in a symbolic language that is fourth and fifth dimensional in nature and does not have time as one of its boundaries, so time is not required. In this format you are collecting information consciously with <u>all</u> your senses <u>and</u> sensibilities. Time only comes into play when you interpret the information for the client, or journal it for yourself.

Time is important to this three-dimensional reality only. Look at the dream state of Consciousness. Most nocturnal dreams last only a few seconds, and yet when asked, most individuals would say they had been dreaming all night. Imagine, all that activity crammed into a few seconds.

Just as the subconscious mind uses symbols to build dream images, the Akasha relates stored data to the practitioner in symbolic thought form images that excite all the senses. Usually these thought forms are presented in a series of glyphs resembling early writings such as Mayan or Egyptian glyphs that are surprisingly easy to understand. The place inside you that doubts will want to invalidate your knowing these symbols through the belief that you have never taken the <u>time</u> to study their meanings. This is not true. Being an Egyptologist or an expert on Mayan, or any ancient language, would not improve your ability in interpreting the symbols of the Akasha. As a matter of fact it might impede your ability because you would have learned the <u>only right</u> way to interpret certain symbols and would not allow the symbols to speak to your inner knowing.

The Akasha is very user friendly and self explanatory. If you feel overwhelmed ask that the information being presented be given in a form that is easily understood by your current personality. The glyphs will change into letter symbols and you will suddenly be reading the answer to the question just as you might read a book or newspaper. This is not the most desirable manner to get the information but it is most effective in the beginning.

The multi-dimensional format of the Akasha is a cosmic dialog of sorts that appears to be an interactive holographic imaging of data. It appears holographic because all the senses are excited by the presentation, no one sense is dominate. This interaction is very important to the individual using the Records because it demonstrates the flow of Consciousness from one dimension of reality to the next.

I kept this type of interactive rapport in mind when deciding a format for this material. The following question and answer conversations reveal everything necessary to have a basic working knowledge of how the Akasha functions. Once you are in the Records you will have everything you need at your finger tips. When you desire to know more, all you need do is ask the question.

ΔΔΔΔΔΔΔΔΔΔΔΔΔΔΔΔΔΔΔΔΔΔ

On one of your tapes I believe you said the Akasha is available to everyone and that we all are constantly in touch with the Akashic Records. If that's the case, why isn't everyone running around acting like Nostradamus? Why aren't people having spontaneous experiences and why do we have to learn techniques?

The Akasha is the repository of all events and responses relating to Human Consciousness in all realities, therefore everyone is constantly feeding the Records with new data generated by their response to Creation. Each one of us, within our current belief system, spontaneously draws upon this collection of knowledge to guide us in our pursuits and purposes. Some experience this natural bridge into the Records as inspiration, intuition, hunches; others as coincidence, or déjà vu episodes. There are some who have the interest to develop this natural bridge to the Collective Mind into effective tools, such as reading the Akashic Records, clairvoyance, clairaudience, or automatic writing, to name only a few of the more popular forms.

The manner of receiving information largely depends on an individual's core beliefs – the early ideas about themselves that form though interaction with family, friends, teachers and authority figures in this lifetime, and all influencing lifetimes. If an individual wanted to develop a particular ability, such as clairvoyance or automatic writing for example, that ability would have to be in alignment with their foundational beliefs. If not they would more than likely find the inner conflict too distracting and quickly lose interest. Here is an excellent example that happens to be about this century's most noted Akashic Master: Edgar Cayce's conscious core beliefs were regional to central and southeastern North America and included a very strong belief that the Christian religion was the only proper avenue when approaching anything relating to matters of God Creator. It just so happens in his case that a deeper inner knowing coming from several influencing past lifetimes included the ideas of Christianity, and also embraced the mystical realms of reality. Cayce was a Sunday school teacher and southern gentleman. He was also a full trance channel. The information coming through him while he was in trance was one-hundred eighty degrees from his waking notions of reality. Being in full trance while accessing the Records was the only way he could still his inner conflict about receiving such information. Had he been raised in a non religious environment, his accessing method might have been totally different. So would the appeal of his story as being America's *Sleeping Prophet*.

Unfortunately, modern western religions, each with their need to be the only way to

Spiritual realization, have pushed our natural use of the Records into the preconscious and subconscious realms. Accordingly, our natural talents are suddenly defined as supernatural and we are cautioned against the use of any abilities from within this definition by those presenting the <u>only</u> ways.

Instead of being given a full range of knowledge of how God relates to humankind, in the west we are taught as children that God is watching our every move and will one day judge us as to our worthiness of being in His presence for Eternity. As adults many of us realize that the ideas taught us about God were meant to be controls. The inner conflict that arises as a result of this internal Spiritual rift often requires years of work to overcome, and it is because of this that we must learn techniques to unlock the memory of the Akashic Records and once again allow the natural ability to consciously access these realms to be a significant aspect of our daily lives.

The Nature of the Records

What is the nature of the Akashic Records?

The Akashic Records are preconscious and exist within the framework of the Collective Mind, which is 4th and 5th dimensional in nature. (Physical matter and time are 3rd and 4th dimensional.) Entry into the Collective Mind is achieved through an individual's 'Book of Life.' To enter your 'Book of Life,' you must direct your awareness internally to a preconscious state. Many experience this state of mind as a dreamlike awareness. Imagine this preconscious state as the narrow point of an hour glass with the upper chamber as Conscious Awareness and the lower chamber as Subconscious.

Much of our current computing technology is an unconscious out-picturing of our internal selves. For example: imagine a computer programmed to automatically copy and store everything that is inputted, even retaining copies of information and applications that the user has thoughtfully, or otherwise, discarded. Imagine this computer as part of a global network of computers, continuously linked through satellites to share information. This sounds a little like the World Wide Web, only this system is nonphysical etheric energy. Each time a terminal in our make-believe system is used, the main computer learns from the network interface, <u>and</u> its interaction with its user. If you were to visit a home page of this Etheric Network, the computer would automatically link your terminal with everyone who had ever visited that site, and as you explored the information available there, everyone interested would be fed your responses to that particular home page. In short, the computer is constantly expanding its abilities with the data fed from the network and each interaction with its user. This is an over simplification but accurate description of how the Akasha works.

The Records are preconscious. How can I be aware of conditions within myself when I am preconscious? Isn't preconsciousness another term for unconscious?

We are taught by modern science that Consciousness exists in the physical body, the cellular mind. In other words, if you are perceiving with your five senses, then you are conscious. Preconsciousness is experienced in the noncellular mind, the Etheric body, and is not unconsciousness or subconsciousness, nor do you have to become unconsciousness or subconsciousness to experience preconsciousness. You, as a physical form, experience being unconscious when you are unaware of sensory stimulation. You, as a conscious witness to the physical and etheric bodies, are unlimited Awareness and can view creation from as many platforms as you are capable of envisioning.

How do I become aware of the preconscious state?

Accessing the Akasha, like all introspective activities, requires us to momentarily release our external reference points in favor of an internal, worldless, formless state of existence. The more an individual is capable of letting go of his or her investment in the world of form, the more able they will be to enter the nondistracting state of witness Awareness. As Consciousness plays in the physical body it produces waves of rhythmic electrical impulses within the nerve centers of the brain and spinal cord. The frequency of these brain waves has been correlated with certain states of Consciousness. These scales are rough and there is an overlapping of the characteristics between boundaries :

> Beta – At 14 – 35 cycles per second an individual is fully conscious of their senses and sensibilities. Most are fully awake at this level.
> Alpha – Meditation and relaxation produce the 8 – 14 cycles per second that define this level. Most everyone can easily remain fully conscious in alpha. This is not a transcendental state of meditation, nor is it to be confused with certain profoundly relaxed states of consciousness attained while practising yoga.
> Theta – Trance, hypnosis, profound day dreams, wakeful or lucid dreaming and light sleep happen at 4 – 8 cycles per second of brain wave activity.
> Delta – With most individuals this is the level of deep sleep. Individuals who are able to remain fully conscious at 0.5 – 3 cycles per second are considered to be mystics. This is the level of transcendent Consciousness where everything is experienced as One.

Getting into the Records is a matter of remaining fully conscious as brain wave activity moves from beta level through alpha into theta level. At first glance this might seem difficult. It is a matter of being consciously guided through the different levels of Consciousness with symbols or thought forms. This directs your Awareness into the Collective MInd.

The quality of Consciousness as alpha becomes theta is beginning preconsciousness. As you consciously enter theta you are entering the preconscious state. Being fully conscious while in this state of Awareness we see our past and all its many remembered states as a series of "probable events." At that moment, the moment in which we only probably existed, it is possible to release the ego's control of the future with its many "what if" concerns. Here the male aspect of individual Consciousness joins with the female aspect of Collective Consciousness to create the Mystic's mind. Once we have entered the Mystic's mind, a state of mind where duality ceases to exist, we are free to explore the realms of past, present and future as if they were a series of probabilities.

Here is a common concern: the act of dropping duality can be surprisingly unpleasant for many, because it appears as though they are being asked to let go of all that is "real," in favor of something that only looks "probable." Interestingly, you only have your perceptions of a past and present. You may believe you share some of these perceptions with others, but they have their own unique view of you and your journey. In the end all you have is perceptions and the probability of yourself. Look at the phenomenon of planted false memories – if an authority figure from your childhood insists that a certain series of events, or circumstances are true, you will adopt their perceptions as your own regardless of whether or not the general consensus of perceptions supports the planted version of reality. In other words, if a misperception (lie) is told often enough by someone who is suppose to know, others will adopt the lie as a true event. These planted perceptions can be as innocent as an individual's desire to be right about a past event and the ensuing responses, to a government's desire to control the world view of its citizens through the use of propaganda. Then there is also the phenomenon of selective memory.

You use the terms envisioning and probability as though they were the preferred state. Aren't they just imagination?

Every thought you entertain, whether stimulated by sensory input, or "imagined" data, serves as the foundation for this and other realities. There is no such thing as an idle thought. If you would like to "see" what a thought looks like, stand out in a clearing, away from city lights, on a cloudless night and look up into the sky. Every thought you entertain looks like a constellation, a Milky Way. For those who have trouble using their imaginations to the fullest, let me offer this unsubstantiated data from the world of academia.

Duke University[1] conducted a series of studies on subjective and objective stimulation. Two separate control groups of individuals were wired to record physical response patterns. Each of their five senses was repeatedly stimulated and the results recorded. The same individuals returned the next day. They were wired up and stimulated again, only this time their stimulus was to recall the previous day's activities. The results were nearly identical. The only real difference was the variation of intensity from one individual to the next. It seems some of the participants were more willing to use their imaginations than others. Does this prove anything beyond the fact that the senses are used to integrate data into the cellular mind, the physical body? Yes it does.

What we call imagination is really the "power" of the nonphysical mind, the Etheric body. This nonphysical power acts in much the same manner as the resulting force of a group of muscles acting together to accomplish a task. Accordingly, very little is able to be accomplished in this realm unless you are able to exert the power of imagination. How does that popular adage go, "If you cannot imagine it for yourself, it won't happen." It is because of this that many mystics refer to imagination as "dynamic will."

The physical body expresses its will power through repetitive, learned response. Example: if you want to advance in a sport, you must first become automatic with its fundamentals – a certain group of repetitive motions. This then gives you the opportunity to concentrate on the more subtle aspects of the game. In order to go beyond the basics you must be able to see yourself excelling. This "seeing" is done with the Etheric body, or imagination. This separates the average from the excellent.

When "dynamic will" combines forces with the cellular memory, the result is a measurable electromagnetic response in the physical body. This is how the Etheric and physical bodies act as a unified field.

Unfortunately, most of us have been taught that the unseen part of us we call our minds and our bodies are separate. We have been taught to only trust sensory data; if we can touch it, see it, taste it, smell it, or hear it, then, and only then is it real. If we are only imagining it, it is unreal. Everything has its reality at the level it manifests, or at the level that is the most effective to its vision of what is possible for itself. It is important to remember that this system of "realness" is needed when we are about the business of surviving the circumstances of this particular world.

As far as probabilities go, imagine a bundle of three hundred clear plastic tubes each about three inches in diameter, each touching the one next to it, all forming a large circle of openings. Now also imagine that the center tube contains the bulk of your Conscious Awareness. Let's call these gathered tubes a Life bundle. This center tube of the bundle best represents the perceptions of your most dynamic experiences of this world, from the moment of birth to the moment of death. The tubes farthest from the center contain the least amount of your Consciousness and only represent extremely low probabilities of existence within this world. The tubes touching the center tube contain alternate experiences and exist as validations and invalidations of the center tube's experience. Any one of the surrounding tubes can become our core experience if we are somehow displaced from the center tube. We can become dislodged from the center tube through deep emotional or profound physical traumas, extreme alterations of body chemistry, or any sudden shocks, such as a great personal loss. These other tubes are considered by many to be probable dimensions. The Records show them to be aspects of the core identity that are important to the setting of imagined mental, emotional and physical boundaries. Without these validating/invalidating probabilities we would have a difficult time sharing perceptions and a seemingly common experience of this world with our fellow travelers.

Each individual is a dimensional reality, and there are other dimensional realities that truly separate our reality from that of our fellow Cosmic Universe mates. Also, each incarnation is considered a different dimensional reality, because it is outside the validating/invalidating points of reference we refer to as our time and space. Why all the many different layers of reality? We need the separation of dimensions to fully individuate our Consciousness from its Source. This allows us, as individuated forms of expression, to respond to Creation without interference from Source. This noninterference gives Source its greatest experience of Itself, and we rapidly evolve through the many layers of Creation.

Are there any other conditions that can influence experiencing the 'other' selves that you illustrated with the example of the tubes?

Imagination effects our ability to relate to these other selves. In other words, probabilities can be influenced by our ability to imagine other probabilities. These other probabilities can be very useful to the core self in that they may contain "real" abilities that are lacking within the core self. In the center tube, for example, you might have developed a wonderful artistic ability that leaves you lacking in business skills. One of these "other" probable selves might have that skill. To tap that "hidden" ability all you would need do is sit in a deeply relaxed state, then with your imagination communicate with that imagined aspect of yourself. Sounds crazy. And it works. Many actors use this technique to get into character.

This might be of interest: a client came for a private session with the desire to discover her purpose for being here at this time. In the session it showed her purpose to be that of a healer. The word "healer" meant nothing to her. The idea that she was to be a healer was confusing to say the least, and in no way validated her preparation for her future as an attorney. I immediately looked into the early childhood influences of this lifetime to determine why she had stepped off her choosen path to become an attorney. The Records showed her as a child playing nurse and envisioning herself a doctor. Then at about the age of eight her father passed the bar and went into private practise. It showed him helping those unable to help themselves. By the time she was twelve he had become well loved in the community as a champion of the people. Wherever she went people would recognize her as the daughter of that wonderful man whom many felt was a "life saver." From about fourteen on she was captured by the idea of helping the less fortunate through law. She literally blocked her early desire to enter medicine, and concentrated on being just like the man she loved the most. Her father was a wonderful example to emulate. Many of us do the very same thing. But what about her purpose to be a healer?

She left the Akashic session confused as to her real mission in life, but promised to let me know if anything unusual came up in the next several weeks now that she had been reminded about her early love for medicine.

Several months went by before I heard from her. We visited for about half an hour before she revealed her recent decision to shift her major to medicine. To become an attorney she had shifted the bulk of her Consciousness from her destiny path and core experience of healer to a parallel probable experience that followed the path of her father. She would have made an excellent attorney because she could fully imagine herself as being like her father and therefore tapped into a parallel self that was travelling that path. The one thing that really surprised her was her family's reaction to her decision – they were jubilant. Her mother always knew she was going to be a doctor, and her father told her how much he had loved watching her as a child when she would heal her dolls and stuffed animals.

With this individual there are several strong probable selves that could play out in this time and space – healer, lawyer, writer, artist or actor. With such strong probabilities it would seem difficult for her to be clear as to her destiny path. We always know. If we get off track something or someone will remind us.

To have access to these probable selves is just a matter of being able to imagine them. If you can't imagine a certain probable path for yourself, it is more than likely that you do not have that as a probable aspect.

Accessing the Records

How do I gain access to the Akashic Records?

There is a certain field of thought energy that once attuned to allows direct and conscious entry into the Records. This field of thought exists within you as a preconscious channel through the Higher Self to the Over-Soul. The illustration at the beginning of this chapter is one of several[2] that can act as a visual key to bring your Conscious Awareness into this channel. There are also the meditations beginning on page 122. Once your Awareness is at the surface of this energy field you will automatically move toward your intention. If your intention is to view the Records, you will. Intention drives the process.

How do I attune my thoughts to these specialized fields of energy?

By dramatically changing your response to the world. It is a simple process you only need to practice while getting into the Records. Unfortunately, it is not as easy as we'd like to think. Unlearn the relationships you have with this world. Unlearn that two plus two equals four. Change your points of reference. Give up the need to be right. Allow for other possibilities. Attune to Cause instead of effect. Relinquish the behavior of choosing success or failure patterns of thought. Become a Mystic instead of a scientist.

Is there a technique or certain way of viewing this that could help me?

The *Course in Miracles*[3] is an excellent place to start. The only drawback is the lessons are spread over a twelve month period of time and require a good amount of diligence. A year is a long time to most.

Here is a more immediate formula: to paraphrase the poem attributed to Saint Francis of Assisi, *"Where there is doubt, also restore faith; where there is indifference, also sow love; where there is injury, also grant pardon; where there is darkness, also command Light; where there is despair, also impart hope; where there is sadness, also bring joy.*

"Do not seek so much to be consoled, as to console; to be understood, as to understand; to be loved, as to love. For it is in giving that we receive. And it is in receiving that God shares Creation with us."

This is a True Way, every aspect existing in each moment. Fully Unified Consciousness. Ultimate Cause – Selfless Self.

Profound feelings of gratitude open these channels to the Over-Soul. This may be the most difficult path to take because it requires us to constantly identify with the receiving force within Creation. Most of us find it difficult to receive without feeling we must give back in equal share. This blocks gratitude. To reverse the effects of this we must be willing to receive without the obligatory feelings of having to give. Gratitude is the key.

Akashic State of Mind

It sounds as though you're describing an Akashic state of mind. Is there a certain mental or emotional posturing necessary to enter the Records?

Yes. A state of openness and observation is most preferred when in the Records. In times past, those who dealt in the knowledge of the Akashic Records were considered mystics and found comfort living outside the main stream of life. Even though the wilderness posed its own threats, it was safer for an enlightened individual to live in nature than to cast lots with those who lived within city walls. Mindsets have changed with sciences disproving many deadly superstitions. For instance, we went from believing someone a witch if they survived bathing on a regular basis, to believing cleanliness is next to Godliness. For the most part, the mystics of today live beyond the fears of the small minds and suspicions of those unable to comprehend a greater reality, and now find safety within the main stream; some even enjoying celebrity status.

This is the age of the suburban and corporate mystic. The outward appearances that used to define spiritualists and teachers of esoteric lore have given way to designer jeans and corporate uniforms. The images that once defined those on the mystical path are gone. Some of today's mystics lead billion dollar corporations, send probes into outer space, deal in quantum physics, facilitate healing, keep homes, teach, compose music, parent, dance ballets, repair autos, collect refuse, paint, landscape, build, conduct transportation, sculpt forms; the list is endless.

The Mystical Mind Set

What then constitutes a mystical mindset? What defines mysticism?

Witnessing existence from a non-duality, non-plural frame of reference allows the perceptions of a mystical mind. The mystical mindset[4] is achieved when we blend Mastery Awareness (the known), into the Mystery (the unknown). When we are willing to let go of the past (guilt orientation) and the future (fear orientation) to live in the NOW. When we are willing to become the performance in each new moment. When we are willing to expand into the greater dimensions of Awareness as Witness and lose our self consciousness. When we are willing to remember the faces and allow individuals the freedom to recreate themselves with each new moment, instead of holding individuals to what we or they might have thought themselves to be in a previous moment. When we are willing to accept this world as a realm of probable layers of reality, as opposed to something carved in stone to be fought over. When we are willing to release judgments and move our Awareness back into the childlike attitude of being in awe. When we are willing to give up hurt in favor of joy. Then we have Mysticism.

The ability to access Collective Consciousness is hardly a gift handed down from on high, nor is it something learned in a secret order. The initiate is determined by a willingness to look beyond the safe and familiar concepts of the immediate world. Even though this movement away from "doing" toward "being" requires certain skills and understandings, it, like so many other things in our lives, is actually about willingness.

What is a good example of a person coming to the moment of mysticism?

The prayer of Saint Francis of Assisi examples the moment when an individual comes to unification – the Mystical experience. Most who achieve conscious entry into the Records and integrate the ability into their daily existence, do so when they have fully understood the intention of Unified Mind/Body/Spirit. The intention of Unified Self Expression is to bring Glory to the All, the "I AM," through the recognition of the Wholeness within each individual. The intention is never to bring self glorification.

The good news - entry into the Records hardly requires us becoming Saints. And if you should, so much the better for you and the Collective Mind.

How does this mystical state of mind effect life's circumstances? Will I suddenly want to run out and buy a robe and live in a cave?

In past cultures, those who gained access to the Mystical realms set themselves apart from the village, living outside the security of the walls and protection offered by the warrior class. The images offered in western history books leave us with mental pictures of the Oracles of Delphi as old hags, or the Myrdwyns of the Druid culture as ugly old men. These individuals were more often the elders of their culture. They lived full, meaningful lives within their culture, then moved beyond the notions that defined the individuals within the walled cities. Their role as Seer was very important to those remaining within the walls. It was the Seers who served as the eyes and ears of the Gods to the villagers. The Seers foretold coming events. They also instructed the villagers in rituals designed to give a deeper meaning and understanding to the mysteries of life. Early rituals of human then animal sacrifices allowed the priest and priestess to evoke forms created by certain thought fields associated with death, to effect conscious change within the Collective Mind of the village or culture.

How did the idea of Seer become unpopular?

Interestingly enough, it was the Seers who sought to mystify their place within history. The role of Seer lost its importance with the arrival of the Christian monolithic God. Early church leaders convinced the masses that it was the Seers who were at the root of their daily problems. The Seers were very much aware of the coming religion. Instead of fighting the church, they cloaked their ways in mystery. This allowed the leaders of the new religion to create fearful images of the old religion. The Seers envisioned a time when they would be hunted like animals. History tells us they were. They also foresaw a 'time' when Truth would once again be upon the lips of all who sought it. We entered that 'time' right after World War II. The etheric energy released at the time of conscious death transforms the Collective Mind. Many individuals marched off to war knowing they would perish in the chaos. If you look through history you will see a pattern of expansion within Consciousness immediately following periods of war.

Through Imagination to Experience

How do I know when my experience in the Records is real and not just my mental wanderings?

It is hard to tell immediately because your initial encounter with the Records is dominated by attuning to certain levels of thought. If there were another way to move conscious Awareness into the Collective Mind, it would be preferable. Not because using thought is somehow wrong, but because of the stigma attached to the use of thought in an imaginative manner. We are taught if something is imagined it is not real.

Also, the beginning experience for many is that they are somehow dreaming at a very high level. This is due in part to the quality of energy found within the preconscious areas of the Collective Mind. This energy looks and feels very much like our dreamscapes and dream bodies because it responds so readily to our combined thought/feeling projections. Initially, many seekers feel they are asking the question, then dreaming up the answer. And because of the dreamy quality of Consciousness at the theta, or preconscious level, they are convinced they fell asleep and dreamed it all – questions and answers. This is where most individuals who are not serious about attaining this ability stop attempting to enter the Records. They feel it is impossible to break this barrier. It is not, and really only requires a little more effort.

In this body of work we are dealing with the Collective Mind, not the Collective Unconscious or Subconscious Minds. The trick here is to remain fully cognizant and very attentive while entering, and moving through the alpha then theta or preconscious levels of Consciousness. This is the only way to move Conscious Awareness from the imagined images of the Records into a full experience of the Records.

Again, our link to the Akasha is through what appears to be our minds. Because of this, it will always feel to some degree as though this is happening in our heads. Our cellular mind, or physical body, is where we integrate and store the information being received by the senses. Sensory data is how we build our Awareness. It is through our Awareness that we imagine this world; it is through our imagination that we are able to use our senses. This is a wonderful loop, designed to support itself. We rely on this system for our very survival. It is when we have developed sensibilities other than the five senses that more elevated probabilities interrupt this cycle of stimuli integration and response. This is the doorway through which we move our Conscious Awareness into other dimensional realities.

The question of imagination versus experience is important. Validation as to the authenticity of the information being gained through the Akasha is critical to the continued use of the Records as a means for guiding yourself through life. Validate your experience as often as you can. Ask questions about the near future – the next few days. Let time tell you if it is your imagination or actual future information. Get information for friends. Their feedback will quickly inform you as to the validity of your experience. This is the easiest way to remove this doubt. At some point the external validation will have you believing in your ability to read the Akasha and the desire to get immediate validation will be replaced with a profound knowing. This knowing is experienced by everyone who gains entry into the Records.

Obsession or Intuition?

What about the idea that we attract to us the things we fear the most?

A popular concept coined by the New Age movement and hardly a Law. I love the cartoon where a mugger has a gun in one hand and the wallet of his victim in the other and is asking the man he's robbing, "What did you do to deserve this in your life?"

We are all in touch with the Records all the time. I've known many an individual who has accurately intuited negative future events. So the question might be, "Do we attract negative things our way by obsessing about them, or is our obsession a response to an intuitive feed from the future that is putting us on notice to be aware?"

Let me illustrate with a story. During the time I was in business, I met a man and we became instant friends. I'll call him Bob. We were both of the same ilk – determined, successful, lovers of life. The only real difference at the time was he was recently married, I'll call her Betty, and they were newly pregnant with his first child, her third. I was newly divorced and the father of two growing young ladies. Other than that we were one in our pursuits. We both had our own businesses and were both applying Spiritual concepts in the work place.

One day, about a year after we met, Bob and Betty, and two mutual friends and I were all sitting around socializing when Bob suddenly asked for a reading. I sat quietly for a moment, then asked for his full birth name. Suddenly I saw Bob driving at a very high rate of speed down a country road. At first it was unclear to me if the images were symbolic or actual. Mainly because some of the details were not as I knew them to be in reality. The images of him in a car that was different from his own, were of a frantic nature. He seemed manic. The Bob I knew was always together, smooth. Then I watched as my friend drove the car over a cliff. He killed himself. I started crying. Everyone in the room cried as I told them the details. It was difficult to believe what I had seen. My mind did the normal inventory of his life. He had everything a man could ask for, a beautiful wife, a child on the way, millions of dollars, all the things society holds dear. What could be so wrong that he would want to kill himself.

After we finished crying, Betty revealed Bob's life long tendency toward addictions and his constant struggle whether to stay here on the planet or leave. Betty then revealed that he had tried suicide before. I had no idea. So much for being psychic. I was stunned. Betty asked when it showed this event as happening, I answered in about three years.

About two years later Betty began to call for counseling on a regular basis. Bob's depression was getting worse and he was taking it out on her. Interestingly, Bob became less available because of a new business venture, so there was almost no contact between us at this point. Betty worked hard to understand what Bob thought was so wrong with his life. It became more and more difficult for her to stay centered with Bob's insults and assaults becoming a daily ritual. I reached out to Bob, and found him angry at my attempts. It was very confusing.

I was living in California and had scheduled a trip to their city. Betty and I set up several counseling sessions for the time during my stay. By this time Bob was steadily projecting his inner pain on others; and his anger was alienating many. On the night of our last scheduled session, Betty called to say Bob had gone to the country in a relative's automobile. When she told me the make of the car, I knew this was his time. She told me Bob had said he was glad I was in town because she would be in good hands. Betty and I were both frightened. We both knew it was about to happen and were both unable to effect a change. I cleared my schedule for the next day to make myself available to Betty. Later that evening Betty called to let me know the police had just come to inform her that Bob had been killed in an automobile accident. It seemed the passenger's side front tire of his car had caught some soft dirt and had thrown the car off a small embankment, into a bridge support. While it was true he was going rather fast for that particular stretch of road, there was no indication of anything other than an accident. Officially, Bob left accidentally. To the world his death would be seen as untimely. There was no disgrace.

Was Bob's obsession with suicide fear based, or was he simply intuiting his future and acting out what he felt was the inevitable? He had tried different ways in the past. Was my role to give him the correct formula for carrying out his desire to leave? If I had kept the images to myself that day would he still be making botched attempts? I struggled very hard with many such questions over the months that followed Bob's death. Betty and I have kept in close contact, and often wonder about our roles in the drama.

My conclusion: we are constantly intuiting coming events that we in turn act out in one way or another in current time. On this side of enlightenment, these intuitive "hits" from the future excite fear or engender hope. We all have well defined roles to play with each other. Many of our future concerns and fears are intuitive impressions of what lies ahead in our journey. If we remember that it is our response to events that determines the outcomes, we remain sovereign Souls. If we get lost in the fear, we are lost in the fear. In this condition little is possible except to be effected by our small responses. Being able to access the Akashic Records allows us to view what is ahead much the way headlights illuminate the dark road ahead of us in the night.

Do you think your role was to give your friend the final answer?

Yes. I've gone into Bob's Records many times since his departure to check and double check the question you have just asked. In the moment just before the impact, he gave up his emptiness. His addictions dissolved in that moment. My role was to help him find the permission deep inside to die by his own hand. There was no judgment from me about his leaving in this manner, only my sorrow at his going so far away from my physical senses. Bob had struggled with this question from the time he was twelve. Over thirty years.

After the reading and before his death, Bob and I would take many Fridays and do whatever came to mind – drives in the country, visits to Civil War memorials, walks for hours on end, movies or just sitting and talking about how empty his feelings of addiction were. It was during this time that I found out my friend was an incredibly sensitive individual, empathic in fact. As such, it was very difficult for him to know his boundaries. He so closely identified with everyone it was natural for him to lose himself in the process of being their friend.

Suggestion

Could offering information from the Akashic Records be a form of suggestion? Is there a higher degree of accuracy for positive information than negative?

The last question first: the Records do not list information in positive and negative categories. However, because most readers are human, there will be a natural tendency to interpret the data from the Records in a manner that seems positive or negative.

Yes, to your first question. Individuals who form the core of mainstream society would say suggestion is why any psychic prediction comes true. Actually, there is a lot to consider about the role of suggestion in any reading, Akashic, psychic or otherwise.

I have studied hypnotherapy and I am quite aware of the power of suggestion. As a student of metaphysics, I am also aware of the power of the spoken word. When an individual comes for a session they are already in a high state of suggestibility. When we visit any authority figure, the boss, the butcher, the doctor, parent or teacher, we defer our position of authority to theirs. This is suggestibility. How an authority figure addresses this power is very important to the outcome of his work with the client.

Over the years I've noticed within myself a desire to focus only on what works. This has impacted my readings, in that I tend towards interpreting in a positive manner. If asked I will look for any negatives, but for the most part I hang out on what I would judge as the positive side.

Why?

Keeping in mind that we are judging here, the positive side, contrary to popular belief, is far more powerful in its ability to manifest than the negative. Actually, the only aspect of the negative side we might consider powerful would be control. Control is born out of fear and tends to bring separation. The illusion of manifestation emanates out from the assemblage point of thought and feeling – Unification. I really enjoy the illusion of instantaneous manifestion, like watching Sai Baba in India. It breaks down the superstition that we have to do something to get something. Those in control, the ones with all the rules, get extremely upset when an individual demonstrates an effortless life. Effortlessness is quite confrontational to most individuals of this day and age. So much stock is put into doing and Mastery. What of the Mystery?

If a person knows about something in the future they can change it. Is there more to this than just suggestibility?

Yes. Once an event is observed the outcome begins to automatically change. This is a form of time line pollution – the event happens and because of prior knowledge the outcome is different. Everything seems to have been altered, including the nature of the event. If prior knowledge allows your response to become more fluid, more expansive, then the timing will also change. The more expansive our response to a <u>coming</u> event, the more <u>condensed</u> the time is between the knowing of the event and its manifestation. The more expansive our response to a NOW event, the more elastic and consciously manipulative time and form will appear to be.

Time Line Pollution

I heard once that when you look ahead you pollute the time line. How does this pollution effect the cycle of birth and death?

Yes, it is true from this side of enlightenment that when we look forward or backward we leave response impressions of our current selves along each path that slightly alter our 'then' experiences. These response impressions effect our other selves in much the same way an opinion of someone we highly respect effects us. With that comparison in mind, you can imagine the powerful impact these trace impressions leave. And yet, an individual must be very conscious in each moment to detect when these are present. This is the pollution teachers have spoken of when they have warned against living anywhere else but in the NOW. As to the effect on the cycles of birth and death, there is only one – the more we know, the more awake we are from the dream of this reality. This wakefulness will lead you off the wheel of birth and death. Death is a response, not an event.

Why teach others how to look into past and future lives if you believe we can cause pollution?

I believe that the amount of pollution is insignificant in light of all that is gained through seeing clearly into the past and future. Our ability to respond to life is greatly enhanced when we are no longer afraid of the unknown.

Besides, there is little "real" world time left. We, the Collective, must use every method necessary to bring about the moment of individuals experiencing themselves as Ultimate Cause, Selfless Self. This awakening to the True nature of individual Self-Expression will cause each time line to Unify, sending a wave of liberation from illusion throughout Human Consciousness. Knowing this outcome lessens my feelings of conflict over the paradox.

The second part of your first question was, "How does this pollution effect the cycles of birth and death?"

Thirty years is the average number of years between incarnations at this point in time and space. Three hundred years ago it was more like an average of one hundred twenty years between incarnations. If too much Earth time passes between incarnations during a period of high renaissance, such as now, the individual incarnating will feel out of step, or at the very least, as though they belong to another time. Looking ahead on the time line shortens the time needed between lifetimes by allowing the individual opportunities for resolution that would normally only be done in the reality between death and rebirth. The more aware we become at all levels, the less time is needed on either side of the veil that separates the world of the living from the world of the Living.

Without a doubt, NOW is where we belong. Adventuring into the future can cause distortions in the time distance between events. Once we have seen the past or future we enlarge the range of our response to events, diminishing the time/space between events on all observed time lines. This type of distortion can leave one's personality self feeling a little overwhelmed by the number of major events spaced so closely together. This could be considered negative in that being overwhelmed lessens our ability to integrate data into our cellular minds. In the bigger picture the only real data we need at the cellular level is the automatic responses that keep the body alive.

How do you work around this problem?

It is more a question of understanding what type of pollution is present, than an issue of working around it. I'm using pollution here as a way of defining something unnatural in a particular dimension or time. Let me finish with the last question before moving on.

From the macro view time is simultaneous. The lifetime you are living now is the only lifetime you will have. Birth, more than death, has an amazing effect upon the personality self. In death you have dropped the physical form. Little else changes. Then, if you have more to finish on Earth, you take a new physical body. In the womb you are in a wonderfully unimaginable existence. A heaven perhaps. Suddenly, and without much warning, you are thrust into a dimension of time and space completely different from anything you've ever experienced; a dimension filled with one urge after another. Layers and layers of urges. Nothing can adequately prepare your personality self for the transformation from the Etheric mind, dominate in the womb, to cellular mind, dominate after birth. As you learn your new world, you start the climb from body mind to intellect mind.

By the time you are five years of age most of the old you, the previous lifetime you, will have been dropped in favor of a more appropriate you of the current time and space. A few things will seem the same. Most everything else will have changed as you learn to manipulate your new physical form and its circumstances.

How do I work around the issue of pollution? I work from the micro view with influencing factors – mainly karmic issues from past and future lives that are naturally polluting the time line. So you might say my main focus in a reading is to ask for information regarding influencing factors from other lives. Here I can act as a telephone operator, connecting the influencing lives to each other through the switchboard of the Akasha.

If an individual is unable to make an emotional connection with past or future life influences, they will remain in denial of certain characteristics that shape their present response. One form of time line pollution: diametrically opposed influencing lifetimes. Say you're a devout communist in your current life and inadvertently find out that you were in fact one of the signers of Declaration of Independence of the United States of America. To further complicate things you, as the signer of the Declaration, spontaneously become aware of the "you" who is diametrically opposed to democracy. Talk about pollution. Imagine what could happen in both time lines. Here you struggle with the knowledge that you helped to create your enemy. There you find yourself dis-eased by the constant inner battle over which system is indeed the best for the people. Pretty intense!

Another common form of time line pollution is the historically important personage. If an individual wants a reading to find out all the famous personality selves they have been, I send them to someone else. And I've met too many people who have been told they were Cleopatra, or Thomas Jefferson, etc. to believe in readers who give out this kind of information. I seldom get names from past lives. It's because I'm more interested in quickening the state of Enlightenment than I am in personality selves and their successes and failures.

We have all tried <u>everything</u>. Eventually we find a place of comfort within our Soul group, and incarnate over and over again in that genre. Few of us have been important to history, but then history, for the most part, only favors those who are important to the viewpoints of its writers. That would mean elite white males for the past two millennium. Only the elite from one race – a pretty narrow view I'd say.

I have a friend who went into the Records and found out he was indeed a very famous individual, and not just with the elite white males. This incarnation was known almost world wide at the time of that incarnation. His accomplishments were very impressive. Here is where the problem presented itself. This individual was not achieving even a small fraction in this current life of what he had in that past life. My friend was keenly aware of the concept of simultaneous time and set out to borrow some of the genius from the previous incarnation. A form of simultaneous inter lifetime competition began that exhausted both incarnations. The past life personality became very aware of the future personality's jealousies and attempted to break off any contact with the future self. This can be dangerous because an individual may suddenly feel fragmented and lost. I asked him to stop obsessing about the differences between the two lifetimes and to concentrate on how he could help the past self achieve even greater affluence. It was extremely difficult, but he managed to shift his attention away from what he seemed to be lacking and got behind the success of his other self. He not only improved his mental and emotional selves, he suddenly found himself in a wonderful period of fulfillment and worldly gain. What we wish for others we wish for ourselves. This includes past and future incarnations of ourselves.

Past Life Influences

How do past lifetimes influence present life?

Let's take a moment to look at what 'triggers' past life memories and influences: overlapping response patterns from the past and future that appear as uncharacteristic behaviors; similar circumstances, such as living in a town or village where you have had another life, having the same line of work, presently incarnating with individuals from another life, having a Soul mate suddenly show up in your current life; or incarnating with the specific goal of finishing something that was begun in another life.

For example; I did a reading for a young man about five years ago who was about to begin his college career. He was a little uncertain as to where his life was going. He said he had many options available and was lost as to his true purpose for being here. When I went into the Records I asked for any influencing conditions from other lives. This is a good place to begin with most new clients. This individual had been an architect many times in the past, from ancient Egypt to modern Greece and everywhere in between. He was truly gifted and dedicated to architecture. So much so that in one lifetime he had been the original designer of a cathedral, then as an artisan in his next incarnation he had put the finishing touches on the same building.

I asked if he had ever entertained the idea of being an architect. He said his father was a well known architect and that they had never gotten along, especially not the past several years. I asked if he was going to let that stand in his way. His final answer was no, but I could feel his deep dislike for his father was still blocking a commitment. Just before we ended the session I asked what had been the turning point for him and his father. It seems the father had become upset when the son had won an art competition at school. It happened that the local newspapers had gotten wind of the accomplishment and put the young man's face on the front page along with the story. The father had become irate and told the youth he was never to enter any other competition.

I asked my client to give me his father's name again. I wanted to see where they had been together in past lives. I was shown the pair in Italy. Both were artisans of fine reputations. They were competing for a prized commission, one that would mean instant fame and recognition that would extend well beyond their home town. The individual who was the son in this current lifetime had easily won. The father of this lifetime had vowed in that past lifetime, never to forgive him for taking his prize. It seems the competition was more political than anything else. The winner had been well connected through family. The loser was the better artist, but had come from a poor family.

Obviously little had changed. The father in this lifetime had come from a poor family and had to work very hard for everything, while the son, by virtue of his father's hard work, was born into an upper middle class family. Interestingly, the father in this lifetime was supplying the son with the proper connections, because the father did not want his son to work as hard as he had. I suggested he let his father hear the tape of his session. He didn't think the father would support his decision to come to a reader.

I later heard from him. He had decided to go for a degree in architecture. He reported that he and his father actually had come to blows. It seems the son had aced the first term architectural exams his father had just barely passed. Because of their rift, he took an intern position with a firm in competition with his father's. The young man vowed in his letter to me to never forgive his father for how he had recently treated him. I looked into the future and saw the two of them at it again. The sad part is — working together they could be an unbeatable team.

Another example: an older woman came for a reading wanting to know about possibilities for romance. She had been without a mate for some fifteen years and was now tired of being alone. She was very intuitive about the coming events in her life. When I explained that not only would she have her Soul mate, she would also have his entire family, she almost fell off the chair. It sounded horrible to her. She cherished her alone time. She left the reading worried about how she would cope.

Several months later she called. "I've just returned from Rio. I met him. It's unbelievable. He's half my age. What am I going to do? This is crazy! I know it's him. I knew it from across the lobby of the hotel. It's crazy. What will my kids think. He's only two years older than my oldest son. This is cruel. Did you know he was going to be a mere child?"

"Age is only important on this side of the veil," I explained.

"We're already talking about marriage. This is nuts. Everyone will think he's after my money. The oddest thing was when we made love, I didn't feel older. I wasn't concerned about my body sagging or anything of the sort. He was incredible with me."

"Does he speak English?"

"What? Yes. He even speaks German. How do I handle this?"

We spent the next hour working on her feelings about how others would perceive her relationship with this young man. I had the luxury of watching this unfold over the next several months. It was rather dynamic. Two years later they are both very happy, and she has brought his family up from Brazil. Eight of them live in a condo she had purchased as an investment. She and her new family have decidedly different interests than the members of her first family. Her oldest son has all but written her off as a kook and has filed lawsuits trying to block her from spending any of the money left to her from his father's death. This meeting of her Soul mate has created influences that have far reaching implications.

Selecting Data

How selective can you be when asking for information in the Records?

You can isolate any information that is stored in the Records. The subject of your search can be as selective as subatomic particles, or as general as the geological history of this world. The only limitation is your awareness of the subject's existence.

What if you only want to focus on the positive aspect of any given subject? Say you only want to know about the happy events in the future that will be effecting your family members?

Your concern is shared by many. The criterion used in storing the information is beyond the concept of duality – good versus bad, positive versus negative. If knowing the whole contents of certain subjects is not what you want to experience, simply stay out of those areas. It's really as simple as that. If you are overly concerned about getting 'negative' data from the Records, I would suggest discovering the source of your doubts about yourself as Cause.

On the odd chance of repeating myself - I believe that when we are aware of the major events of the future we relinquish our fear of the unknown, and in doing so become fully

Conscious of what is possible for ourselves. In this state we enlarge our range of response, which influences time, outcomes and circumstances. Fear of physical, emotional or mental pain would be the only deterrent to viewing the Wholeness of Creation. And yet, if we are unaware of what's coming, there is fear. It's a catch twenty-two for some individuals.

Storing & Retrieving Data

Exactly how does the information get stored in the Records?

The infinitely compressed bundles of information contained within the Records enter the system through our senses. Thought and emotional energy combine when our cellular minds (physical bodies) are stimulated. When these energies combine, their individual properties are transmuted into geometric forms of Etheric matter. This focused energy is stored in multi-dimensional layers in your individual Book of Life. Your Book of Life is a single cell within the Akashic Records that indiscriminately shares its data with the Collective Mind.

Maybe it would be easier to explain if we were to approach it from how we retrieve information from the Records.

As was stated earlier, when you first enter the Records the range of presentation can seem a little overwhelming. Not only are you dealing with new images of language, but you are also getting multi-dimensional impressions at a very high rate of speed. This happens because each sense activates spontaneous presentations from 'other' stored sensory data. After all, every moment of every lifetime is stored within the multi-dimensional energy fields of the Akasha, even the data your ego Awareness missed. This missed data, such as empathic sensations, intuitive impressions, clairvoyant images, the spectrum of Light energy which includes auras, etc., is fully present when information is retrieved from the Records. This non-sensory data is mixed with sensory data to give you the most complete answer possible.

The information for each of the five senses is always presented within a primary range of forms. For example: when you ask about a past life influence you may get the information first as a sound, then suddenly it would appear as though the sounds were creating images. The sense that is being stimulated first is the primary data genus for that given moment, or influence. In our example sound is the primary data path and light, as images, is secondary. You might find that in a given lifetime one sense dominates the others, or you might find that in the beginning of a past lifetime one sense is dominant, while in the later years of that lifetime another sense is the primary data path feeding the Akasha.

Each presentation in the Akasha is a complete recall of a given moment, or a combination of moments. If you were to ask a general question about sound, such as, "Present the combined lifetime data from my Book of Life on sounds that would create the deepest emotional release for me in my current state of Consciousness," the holographic fields of the Akasha would literally wrap around your cellular mind (physical body) and stimulate each cell of your body creating a holographic like experience of the data being retrieved. This stimulation would cause your emotional body to shift its resonance and you would experience a deep energetic release. As stored emotional energy began to release you would not only experience the sounds coming from the Akasha, but would also begin to see images from those past life experiences influencing your current state of Consciousness. After a very short time, taste, smells and touch sensations would also be present as secondary streams of data. You would call these combinations of data a full past life recall. This would all happen within a few moments.

As has been stated, each primary data genus is accompanied by secondary paths that give a wholeness to the data being retrieved. Example: if you were to ask the Records for data about the sound an extinct species made, the primary answer would be presented as a sound form, but would also have a series of smell, sight, taste and touch forms attached. These secondary information forms would appear less solid than the primary sound form, but are needed to give the whole picture to your Consciousness. Actually, this is the same manner in which information is presented in our "real world" but we are taught to discriminate against the lesser data, favoring the most "real" sensory forms. The same applies to a sight form, i.e., there would be sound, smell, taste and touch data forming a backdrop to the primary visual forms. In certain indigenous peoples, such as those in the Amazon Rain Forest and the Aboriginal people of Australia, this ability to get the full spectrum of data in the same manner as it is presented in the Akasha is still intact. In our civilized state we ignore this other information, treating it as being superfluous to what is important and therefore unnecessary to our experience. We consequently have given up conscious Awareness of the lesser information forms attached to the primary data stream and only get a piece of the big picture. This is truly Micro Awareness.

Hallucinogenic drugs, such as LSD or natural hallucinogens such as mushrooms and peyote, allow these secondary information fields to once again be available to our full Consciousness. We only think we are "seeing" things (hallucinating) because we are no longer discriminating against the lesser data streams. In profound cases of hallucination the lesser data streams become as dominate as the primary field and the individuals lose touch with their prioritized dimensional reality. This is why an individual is allowed a full range of data when under the influences of mind altering substances. Every culture, past, present and future, has used mind altering substances to get at the big picture – Macro Awareness. The writings of Carlos Castaneda give the uninitiated a glimpse into these realms of multidimensional reality in a very meaningful way.

Getting data from the Records sounds a little complicated in light of the primary and secondary data streams mentioned above. And you will immediately begin to impose your ideas of reality on the Records by aligning the data in discriminating values, so that the data streams come together much in the same manner as they do in this world. For example: you are sitting in a theater with your 3-D glasses snugly fitted to your face. The lights begin to dim as a three dimensional image of a field of wild flowers comes into focus on the screen. There is no sound as your eyes search the image. Red flowers. Blue flowers. Green blades of summer grass being pushed by a silent wind. Now a butterfly. A bird. A child breaks the horizon pulling a wobbling kite a few feet in the air behind her. Suddenly you hear her laughter. Now there is another dimension – sound. And because the theater owners want you to have the greatest experience possible, they've arranged for a full range of summer smells to fill the screening room. First the visual images; then the sound and now smell. They want you to be aware of each sense so they are adding the sense elements one at a time. This way it's more dramatically entertaining.

More human images are added to the scene. This is a family. The mother and father each grasp a handle of a large picnic basket. It must be full of wonderful foods to be so heavy it needs two adults to carry it to its resting place. Digestive fluids begin to make their way into your mouth as you remember the tastes of picnics past. You watch as the contents are unloaded and carefully placed on the colorful blanket. Your whole attention is on the food. Smells of fried chicken, potato salad, buttered corn, and your favorite of all things, apple pie blends with the smells of flowers and grass. At this exact moment a special device in the theater stimulates your taste buds. Another element is now entering your experience – tastes.

The images on the screen are so real now that you find yourself reaching out for a piece of pie, half expecting it to appear in your hand. Suddenly the sensory data stops, the theater is flooded with ordinary light and you sit stunned by the reality of where you are. You were there in the images of the family picnic, and now you are here in an air-conditioned room.

The invention of virtual reality, with its multi-dimensional forms, is the closest description of what it feels like to be in witness of the Records. What I'm trying to describe is a multifaceted experience with one dimensional symbols – words. The three-dimensional images viewed in the Records are impressions of sensory data released back to you in three-dimensional forms that appear as holograms projecting out of a blackened theater screen, a deep void. As you gain experience in the Records these symbols will engage all your senses and will appear truly holographic in their structure.

Other Akashic Records

Are the Akashic Records only for the human experience?

Yes. Other systems have their own manner of sharing experience through a Collective Consciousness repository. Many are very much like the Akasha in how they function, and there are Human individuals who can interpret symbols from those systems. I know individuals who can read the Records of animals, and I have also heard of another individual who can access the Records of plants. These are not my area of expertise. Although I was once asked to give the past lifetimes of a pet cat for a client and was amazed at the amount of data being released back to me in response to my question.

Are there other record keeping systems for alien worlds?

Right. Each of us comes to this world from another system. We bring the knowledge gained through our experiences in these alien worlds and share the information of our journeys at a Collective level with the Akasha. There are a number of us who alternate incarnations between this world and other realms. Many of the alien influences found in this world have been brought here in this manner. Are those bringing the alien information always conscious of their roles? No. Unfortunately our world culture is still enthralled with the micro science view of Creation and invalidates early memories of other worlds by relegating their accounts to the realms of over active imaginations.

Can we explore our "other" world adventures when we access the Records?

Yes. And this requires a concentrated effort. Usually the first inquires into the Records are about cleaning up how we're playing the Human Consciousness game here on Earth. We want to know about our Soul's purpose, life themes, past life influences, karmic debts, etc. Once we have satisfied our need to know about this reality we can focus attention to "other" systems of past or future incarnations. You will find the number of systems you have played in to be many. Ask specific questions, such as, "Did I have a series of incarnations in the Orion system?" If the answer is yes, then ask, "What was the overall theme of the incarnations within that system?" You could continue by asking to be shown the physical form you inhabited in the last lifetime in that system. That data will lead you to other questions.

In Macro reality, we all have as our Ultimate Source a Star – a point of Light in the great void that is the Source of our Conscious Existence, a point in "reality" where only we exist. We emanate out from this Source to join with others of similar characteristics. In doing so we take many different forms, in many different worlds. Creation is our playground, our sandbox. This Star Source is our one true manifest expression. Eventually we return "home" to this point of Light to Create within its matrix.

I have a client who could care less about this world and is using the Records to explore his patterns of incarnating through other time and space realities.

So we can explore our adventures in past civilizations here on Earth. Does that include the civilizations that existed prior to Lemuria?

Yes. Every major civilization is recorded in the Akasha, from the first civilization called Noh-AH, to Lem-Ura, to Po-Seda, to At-Latia, to the current civilization referred to in the Records as Ur-Antia. Each civilization has its own characteristics projected from a Collective Mindset, just as each culture and race on the planet today is a subset of the Collective Human Mind. Once you are within the Records of a past civilization you will be able to read the Collective Response as it relates to each of your incarnations within that dimensional reality, as well as your individual event/response patterns, and lifetime themes.

Out-Of-Body Entry into the Akasha

You also teach that we can enter the Records while out-of-body. What exactly is the difference in experience between going to the Akasha OB, and going through the mystic's mind? Is there a difference?

There is a very important difference. When you enter the Records in the disassociated state necessary to achieve an out-of-body experience (OBE) the immediate integration of the information into the physical body is interrupted. This gap will deepen the dreamlike quality already present in the Records. Also, if not properly done much of the information can be lost during the transfer of Consciousness from the Etheric body back to the physical body. This would create a feeling of unrelated images. This is not the preferred state for someone who is a beginner in this type of work. It is interesting to note that everyone who enters the Records feels as though they have had an out-of-body experience. This is because of the disassociation of Consciousness from the physical senses.

When you enter through the Mystical, the information is instantaneously experienced, integrated and retained. In the Mystical there is a quickening of the flow within the Collective Sub and Super Conscious Minds. This quickening assures full retention of the data. It is truly amazing how much data can be recalled and how little time it takes.

Can you alter the past or future by finding an event in the Akasha, then going OB to the time/space and changing your response to the event?

Interesting question. Macro – everything is simultaneous, so the answer must be only if it is already part of the big picture. Micro – life is progressive. Why go back when the event is over and the lesson learned. In a manner of speaking you do this quite naturally anyway. Every time a past hurt has been healed or a hatred has been resolved in the NOW, you've automatically changed your response to similar situations in other time lines. It's really an exaggerated effort to look the problem up, then go OB to the time and space of each transgression. In what you're suggesting, an individual must fully understand the idea of parallel universes of time/space, or at the very least the concept of non-linear reincarnations. Then that individual must learn of the Akashic Records and how to get there. Then there is the question of achieving a conscious OBE.

Time is truly like a ball of yarn, instead of a string of yarn. At every overlay is an event, a lifetime, a happening. Each one touching the other. Touch one and you touch them all.

Blocks Along the Way

What will keep me from having an experience of the Akashic records?

There are only four elements found within the Collective Human Personality that will stand in the way of successfully experiencing the Akasha.

One: the fear of what is to be found in the past or future. There will always be a certain amount of fear as to what immutable events are "lurking" in the misty images of the future. That fear will color your interpretation of the information, even after years of successfully accessing and interpreting the Records. You will soon learn when this fear is present, and will find effective ways to allow for its distortions. I believe a certain amount of this is "healthy." The only way this can block the experience is when the fear is greater than the intention. The greatest distortion this will have on the information is in the ability to determine the actual timing of events.

I know a young lady who began working with these techniques and was very successful, very quickly. She reported that every time she saw an event she wanted to happen, and feared it wouldn't, the timing she was first given would change. The event would be pushed away. The opposite held true with events she didn't want to happen and knew would. Her fear of the eventuality seemed to rush the event toward her. This distortion has been noticed by many who do not have the advantage of having a Spiritual practice that is focused on the concepts of Unity, or the absence of duality. Unity allows non-judgment to prevail.

As for the fear of what dastardly deeds you've performed in the past, that will diminish as you gain the knowledge that we have all played every imaginable role possible.

Two: judging the Records as to their accuracy. The information offered in the Records is never wrong, and our interpretations can be off by a country mile. Judgment alters the interpretation of the information being offered.

When you look into the Records to review the past years of this current lifetime, you might be in for a surprise. Most of us have very selective memories when it comes to the roles we've played in current life dramas. Naturally we have our own point of view as to what transpired and who was at fault. We also have our need to be right about our position. So, there is a tendency to "make wrong" the information being presented in the Records when it is contrary to our selective memory. This blocks the experience because you will choose your memories and invalidate the presentation from the Records.

A great many of us have repressed and/or completely forgotten many of the unpleasant experiences of our past. At this point interpreting the Records can be a little tricky. If you are extremely positional about a given area of your past, say your relationship with an adult figure, or a sibling, stay out of that part of your Records. Using the Records to resolve past disputes is of little value. The information in the Records is very non-positional. If you happen to use the Records to view past dramas, you might find you had more of a contribution to your suffering than you previously considered. The need to be right is a big trap in any dimensional reality. Being right has no value in the Records. In fact, the less invested in the accuracy of the data you are, the more accurate your interpretations will be.

If you uncover something from your current life past that becomes overwhelming, get help from a professional, someone trained in supporting individuals as they sort out unresolved feelings. Be smart. We are never alone here on Earth. At the very least we have each other from whom to draw strength and support.

Also, treat information about your future as you would treat information from your past. If you see an event in the future that you have no skills to manage, get outside help. The same applies to the past.

Three: doubt that what you are experiencing is really the Records instead of just your imagination. When we first start viewing the Records it can appear as though we are directing the information instead of just allowing it to form in front of us. We ask a question, suddenly a great deal of activity happens within our minds. Thought forms then appear around us as a multi-dimensional series of images, complete with smells, sounds, and physical sensations. It is wonderful to experience, but we ask, "Did I just make it up?" In the beginning it feels like we somehow created all we witness in the Records with our memories of the past and our hopes for the future. This can block your experience because you doubt the source of the data.

Four: doubt concerning your right to view the Akasha. The Akasha is there to use just as we would use any research or reference tool. You have every right to the information contained within the Records. You helped put it there. Also, there is an agreement within the Collective Mind to share what is in the Records. This sharing is how we as Human Consciousness are able to evolve so quickly and dramatically.

Fear, judgment, and doubt truly muddy the ethers and foul the mind, keeping us from joy. This is an important lesson. One not easily learned.

What could stand in the way of accurately interpreting what I'm seeing in the Records?

It is difficult to interpret the symbols in the Akasha accurately through the veils of worldly concerns. If we inject the limiting view of right versus wrong into the Akashic Records or Book of Life, we will go for the personality's interpretations and miss what is actually being presented. The images in the Akasha are holographic, geometric shapes created by the energy of Unified thought fields. To interpret accurately it is important to set aside personal beliefs. While in the Records you are no longer an individual, you are a Seer.

How we interpret the symbols in the holographic forms of the Akasha reveals our level of understanding. That is to say, every serious student will improve with experience, and there are those who will immediately know all there is to know about the Akasha. As far as clients are concerned, what they do with the data disclosed through your interpretations reveals their intentions and level of understanding. You are not responsible for the use of the data.

Your End Most Lifetime

What if this is your last lifetime?

A female client came for a full day of sessions. The goal she wanted to achieve was to chronicle all her past lives. This was particularly interesting to me, mainly because most individuals only care to hear about one or two past lifetimes, then focus the rest of the reading time on what will happen in the future.

The first step was to map the boundaries of our inquiry, so I asked the Records to show the stats of her first incarnation. Images of Lemuria, some 25,400 years ago, flashed in front of me. She was in a male physical form, a technician of sorts and lived her existence in an area of land now submerged off the western coast of South America, off the coast of Peru.

I immediately checked her manifest orientations: her Soul was dominant to masculine. Her Will was dominant to healing. Her Purpose was dominant to power as a leader. Her Home Star was in the Vega system. Her entry into this system was through the Urantia Star, our Sun, and her exit would be through the planet Venus. The next boundary to establish was her final lifetime: The images surrounding me were only a few years away. This was to be her last incarnation. Feelings of Unity and images of Clarity filled my physical and Etheric bodies as I witnessed her final days.

It is impossible to describe her joy as we continued chronicling her incarnations. Names, dates, life's purposes, life's themes, Soul groups and mates, cultures and countries. She listened without judgment as we listed each life. The more information she had, the greater her joy. By the time we finished she was beaming. Just before she left she informed me that she had known since her childhood that this was to be her last time here on Earth. She was told so at the age of three by one of the Angels, the taller one, who use to stand at the foot of her bed while her body was sleeping. She went on to describe a life charmed by miracles and impeccable Human mentors. It was a joy to listen to her stories.

Seldom do I read for an individual who has such a profound final incarnation. Most ending lifetimes are filled with last minute business. Some are even more difficult than first incarnations.

After a while, a few hundred lifetimes or so, we all come to love this world with all its sensory tricks of illusory manifestation. Here we come to know ourselves. We've ripened, like a melon on a vine. This world is so familiar in our final lifetime, and at the same time it has become strange with all its struggles and hard edges. In our concluding lifetimes we are no longer a part of this world's systems of control, and yet, we are in the midst of its forces of manipulation. We have awakened; we are in the final moments of our realization, and know deep inside our Souls that our moment of Awakening is leading elsewhere. What a paradox; to love something so completely, and to want to be free of it at the same time. This is bittersweet: to be a guest in your own home, to be a passerby in your own neighborhood.

Concerning families and friends: individuals in their end lifetimes usually have difficulties relating to family members. They often choose dysfunctional families so that the bonds of affection are not too distracting. They also find it difficult to join groups. They have friends and family, and feel no sentimental attachments. In fact, most individuals in their end lives have a deep feeling, usually from very early on, that they are strangers within their own folds.

Career: usually, in the last lifetime there is no mission or great purpose to complete. The contribution has been made. This often leaves the individual with a sense of having little if anything to do, while having a great range of abilities. The good news is with this setup we can experiment with greater clarity than ever before.

Many individuals have the misconception that all concluding lifetimes are expressed in profound Spiritual Awareness, such as a Buddha, Mohammed, or a Christ. While this has been the case in some instances, it is certainly far from the rule. Usually an individual who chooses such a lifetime is in their bonus round as opposed to their final round. They do this out of enormous compassion for their fellow travelers. Here they are expressing as Ultimate Cause, Selfless Self to inspire others to Wakefulness. This type of lifetime is decided after the Earth career of an individual is over and is offered to the Collective Mind as a celebration of the Human experience.

Macro Awareness sees culminating lifetimes in the same light as the first. This is the Alpha and Omega in simultaneous expression. The seed and the tree are at the same time. There are no seasons. No progression. All exists as one.

Our Grand Finale

What happens when we are in the last moment of the last incarnation? What happens when we have evolved to the culminating moment?

When we are through with this world we begin a new series of adventures in another system; when we are through with all the systems, we express as God Creator. I'll try to put into words what is indicated in the Records: at our crescendo we move back into the void to our Source Star, turn inside out and manifest every thought, every feeling, every response, every performance, every moment ever encountered in our entire journey through Creation as individuated Awareness. Now, as Creator, we are the Source for those individuated forms. We are the medium. Every manifested form that moves out from within us proceeds on a journey to their Self-Realization. Our Creator journeyed through systems and incarnations gathering us as its impressions. In our Creator's final moment it turned itself inside out freeing every impression it had known into individuated entities – Us.

Are We Ready to Know

Are people in general ready to know about the Akashic Records? How can you be sure that someone might not get into the Records as a result of reading your book, or taking a seminar, then promptly misuse the ability. 'Isn't there some Spiritual preparation necessary to become a Seer?

Yes, to the first question. We live in a time when individuals want to know the Truth, their Truth. The Akasha is not concerned with how the information is used. We are judged by ourselves through our intentions. If our intention is to Wholeness, we will experience Unity whether we are working for what might be called the Light or the Darkness. Remember, there is no judgement in the data stored in the Records. The only time an individual sets conflict into motion is when they intentionally use the data in the Records to create conflict in others. The best that can be wished for them is that they meet themselves on the road. This is the best we can wish for anyone. Meeting yourself on the road ultimately leads to Self-Realization.

Devoting time to cultivating just the right students is a luxury this dimension no longer has to play with. We are truly at a time when we must act immediately. In the old days we had to walk a very straight and narrow path and were only selected after many years of observation. We were then given to the priesthood. The priests gave us many chores and tasks. We were watched at every moment for indications of our true nature. Only after we had shown certain qualities were we allowed initiation into greater understandings. Once in, we had to prove ourselves in the face of every imaginable form of distraction.

There were many rules that began with, "Thou shall not." Many of us have walked very straight and narrow lifetimes in preparation to being here and NOW. We are now in the age of, "Blessed are those." More preparation is unnecessary. We have come the distance and are ready to demonstrate in this New Age.

What if someone is not ready for certain pieces of information? What if having the information does more harm than good?

Many individuals will say just as they're leaving a private session, "Oh, I meant to ask about...Well, maybe next time." If an individual asks, they are ready to know. What an individual does with the information is completely up to them.

I offer an example. A businessman often called with an address he wanted me to check. He was in the salvage business and would buy burned out buildings from insurance companies that had to pay the claim against the damages. One time he called wanting a session about his personal life. I think he had waited to see my success rate with his business before he trusted me with his personal life. He asked about personal relationships. I gave him the information as I got it: "You'll be married within two years. She will have red hair, one hundred twenty pounds, five foot six. Her name is Carla. You will have a child right away and will love the child in a way unimaginable to you in your present state of mind."

He thought that was the funniest thing he had ever heard. He was a confirmed bachelor who played golf every chance he got. There was no place in his life for a permanent relationship, let alone a child. He never called about his business dealings after that. By his response, it could be said that he wasn't ready for the information about his personal life.

About two years after the reading I received a card inviting me to a wedding. A hand written note in the envelope said, "You were wrong, her name is Carlin."

Another example: a man came for a reading about his career. He was working in the production side of the film industry and wanted some reassurance that one day he'd work again. This is very common in the film industry – you work like a maniac for weeks on end for six months, then have a couple of years off. I looked, and sure enough he'd be employed shortly. But there was a problem. His health. It showed he had cancer in his lower abdomen and would quickly die unless he made some very dramatic changes to his way of being in the world.

I kept my agreement with myself regarding, "If the question remains unasked, I remain silent." The reading ended, and just as he was about to get up I asked, "What about your health? Do you have any questions about your health? "Funny," he said, "I've had something weird going on in my lower belly recently. Right here." He pointed to the exact spot where I was shown his cancer. I immediately responded with the information I had been given earlier. He sat back down. He said by my quick response I must have known prior to his asking. I told him I did. He got visibly angry. We talked. I explained my view of how this system of information works. He accepted my explanation. The next day he was at the doctor's.

A week later he called to say they had found even more, and that chemo and radiation treatments were to begin at once. He thanked me for being so straight forward with him. I offered to work with him on an ongoing basis as he unraveled what was eating away at his body. During the next several months, we uncovered a lot of resentment and pain at his failures. Interestingly, there was little celebrating at the success points in his life. When confronted with this, he explained that celebrating success was in bad taste. To say he revealed a strong dislike for arrogant and proud people would be an understatement. There was also another ingredient missing in his world – Gratitude. "I work very hard for every thing I have. No one has ever given me a thing. What's there to be grateful for, the fact that I had to work so hard?" It had almost sounded surreal the first time he had said it to me. By the time I had heard it several more times there was a stark reality about it.

The reading obviously revealed the disease, but did your subsequent work have a positive effect on the cancer? What happened to him?

We lost track of each other. He wanted something from me that I was unable to give him. I believe he felt that because I had been the one to reveal the disease, in some way it was mine as well as his. He wanted me to get rid of it for him. I am uninterested in being a hands on healer, and I am unlicensed as a gestalt therapist. When he finally realized I was unwilling to take responsibility for his disease, he stopped coming.

Can you always read from the Records? Is there a type of person you can not read for?

Yes, there are certain types I personally have trouble with. And, why program you with my stuff. I've also noticed that there seem to be certain days and phases of the moon when I'm unable to access the Records. Again, why program you with my stuff. I've already said too much. Now some of you will have a watchful eye on the phases of the moon. You will find a pattern with your own ability. Once this pattern is discovered, you can take those days off.

Guides

What about the guides often spoken of by channelers and psychics?

There are several types of guides. We are guides for each other. Many of us travel in Soul groups and often share the role of guide to our fellow Soul group travelers – you might incarnate several times with a cosmic associate, then sit one out and act as a guide to their next incarnation, or visa versa. Here you might be helping your friend with a very Earth oriented task, one that requires the touch of a guide who has been on Earth. This is the most common form of guide.

There are individuals who have completed their travels here on Earth, attained enlightenment, and now serve Human Consciousness as midway guides to the Angelic Realms. In using the term midway, I refer to those off the wheel of birth and death and yet to ascend out of the realms of Collective Consciousness. Many of these guides help in the transition from death to the state of existence between lives. They allow those leaving the Earth plane to project their greatest hopes or fears upon them, playing out the recently expired individual's ideas of God and Creation.

Then there are, of course, ascended Masters who guide the activities of groups of individuals seeking enlightenment. These individuals often incarnate as Spiritual leaders. Also, there are those Guides who emanate from the Angelic Realms. Here there are a great many varieties of Guides, from Archangels to Ascended Masters who have attained the Angelic kingdom, to beings who have never been in any manifest form, on any world.

I find it very reassuring that we have such a support network. It would be hard to imagine being here at the edge of Creation and relying solely on my fellow Earth bound travelers. Fear and greed have a way of altering personalities. This is a world of dualities where anything can, and will happen.

Explain more about us as guides for each other. I find that very exciting.

This information is easy to find in the Records, so I'll encourage you to find it for yourselves by revealing just enough to tantalize. Let's look at it from both the micro and macro points of view – everything is linear and everything is simultaneous. We guide each other, we also guide ourselves through the Over-Soul. One lifetime can be a guiding aspect to another. Example: in a past lifetime I was native to North America. This was prior to the Europeans. My mother died as I was born and my father was killed shortly after by wild animals. The tribe saw me as bad medicine. I was placed in the care of an uncle who happened to be the tribal shaman. I was given the worst of tasks to rid me of the Great Spirit's anger.

In that lifetime I learned a great deal about how the system of Creation works. In this current lifetime I have also studied with an Indian group. As soon as I heard the old language the memories of that particular past lifetime flooded my being, renewing my understanding of the natural order found in this world.

Soon after my first sweat lodge I awakened during an OBE and was inspiring a young man's personality-self in Holland. We were working on an idea he had for a communication device. His direct meditative experience of me was as his North American Indian guide. Several years later I was able to meet him through a mutual friend while on a business trip to Amsterdam.

There are many wonderful books about guides. The Angel books being published right now are great fun. In particular, Terry Lynn Taylor's Angel books are a delightful read.

Are guides transitory in our lives, depending on where we are and what our needs are?

Right. We draw on just the right help, at just the right moment. It is hard to go wrong with all the backup that's there waiting to lend a helping hand, or the occasional foot. The number of guides can change with the different cycles in our lives -- growth cycle, learning cycle, etc.. I once had a client who's guides changed with each new endeavor. The primary guides remained the same, but she would collect a new group of secondary guides to help out with the small details of running her rather complicated life.

Soul Groups

What about Soul groups?

The Books of Life in the Akashic Records are like concentric circles touching each other. Where one circle touches another you find a friend, or a Soul traveler. We tend to travel through Creation within certain families of Souls who are most like ourselves. More cosmic risks are taken and more integration is accomplished when we are with friends, Earthly or Cosmic.

What is the relationship of consciousness to Soul?

Consciousness is the center, the heart of the Soul.

Let's look at the individual Human Soul. The Soul serves to integrate each experience within the cellular (physical body) and noncellular minds (Etheric body). The miracle of this Collective synthesis is rather astounding when observed from the micro point of view. There are 144,000 impeccable cells that make up each individual Human Soul. These Soul cells exist within the physical body and reflect the nature of the Original 144,000 Christ Souls[5] that make up the foundation of Consciousness in this dimension. When a physical form is to be inhabited, these Soul cells lower their resonance and descend into the physical body through the chest at about the thymus gland. These Soul cells carry all the knowledge of each lifetime and distribute that knowledge evenly throughout the new cellular mind (physical body) at the time of their descent. The cells of the Human Soul are the channels through which response is then reported back to the Akasha. Etheric Soul groupings consist of any number of Human Souls and exist as a place of sharing, a sort of Cosmic family for individual Souls. The Soul group exists as an Etheric body for each individual Soul, with each individual Soul acting as a cell within that Etheric body. We feel truly abandoned in those lifetimes when we incarnate without members from our Soul Group.

Footnotes:

[1] I apologize for the lack of documentation of this study, and its results. This was related to me by a friend, then related to me again by a different friend who was unaware of the first friend. This second friend had even more of the data. I trust these individuals and have yet to find this study printed in any form, so I am flying blind here. If anyone has access to those who conducted this study, or a copy of the study itself, would you please inform me at the address in the back of the book. I have gone out on a limb using this information without hard data to back it up.

[2] The illustrations at the beginning of each chapter can act as mandalas when used in meditation.

[3] The *Course in Miracles* is a series of disassociation lessons that were dictated by the Holy Spirit through Helen Schucman. This is a very effective approach to unlearning misconceptions and superstitions.

[4] Investigate Rupert Sheldrake's works on morphogenetic fields, the invisible forces shaping Collective Consciousness.

[5] See page 8

The Ultimate Expression

You as a Source for this World

Most seekers are consciously traveling a path toward Enlightenment or Self-Realization. They see enlightenment as the culminating experience of their journey here on Mother Earth, and the first step toward becoming Cosmically Aware and One with the Creator. The beauty of the Spiritual journey as it is defined within this dimension is that it really does not matter whether an individual is a fundamentalist Christian who experiences God Creator as a personified savior, or the devotee of an enlightened guru who lives silently in a cave. The objective is the same – to live a harmonious life with Creation and to be a Source of comfort for others who seek shelter from the illusions of this world. No matter what our orientation to the realms of Spirit, we are all heading to one enormous Collective moment of Realization.[1]

As you begin your journey into the dimensions of the Akasha be aware that each moment you spend in this endeavor brings you closer to the Ultimate expression of Human Consciousness – To Know thy Self.

Enlightenment

To become illumined, or enlightened, is the very point of being here in this dimension. To steal a line from the movie, "*Dune*," "*The dreamer has awakened.*" Individuated self expression. Unified Mind. Self-Actualization. Self-Realization. Ultimate Cause – Selfless Self. The inner conflict is over, the critical voice is silent. You are no longer self conscious; you are no longer concerned about you; you are no longer the center of the universe; you are no longer insane with guilt, shame, jealousy, self pity, doubt, etc. You have come full circle and discovered the fine line between transcendence and psychosis. Your questions have suddenly turned into Answers. You Know who You are.

We come to the condition of enlightenment, or Self-Realization, by allowing Realization to happen within us. The majority of individuals I meet are hard pressed to imagine becoming enlightened. They feel it would take a miracle, or at the very least an intervention from the Holiest of Holies. Or, if not an intervention by God Creator, then an enormous effort and sacrifice on their part. In the past this has meant going off to a quiet place free from the distractions of the world. In the quiet, it is believed, we can unburden ourselves of the weight of civilization and social Consciousness. This is the image most people get when they hear the word enlightenment: isolation, aloneness, painfully simple meals, much meditation and introspection, little sleep, silence, giving up all the wonderful things they have come to love. No chocolate.

We have all heard the stories where the teacher gives the student something very dramatic to do: fast forty days and nights. Walk for one thousand consecutive days. Sit in a five foot circle deep in a cave with no food, no water, no clothes, no light, and no sleep for three days. What the teacher is doing is helping to create an awareness of Self within the activity. The details of the activity are unimportant. It's about who's doing the activity. The activity helps to bring you to Yourself.

The simple fact is, there is almost nothing we have to do to become enlightened. We are Spiritual Beings first, human beings second, so ability is hardly the question. Enlightenment is about willingness. The fact that many seekers have been taught that enlightenment is a process, as in precept upon precept, line upon line, only serves to insure the lineage of teachers. Also, this helps to reassure seekers that they are on their way to becoming enlightened by virtue of the fact that they have at least recognized the enlightened state in another being. A teacher's role is to encourage and to console the Whole Being of the seeker. Most of us seek to be consoled along the way by the idea that it is we who are really doing something to bring this desired state into our existence.

Interestingly, we are against enlightenment the moment we step out of our role as Sovereign Witness to this world. Every time we prefer duality over Unification; every time we look outside ourselves for the answers; every time we judge; every time we...well, we could spend all day just listing how it is that we fight against our moment of Awakening. The good news is, when we witness our exact moment of Awakening in the Records, the struggle of our negative egos against enlightenment is relinquished. This happens because the negative ego's illusory perception of reality is seen for what it is – a dream. The effect this realization has on our physical world Consciousness is a dissolving of immutable events and the collapsing of the illusion of time.

Finding our exact moment of Awakening can be a little tricky when we first get into the Records. The images may seem a little sketchy at first. Our negative egos will attempt to discourage us by insisting we are not capable of accessing the Records. In the Records we will come across past lifetimes in which we appear to be decidedly more enlightened than others. The truth is, we are constantly demonstrating degrees of enlightenment.

Micro view – we move in and out of enlightenment every day. Some days we have more enlightenment than others. There is one moment, in one lifetime, when a shift happens. This shift is unparalleled in all other lives. There is no other like it. Then the dreamer awakens. All the events already scheduled beyond the shift into enlightenment come crashing into the NOW of this awakening. Now we can Create. Before we only had the event/ response loop. Now we Create.

Macro view – time is simultaneous. We are already and forever Self-Realized, Ultimate Cause, Selfless Self. End of story, beginning of story. Beginning of story, end of story.

Several years back a friend discovered in the Records that her moment of enlightenment happened in a previous lifetime. My response was to remind her that incarnations are not linearly progressive in time and that her past life enlightenment might be where she was headed next. We both checked and found that indeed this was a past life enlightenment and that she had returned to be of service to humankind.

The idea of reincarnating in a relatively unenlightened state after reaching enlightenment was a new one on me. We both were extremely intrigued by this discovery, and spent much out-of-body time in the Records over a two month period searching through the finest details of the Records to get the answer. The Records showed this type of experience to be unusual in present history, but indicated it occurred with regularity prior to the split of Collective Consciousness in Atlantis. The reason for this was that after the division in Atlantis a Soul undergoing such an incarnation was too vulnerable to the violent polarized undercurrents within the Collective Mind. When a Soul is fully awakened within the physical body, the personality of that individual becomes completely innocent, leaving it unprotected and extremely subject to the thoughts and feelings of others. This is one reason why there have been a few who have been ready to incarnate after fully awakening. The Records also showed that because of their profound sensitivity many of the individuals were used by their cultures as mind readers, clairvoyants, mystics or hands-on healers. In this age of broadcast communications these individuals not only experience the influences of other individuals, they are also bombarded with electromagnetic transmissions of microwave and radio wave frequencies.

It indicated in the Records that individuals would undergo such a journey to move into the level of "Love as Existence." Their complete vulnerability and their innocence was meant to inspire; to celebrate Human Consciousness; to help guide others to Completion. Once you make the Holy Shift, you are never the same. Even if you choose to come back unaware of yourself, you would appear as a bright light to others. Others will see you as an example of how to Be.

There are several wonderful examples in the Records of individuals who have returned under these circumstances. These individuals are very passionate about the Human experience and it shows in the Records that they are almost always healers. There have been accounts of those who have become enlightened, incarnated in the next lifetime unenlightened, only to gain enlightenment once again. At this point these individuals are considered by those in the realms of Spirit as co-Creators. Nothing, but nothing is left unfinished. There are no more events perfectly scheduled to help bring them to enlightenment. They have arrived. Now all the energy they were using to "figure it out" is directed toward spontaneous Creativity. When we become enlightened we are in fact Conscious Creators. All the energy devoted to "doing" enlightenment prior to Self-Realization is now used to Create through our "Being." When we are Self-Realized, we are Awakened from the dream of self-importance and begin to fully Create from Selflessness. In Self-Realization we are no longer the center of the universe.

What I mean by the statement that we are no longer the center of the universe is, we no longer define the world around us through our doubts and concerns, or by past events or imagined future moments that have us responding in one way or another.

Prior to enlightenment, in the self important human, there is a need to be right, i.e. wear the right clothes, say the right words, live in the right house, be in the right place at the right time. If We, the Collective Mind, are indeed the Creator of anything, it is the need to be right. We equate being right with being accepted, validated and loved. To be right is to be loved. This is self-importance.

Self-Awareness, Self-Realization is to BE love, acceptance and validation. In this state we Create. Prior to this we replicate the old. Nothing new is created. On this side of enlightenment response brings outcomes, which in turn attract circumstances. Many have the belief that circumstances create us. Circumstances reveal us. We are in no way at the mercy of circumstantial influence, unless, of course, we want to be. And that is truly the question.

As for social consciousness treating us differently, it is inevitable. As an Awakened individual we are no longer a part of the Collective Mind and its subset, social consciousness. If we are not with them, many will see us as being against them. We will become the enemy to some and a bright light to others. Look at the past, from the stoic philosophers to Jeshua Ben Joseph, from the prophets of the Old Testament to the oracles of Salem, Massachusetts.

Unity

In the exact moment of Self-Realization there is a sudden, unstoppable Unity. Enlightenment brings Unity. Unity is our natural state of Being, a condition brought about through the closing of the gap between polar opposites, such as thought and feeling, event and response.

All the ideas and corresponding behaviors that exist in our mind/body are there as a result of our sensory encounters (response) with external happenings (events). In our natural state, when we are physically, emotionally and mentally balanced, the integration of sensory data lags behind the event only by a minutely discernible measure. In this state, event and response, thought and feeling, doing and being are experienced as simultaneous. This is an individual who is unaware of the concept of self consciousness; unsophisticated to the nth degree. This is the state of mind that is Unified Self-Expression playing in the manifest world. Life is pretty simple to these individuals – event/response, thought/feeling, doing/being, male/female, Mystery/Mastery. Unity.

As was stated before – we come into this dimension to experience separation. As we experience this duality we become bundles of stress waiting to explode back into Unity, into Authenticity. Pressure builds from deep within urging us to make this jump back to Unity. And with each moment, with each lifetime, we feel ourselves getting closer and closer. The light at the end of the tunnel dimly winks at us through the pollution of our misunderstandings about the nature of duality. After we have had our fill of the push and pull, the urge to unify body with mind, thought with feeling, male with female moves through us like a fifteen point earthquake.

Our current world condition is actually bringing us, the Collective Mind, closer to Unification. When we are under stress the minuscule gap between event and response widens, causing us to become painfully aware of the nature of our condition. This is the good news and the bad news.

The bad news first: on Earth we become overwhelmed by the amount of information wanting to be integrated; the more externally oriented we become the more aware we are of the gap existing between thought and feeling, event and response, desire and manifest form. For the majority this exacerbates their condition until they find themselves unable to fully respond to anything due to the overwhelm. Some learn how to use the energy of confusion and indecision to broaden their response. Others simply crumble under the seeming weight and go numb. They follow whatever idea seems to support their general belief system, and as long as those leading the way deliver comfort and promises of a brighter tomorrow, they remain asleep.

The good news: we need this angst. It is in those profound moments of overwhelm that we decide to return home to non-duality. In his book, "*Hidden Journey*," Andrew Harvey writes, *"the soul has a power to transform every horror into bliss and that horror is the deepest friend of the soul because it compels it to find this power. It is with this power that the transformation will be done."* (p. 165)

Prior to enlightenment, most individuals move between pleasure and pain. They integrate their findings as they recover from the pain, then move to a slightly higher level and repeat the cycle. In this approach a great deal of energy is spent on the manifesting forms of pleasure and pain, success and failure. This dual experience is important because one side of the equation validates the other side. In this state of being, validation and the need to be right rule with a vengeance.

After Enlightenment, the individual moves from peak experience to peak experience. Pleasure and pain take a formless appearance because the focus of the journey is Cause, instead of cause then effect. As Sovereign Cause, we are uninterested in looking back to see the effect. Our focus moves from the Creative to Creative; from Everlasting unto Everlasting. There is no "How am I doing" in mind. No game is being played. Just Creation.

For those of you who want to know how to tell whether or not you are operating out of Unified Mind, take an inventory of your life. When what you have matches what you want, you are Unified Mind. When desire is no longer present, then you are Unified.

Ultimate Cause, Selfless Self

While most enlightened individuals express Unity through Selflessness, many have yet to consistently express Consciousness as Ultimate Cause. In the beginning stages of enlightenment most individuals are captivated by the effects of being Self-Realized. This captivation allows for external influences, such as adoration, to distort the sovereignty of the enlightened state. It is when we move through enlightenment (Ultimate Cause) into mastership (Selfless Self) that we are no longer subject to any external influences or distortion of reality.

Interestingly, the you who desires to experience yourself as Ultimate Cause, Selfless Self will be unaware of the moment You become Selfless Self. Others will say you have become enlightened, then Master. You will be, for the most part, unaware of your state of Being. True paradox.

†Σ†

Footnotes:

[1] The Akashic Records show this Collective moment to be in the very near future between the years 1997 and 2001, with the year 2026 as the culminating Unification of Human Consciousness, and the beginning of the 1,000 years of peace. The lack of clarity in interpreting the symbols of the exact timing stems from the symbols themselves. Instead of the dates being presented in modern numerical forms, they are depicted in what appear to be ancient glyphs. You can get more information about this subject from the Records by asking for all data on the Twelve Days of Light. See footnotes on page 98.

Metaphysically Speaking

Discoveries Within the Akashic Records

Entry into the Records requires very little in the way of New Age metaphysical understandings. In fact, it is easier to enter and interpret information from the Records when we have unlearned most of the concepts we believe are Universal Truths. Why is this? Most of those who enter the Records quickly realize a number of the 'Cosmic Laws' they have used as guidelines to Self-Realization are little more than notions born out of our need to define our role here.

The ideas brought forward in this section are merely intended as a point of reference to the understandings found within the Records. It is not necessary to adopt these concepts as a guiding philosophy to gain entry into the Akasha. However, our beliefs about Creation form our ability to interpret what we experience in the physical world, as well as in the Akashic Records.

It is from this point of view that the following conversations are offered.

ΣΣΣΣΣΣΣΣΣΣΣΣΣΣΣΣΣΣΣΣΣΣΣΣΣ

Original Thoughts

You have said that we do not have thoughts, but experience thoughts much in the way a radio picks up radio waves. If this is true, while we are tuned to a particular band do we use those thought waves, or do they control us? I ask this because my thoughts feel very deliberate, yet it feels that I have little control as to what I'm thinking.

We, as Awareness, are not at the mercy of bands of thought energy. However, we experience any given range of thoughts because we have been programmed to do so through the Collective Mind, genetics, instinctual relationships, extended families, environments, cultures, and even the Consciousness of the planet we so lovingly call home. By virtue of this arrangement we sometimes feel at the mercy of certain thought patterns. This changes when we awaken to the knowing that we, as Spiritual Beings, are beyond these influences. Once awakened we, as Sovereign Beings, have the ability to go beyond these Collectively imposed limitations and, as such, are able to entertain certain thoughts without being in their control. We are in the world, not of the world.

Thought energy behaves in the same manner as Light energy. It exists both as waves and particles. Waves, in that we can experience Whole concepts; particles, in that we can attune to a singular aspect of any Whole thought. Wave is macro – everything exists simultaneously. Particle is micro – Consciousness progresses along predetermined paths, evolving to greater circles of influence, as it analyzes the many different layers of thought energy stimulated by the physical senses.

Let's look at a few examples of thought existing as a wave. Television was simultaneously developed by several different individuals, each unaware of the other's work. Radio was the same; computers the same; medical advancements the same. How is it all these individuals had the same thoughts unified with the exact same feelings that led to the simultaneous discovery and manifestation of these inventions?

On the other hand, the development of religions has been progressive. Here we have thought energy as a particle with each subsequent ritual and concept building on the last, all progressing toward a monolithic God. While it's true that we have more than one religion, it is also true that each religion has progressed from earlier concepts of God. Religions seldom take great leaps in new directions.

Another example of thought energy existing as a wave or field is telepathy. How is mental telepathy possible? Individuals of a certain mindset are attuned to one another through pre-determined waves of thought energy. The pre-determined pattern of these waves might be genetically based, culturally founded or Soul Group in origin. This pre-determined quality is experienced largely as subconscious impulses and allows individual Consciousness to manipulate the particles of energy existing within a particular field of thought without having to "think" about it. This happens much the same way the vibration of our voices effects the particles found within the atmosphere of our planet. Many of us do this naturally and find ourselves in relationships with others who communicate in the same manner. This is evidenced in cultural or racial groupings. Without this telepathic link there can be great difficulty in one group fully understanding the other. When we encounter others with whom we cannot share this type of communication we feel immediate conflict. The feelings of polarity that follow are at the base of our instant likes and dislikes, or biases.

Much of our experience of duality, and the ensuing conflict, is a result of segments or bands of thought energy touching one another within our Consciousness. When we look at Light energy we can observe a rainbow effect of colors. Where red touches blue we observe purple. Where yellow blends with blue we see green. Unfortunately, this same phenomenon does not happen with bands of thought energy. If it did, we would experience the blending of thought energy as harmonic geometric forms each expressing qualities of the other.

Unfortunately, thought energy is not only separated into distinctly different bands, each band has its own blend of polar opposites. One example might be: greed at one end of a band within the spectrum available to Human Consciousness; gratitude at the other end of the same band. Where these polar aspects touch within the band a sense of inner conflict arises within the individual's Consciousness. One minute the individual is tightening his hand, hoarding, the next finds him emptying his wallet. In the next moment he is admonishing himself for being so generous. Passive aggressive behavior is often the result when an individual swings between the polar aspects of a particular band of thought energy.

Other examples: wellness is one end of a particular band, illness is the other end. Peace at one end, war at the other.

The entire range of thought energy, taking in all dimensions of time and space, including those dimensions unrelated to Human Consciousness, is enormously vast.

In the Mystical experience you command the full range of each different band of thought energy. This is macro thought. Science and religion are micro. Science wants to examine each and every particle of thought very closely to prove its position or hypothesis. Main stream religions exaggerate the existence of an evil force to prove their righteousness. Interestingly, the mystics of four thousand years ago knew that matter is all comprised of the same basic substance, and that God Creator is indifferent to our concepts of good and evil. These mystics were also aware of the greater cycles that influence the Collective Mind of Human Consciousness.

There is an energetic influence in Creation which, for the most part, cannot be detected by science; mainly because the instruments science relies on are designed to detect relatively gross forms of energy. This influence emanates as waves of thought energy from the very center of all Creation and is experienced by Human Consciousness as Ages of Enlightenment. If you were an archeologist you would be able to produce a rough map of the intervals and intensity of these rings by the many sudden appearances then disappearances of the Earth's historical civilizations.

Center of Creation

How do these bands of thought energy help to create the different ages of enlightenment?

Imagine a point so small it compares to the Whole of Creation as one nanosecond compares to a trillion years. This is the exact moment of Creation, the Center of all that Is. Emanating from this unknowable place is the very energy that brings Consciousness to Awareness then manifest form. We experience this energy differently as we evolve through matter. In the beginning there was a simple urging of cells to join. Now that we are reasonably advanced organisms, the energy once experienced as a primal urge is, on the most part, encountered as creative reason. Each time a new wave from the first moment moves through Human Consciousness we reinvent the wheel, or anything else that might get in our way. (See the Twelve Days of Light information in the footnotes on page 98)

Ask yourself: why does history show the rise and fall of civilizations and cultures? Once a technology is known, why does a period of intellectual darkness follow? How do we explain the wonders of Mesopotamian, Menonian, Greek, Egyptian and Roman technology, followed by the Dark Ages filled with profound superstitions?

As each wave passes, those who GET IT lead an age of innovation that may span several lifetimes. After they become realized through their discoveries, they consciously move off the wheel of birth and death. This is when the new technologies become misunderstood and fall to neglect. This is because those who innovated and fully understood are no longer incarnating to be custodians or reinventors of their past discoveries. Those who GET IT attain Self-Realization and move on to other systems of reality more in keeping with their new Awareness of reality. Those left behind lack the wisdom to use what was left by those who had attained.

What do those who 'get it,' get?

They get that thought (Consciousness, vision) and feeling (energy, matter) are the same - identical in every way, except to the five senses. They also get that the waves of energy moving from the center of Creation amplify this relationship, making it easier at different intervals to manifest each thought instantaneously into matter. At the exact center of each of these bands is a defined period in which every thought is made manifest, instantly. It is at such intervals that those who are Aware of the reality of Consciousness and energy make their transition from this dimensional reality. We entered such a wave about 496 years.

Do those who attain always leave, or do some stay behind to help?

There are those who are sensitive enough to feel the leading edge of each new wave long before the majority of individuals feel its effect. These innovators lead humanity through each subsequent wave by experiencing Consciousness and energy as they truly are – Unified. They incarnate during those times when their creations within the energy are most likely to be understood by the greatest number of individuals. Are they always conscious of their role? No. Few who have been born to the mystical path have actually been leaders.[1] Many Human leaders, however, have relied heavily on the visions and manifest forms conjured by mystics.

Now, there are many "things" influencing our ability to intuit the subtle energies of those waves emanating from the center of Creation, the least of which is our biochemistry. Teachers of the esoteric have given many formulas for attuning to desired thought patterns by altering our body's chemical makeup. They have offered every possible combination of diet, meditation, ritual and exercise. The formulas have been endless. Some have done nothing more than made the participant ill, while others have proved deadly. And there have been those that have worked. Once the proper chemistry is achieved, these desired thought patterns, each with their many manifested forms, quicken the integration of thought with feeling to bring about Conscious performance. Enlightened teachers know that Conscious performance leads to the moment of self as Ultimate Cause, Selfless Self. Ultimate Cause, Selfless Self imitates THE beginning moment, the Center of Creation. Our Teachers know we, as Conscious Awareness, are potential beginning moments, just like THE beginning moment.

The Innocent

What about those who are even less knowing than myself? If every thought is made manifest, won't they be hurt by their self destructive ideas? Who will see to them during the next wave of energy from the center of Creation? Who protects the truly innocent, those unable to fend for themselves?

The truly innocent need not be worried. We are responsible for each other in that we are here to support each other as we move from experience to experience and then finally to Self-Realization. Everyone who advances here does so to experience themselves in this realm of manifest form. We want this experience with all its many ups and downs, its dualities. This vulnerability is alchemical. Here we can feel isolated, alone, even with our Soul Group. Here we are vulnerable. Here we can experience our greatest fear and our greatest glory. When a Soul is new to this place it usually numbers among the downtrodden. Those who are of greater experience will be urged to offer a compassionate hand. Those who are more Spiritually knowing will give comfort by offering food for the heart and mind, instead of protection for the body. The more Knowing an individual is, the more he integrates compassion with wisdom. It is seldom a wise move to interfere with the journey of another.

Do the souls that stay to help after they have gotten it, do so because they somehow feel responsible toward humanity?

No. If they have awakened to their place within Creation, the concept of responsibility would have been integrated into their Being at the moment of Unification. Responsibility has little to do with the Self-Realized. If one of these Beings remains, it is out of their demonstration of Love as Nurturing, or Love as Existence. Love expressed as Giving might also be a motive.

The concept of responsibility has no value to anyone at any level of Creation. Responsibility is an illusion. Most of the world is focused on who is to be held responsible. How can we know who's responsible. It is impossible.

Morality

If no one's responsible, how do we keep social order? If doing what's right isn't the point, then are we to focus on what's appropriate?

Focus on what is needed in the moment to bring clarity to everyone involved and to be a Source for others' experience of this realm. This is the difference between those who truly help, and those who get in the way.

Here's a Hindi story that illustrates the difference between doing what is "right" and what is needed:

A wonderful family lived in a rural village in southern India. This family had been blessed with caring and respectful children. The oldest child was a girl, plain and rather large. Despite her lack of physical beauty, she finally met a young man and was married. Everyone, relatives and towns people alike, was truly happy for them. Immediately they began to plan their family. A year passed, then two and the newlyweds had not conceived. Taking the advice of her parents, they went to the family doctor to see if there was something he could recommend. His suggestions did not produce results. The young woman became totally dismayed. In her unhappiness she began to eat even larger amounts of food. She was soon almost twice as large as when she had married.

They went to more doctors. Always the results were the same; instead of becoming pregnant, she would gain more weight. Finally they decided to see the village shaman. They explained what had been happening since their marriage and asked for his advice. He promptly told them having a child didn't matter because her life was almost over and that she was to die shortly. The young couple jumped up from the floor of the shaman's hut and ran crying back toward the village.

During the months that followed, the young wife remained locked in her room and would not come out for even her husband. Her mother and father were in mourning. The whole town fell into dismay. The well wishers of the couple became very angry with the shaman for his unwise remarks and would often throw rocks at his house as they passed to and from the village. The shaman understood their need to blame.

Finally, after months of isolation, the wife emerged from her death room. She was barely recognizable. Standing before him, the husband saw a stunning beauty, full of life. The two spent the next several weeks together, and after a month announced they were pregnant. It was difficult for anyone to really be happy because of the verdict the shaman had placed on the girl's life.

The parents of the young couple became more and more confused by the change in fortune and went to the shaman for an explanation. Was their present happiness to be short lived? Why would the powers that Be, be so cruel as to take her life now that she was pregnant? There were so many questions. They needed to know.

Prior to this time the wise man had a reputation for always telling the truth, and for always being right. What had happened? If he was wrong about her pregnancy, could he also be wrong about her death? The whole village, with the newly pregnant couple out in front, descended upon the shaman's hut. There was much shouting between those who believed in the sentence of death and those who said there must be more to this than meets the eye. After a short while the crowd settled down and the shaman emerged from his dwelling.

"This young couple came wanting to know what they needed to do to have a child," the shaman began, "Through my compassion for this woman and her husband, I gave the answer that would allow them to be with child." The crowd look puzzled, then someone shouted, "You told her not to worry about children because her life was almost over and she would surely die. You didn't help them conceive the child she now carries. How can you claim credit for their good fortune?" shouted an angry man.

The crowd hushed as the wise man began to speak. "This young couple told me of their problem, I immediately saw the reason for her infertility. She was too fat. The fat in her body was blocking conception. Just as all of you, I have known this child all her life," the shaman said pointing to the newly slimmed bride. "Now I have a question for you, is she a disciplined, or an undisciplined person?"

A heated discussion broke out amongst the villagers, then came the reply, "She is basically a lazy person," one man said with an apologetic shrug toward the father. The father's look was one of agreement.

"What does this have to do with your causing so much grief upon this family?" a lady asked from the back of the crowd.

"The other doctors had told her to lose weight, but she didn't," accused the shaman. "I knew they wanted a child with all their hearts. I also knew she would place her life in peril if she got pregnant with all her fat. I told her she was to die knowing the shock would take her into seclusion, and away from the eating habits that were keeping her from her heart's desire."

"But you told a lie! You have never told a lie. We all thought she was doomed," the father shouted angrily. "How is it that you told a lie this time?"

"I give those who come to me what they ask. These young people wanted to become parents. I gave them what they asked." The old man turned and disappeared into his hut.

The villagers argued about the rightness of the old man's gift to the couple long after the couple's first born had children of her own.

In this case, the wise man knew the couple was destined to have children, he probably saw this as a series of immutable events in their future. He also must have looked ahead and discovered his role in their lives – to help them at precisely the right moment. The shaman was effective in this case because of his reputation for always telling the truth and because he was not interested in the approval of the village.

Predestination

It sounds like you are saying that everything is known from the beginning.

I'm saying everything is known from the macro view of simultaneous existence. Everything: every molecule, every parallel dimension, every form, every element. Every possible Consciousness form, every event that would ever happen in every parallel dimension. Every thought. There is nothing that need be added to creation from the very first moment. Except, of course, our response. The only changeable element that exists anywhere in creation is our response to all the existing events within dimensional realities. By virtue of this it could be said that our response is the unknown. Everything else is known. We give the missing ingredient to Creation. We are the link between the Creator and the Creation, we are the senses of the Creator responding to its creativity. Everything else is known.

Everything. Then predestination is real? What about cause and effect?

Yes, predestination is real in the macro simultaneous time, but not in the micro sense of delineated time/space. Predestination is real when we speak in terms of the events, as opposed to response. We prearranged all the events of each lifetime before incarnating. We do this to insure Self-Realization. In each moment of every lifetime we have placed the possibility for enlightenment or death. This may help: think of the events we have scheduled for this lifetime as rides in an amusement park that has a front and back gate. This is the only hitch – our amusement park is to be experienced in a certain order. We can opt to experience each ride any number of times. The initial order of the rides is the only important thing. We can go back and reexperience previous rides in random order, but we can only progress to the next ride when each aspect of the previous ride is fully experienced and understood. Another thing. The rides are not necessarily progressive from the front of the park to back. The first ride might be in the middle of your park and the next ride could be located at the front gate.

All the rides pre-exist, each one offering a theme; each one promising a different experience; each one leading to greater understanding and illumination. Before our presence, the rides lack the dimension of response. We as response bring life to each ride.

At first we might feel fear at the prospect of some rides. And trying to decide whether or when we will actually get on the ride only postpones the moment of riding, not the inevitability. Once on the ride we may have our fears confirmed or denied. As we experience the same or similar rides over and over again, we begin to fully understand the significance of each ride and the importance of their sequence in our journey.

I like this approach. It takes away a lot of the blame and responsibility of being here if everything is preordained and response is all we are. Does this mean I do not have to plan my future?

Ask yourself. Are you the type of being that naturally enjoys planning for coming events? If the answer is yes, then you will plan for coming events. You will take the time and energy to project the probabilities you can imagine for yourself. This helps you to define what is possible and also allows you a greater response when an event arrives at your doorstep, because you have looked at all the options and believe you have chosen the "right" path. For you, the best way to take advantage of an opportunity is to be prepared. For someone else it is not the best path. On this side of enlightenment it is irrelevant whether you believe your efforts have brought an event into reality or that the event pre-existed. You will live out your destiny. The trick is knowing that destiny.

One way to journey through life is to allow the events to unfold. Another is to look after the details. In other words, we can macro manage, or micro manage. One is visionary/ intuitive; the other sensory/feeling. There are those who have found a healthy blend of western and eastern styles and include the best of both approaches.

Events

You speak so often of event and response. These elements seem fundamental to your hypothesis of our role in Creation. How exactly do you define event?

We could look to Webster's for a common answer such as "a consequence, a result; an outcome. That which comes, arrives, or happens, especially an incident of importance; as in, the course of events. Any one of a series of items in a program, as in, the next event is..."

The macro point of view terms event as that which captures Awareness. By this definition, everything stimulating your senses is an event. This is what the Masters have been telling us forever: Everything, every moment is a grand event absolutely important to our existence.

The micro describes events as individual moments of interaction between Consciousness and energy strung together in a linear construct where each succeeding moment is greater than the last. This sounds like the macro definition, but differs in an important way: this definition implies movement, or integration of data, and therefore an awareness of "past" events.

For our purposes the definition of event as it relates to Human Consciousness is: performances or encounters whether incited by the individual or others, that so capture individual or Collective Awareness as to solicit response. Without Awareness no events exist for Consciousness. In other words, no response, no event.

Within the confines of this definition there are two distinctly different types of events – immutable events placed by an individual into his stream of Consciousness prior to incarnating, and changeable events determined by an individual's response to the immutable events. As you can imagine, most of us are primarily concerned with the immutable events. These moments do not have to involve others in this dimension, they may be solitary in nature and other worldly oriented. There is one thing you can count on with regards to these events; their purpose is to enliven our minds and bodies to the reality of who we are. Often immutable events demand that we stretch our Awareness to include entirely different levels of response.

Then there are the events that are shaped by our response to the big events. These "lesser" events fill in the time/space between the main events and give a certain quality and texture to our reality. These types of minor events often appear as "choices" but are really ripple like responses formed by our perceptions of the main events in our lives.

So the important events are fixed?

Important only in that they are fixed moments of awakening. We place immutable events on our pathway to awaken ourselves, or at the very least, to allow us a course correction. This usually means an attitude adjustment. Our response to these fixed events generates changeable events that fill in the gap between fixed events. Our response to immutable events shapes the outcomes, which in turn attracts certain circumstances. Circumstances determine the level of expectation. Expectation generates the deep emotions of sorrow and joy. When we drop fear and survival as motivators, we enlarge our response. Enlarge our range of response, and we enlarge outcomes and circumstances. Enlarge the circumstances and expectations become less. Less expectation, more contentment. More contentment, greater Self-Realization.

I feel somewhat impotent, thinking every major event is locked into place. Can we ever ask the powers that be to change these types of events? Is there a way to intercede on the behalf of others? Surely prayers must work.

Events do not have the power to determine outcomes. Events are powerless. Your response to immutable events determines the outcomes and therefore your circumstances. Example: when my oldest daughter was thirteen I looked into the records and saw that she was going to be in a very serious car accident. You can imagine my immediate response. I wanted to shield and protect her. I asked her how she would feel if she saw a young lady such as herself confined to a wheel chair for the rest of her life. She revealed she had often thought that even though it looked difficult to be in a wheelchair, it might in some ways be easier for someone in that condition. At least they didn't have to be responsible and think of all the pity they would get from others.

During the time between the reading and getting her license, we worked together to unravel her emotional connection between being pitied and being loved. We also explored the deeper meaning of being responsible to one's self. It was also discovered during this time that she was very shy and was having a problem meeting boys. This new information, and the pre-knowledge of the accident, tugged at my heart strings. Both my daughters are very bright and pretty. I wanted them to have an effortless life as teenagers; mainly because mine was so difficult. I had been painfully shy as a young adult and spent most of my time alone.

The time had arrived for the inevitable auto. I had promised both girls a car when they turned sixteen. What to do? A sensible, Sherman tank of a thing, or something that would turn the heads of young men everywhere. I bought a powder blue MG convertible. Something to match her eyes. I knew in my heart she had worked out the emotional energy around self pity and personal responsibility, and that when the accident happened she would be okay. I got the car when she was fifteen and drove it for a year as I restored it.

My wife, Kathleen, and I were preparing to go on our honeymoon. We were living in Los Angeles, and driving up the coast to my home town seemed like a natural for an easy long weekend. Late the night before we were to leave the phone rang.

"I'm calling from the hospital," Jennifer said as I answered the phone. "I'm okay. And my boyfriend Keith is okay. The car flipped end over end down an embankment, ended up on the rocks in the Chattahoochee River, upside down on it's roof. Most of the glass exploded out of it. We had to swim out of the car. Keith and I have only a few cuts and one bruise each." I just listened as she talked. It was hard to speak. The event I had dreaded for so long had come to pass.

The Records had shown the highest possible outcome if Jennifer had entered the accident with her self-pity and responsibility issues still unresolved. She had worked hard to expand her perceptions of what it meant to be fully responsible, and had overcome feelings of self-pity by allowing someone she loved to love her. The immutable happened, the outcome was different because she had learned prior to the event what would have been learned as a result of the event. Had she remained in the mindset that was present at the time of the reading she would have followed the highest outcome as it was shown in the Akasha.

After Kathleen and I returned from our trip, Jennifer called and related more of her experience of the accident. "I knew it was going to happen that day. Keith and I left a party, heading back to school, I knew this was it. I saw the curve and told Keith to slow down. I felt tingly and warm inside and knew we'd be okay. Just as we got to the corner everything started to happen in slow motion. When the car was tumbling, it was like the car was spinning around me. Then it was over with. The car was filling up with water as we kicked what was left of the windows out. Keith and I stood on the bank of the river just holding each other. The car was totaled. I'm glad we weren't in the MG. And I was really very thankful that I knew about it beforehand."

I have often heard someone describing an accident as happening in slow motion. What's the metaphysical reason?

In the moment of the accident we are in peril. Our senses are extremely acute because we are wide awake, aware of every detail. This is how animals experience reality. This is how we experienced this world when we were really just surviving. Imminent danger brings the normally uninterested witness to the foreground. Most individuals find it difficult to have a point of reference for this type of acuity, so it seems odd. Here's another point: when we are in fight or flight the slow motion effect is absent because we are in action, moving with the unfolding picture. In the car we are strapped into one position and therefore forced into the attitude of witness. Imagine living every moment of every day from this role as observer. Very intense.

What about those who can't remember anything. And not just during the accident, but for days before and afterwards.

There can be many different physical and emotional reasons for this. The metaphysical reason is simply the event is too confrontational to allow the memory. Also, denial of our role in the drama prevents as much of the memory as is necessary.

Is the information they cannot remember stored in the records?

Yes, in cellular memory as well as Akashic. This is one of the benefits of being able to view the Akasha. I've helped many people restore memory lost to traumatic events such as accidents and abuse.

Response

What is response?

Response is the integration of information received through the senses when an event is encountered by our Awareness. Here is where the phenomenon of memory is assembled. It is an electrical dance of energy within the physical substance of our bodies, and most profoundly our brains. Response is our internal reply to the call of the external wild. Micro:

event is the question, response is the answer. Macro: event is the answer, response is the question.

Isn't the world an out picturing of what is inside our being? You're saying 'all we are is response.' Don't we create anything in our lives?

From this side of enlightenment the world is a mirror in which we see ourselves. In that sense it can be argued the world and all within is an out picturing of our inner self. This is a great tool for exploring yourself, investigating just who it is that you are.

In our present condition we are <u>in</u> the drama and <u>of</u> the drama. As such, we are learning how to manipulate the elements of the play to insure desirable outcomes. We see that if we respond this way certain outcomes happen and when we react that way other outcomes happen. We are simply memorizing response and outcome patterns to insure success at playing the game dictated by cultural norms. This is hardly us as a Creative force. It could be argued that an artist creates. This process is more of a commentary on what already exists through the perceptions of the artist rather than an act of creativity.

Free Will

What is the difference between response and free will?

In this world the idea of free will implies we are consciously directing the dynamic conditions behind the formation of the events. We are not the conscious force behind the events of this world; we are the response to them. Response attracts outcomes which unfold circumstances. All we are doing is responding. As response, it is unimportant to figure out each and every detail of the events. That is actually the good news. As fully present response, we are learning to be Creator. On this side of enlightenment we remain unaware of all that is needed within Consciousness to Create. Remaining fully present as each moment unfolds allows us to become Realized. Once Realized, we will have integrated the fullness of our response with our willingness to experience every aspect, every particle of our being as individuated Conscious Awareness. Once this happens we are consciously directing the dynamic conditions behind the events of this world as they relate to us.

So we don't get to create goals and then finish those goals?

We are taught to be willful is to succeed. To succeed is to be loved or validated. Everyone loves a winner. Control is success. We are taught to set goals and to focus our efforts toward the completion of those goals. We believe we are in control because it <u>seems</u> we are <u>creating</u> events and outcomes. The more successful we are, the more firm our belief in a system that has us as the ones creating all the success. If you examine the human experience closely, you will more than likely agree with the mystics of all ages: we are response, the rest is simple attraction. The greater our range of response, the greater our range of outcomes and circumstances. I know individuals who are successful in spite of themselves. Individuals who are in every way successful in business and, according to the experts, have done <u>everything</u> wrong. How can it be that someone could be successful in this way? The formula should work the same for everyone.

What about material success? Are you saying we have little to say about whether we succeed or not?

If it is for you to succeed in this current life, you will. Usually, if you are setting the goals necessary to become a millionaire, it is because you are being precognitive about future events. Most successful CEOs and entrepreneurs will tell you of a moment in their lives when they were forced back from micro managing the front lines. They will refer to this as a turning point, because it changed their ability to respond more fully to their business. When they stepped back from controlling the details, they enlarged their response. The new boundaries afforded by a larger response give them even more of the big picture. Having more of the big picture allows them to envision the next wave of opportunity for themselves and their organizations. This provides an enlarged discovery period and insures their move from opportunity to opportunity, instead of from pain to pain.

So what's the point of being here if we aren't creating our own lives?

There is only one element found in every religion, the only element common to all: KNOW THYSELF. The purpose of being here is to move through the different layers of self expression to Self-Realization.

What is the largest response?

Gratitude is the highest response known in Human Consciousness. This is the mystics path. This is the very narrow path often spoken of by the teachers of long ago.

Choice

Aren't choice and response really just the same thing?

Actually, response is who we are. Many have been taught to believe all we have and all we are is one long series of choices. Choice is flat, one dimensional. Response is multidimensional. Choices can be rehearsed. We are unable to rehearse response. Response is spontaneous, always. Choice is linear. Choices can be memorized. Response is never exactly the same. There is also the argument that if we look back over time a pattern of response shows itself. Patterns are an observable phenomenon in the nature of Human Consciousness, as in all of Creation. The fact that a pattern exists simply means we are rhythmic.

Response is original, authentic. Choice is learned.

We are our responses. If we want to know who someone is, we can watch them respond for a period of time. If we want to know who we are, all we need do is check our responses. The choices a person makes can only tell a limited amount of information about who they are. Their response tells all.

It feels like our choices help to create our responses. If you have the same choice over and over again doesn't that set up an automatic response?

Because social consciousness rewards sameness and consistency, individuals learn to replicate certain behaviors when certain similar stimuli are present. You could describe this as an automatic response. The cellular mind is programmed by repetitive action. Because of this it could be said that our choices have their origins in these cellular programs. But, the answer to your question is no. Response includes information from the total being – you in every lifetime. Choice is more a product of our current lifetime. There are those who believe that ultimately we are the sum total of all the choices made in all lifetimes.

Who is making the choices? Who is replying to the inner urges triggered by external stimuli?

Choice happens in the intellect. Response happens in your Whole being. It involves your head, your heart, your body and your Soul. The idea that a state of choicelessness exists is only troublesome to the intellect. The intellect wants to run the show. To say you are choiceless is to attack the head. The part of you wanting to rebel against this concept can march right out and do nothing but choose until the day the body dies. You are simply acting out a script when you're playing on this side of Enlightenment. You can choose this color car or that floor plan; you can fill in the details between the major events of your life with millions of "choices." You can use your life's energy on becoming an expert at making the right choice at the right time. Choices are a way of feeling in control, of being powerful in the world. Choice is of the ego. Or you can respond to the events of your life, knowing that the details are taken care of by the fullness of your response.

This state of being allows for greater creativity. If you fully understand this concept it will free you from the tyranny of the intellect. The intellect is then free to do what it was designed to do, which is to guide you through a sense oriented world on the most direct path to completion. Once the intellect is given its rightful place you have then become Master. You have then attained that place of witness, and are in a state of Grace.

Complete and utter Grace. In Grace you recognize everything in creation is interconnected; that we are individuated parts of a Whole; that we are God Creator's Self-Expressions. We are the senses of God. When we look at a tree the tree knows itself through us. We are in complete communion when we are in that state of Grace. In that perfect state of communion it appears that we are one with everything. In Grace we are so unopposed to everything. We are in the world, we are no longer attracted to the world, nor are we in aversion to the world. We are in witness. We are the passersby.

Is that why so many Masters are eccentric? Why they seem to have not only their own drum, but their own way of beating it?

Yes. In their full responsiveness exists the true witness which is free of the concepts of choice, free will, etc. In this state we glimpse our own uniqueness.

Will Power

Explain your take on "will power."

Free will is a micro response to this world. Dynamic Will power is a macro response. Free will states, "I know what is best for me, and therefore, I will ensure that my vision unfolds." Dynamic Will allows for a greater witness to Creation by stating, "I am aware of the possibilities within the vision I hold for myself and allow the details to unfold before me. My response is my mentor. I am a sovereign witness of the realms in which I play."

The immutable events of a lifetime can be approached from the micro or the macro. Either is valid and will ultimately take you to the 'same place' – Self-Realization You can be aware of the true nature of reality while on your many journeys through time and space, or you can have it dawn upon you when you arrive at the 'same place.' One is no better than the other. One seems to have less sorrow associated with it.

This is interesting: read the following prayers on page 67. The first invocation is from the Bible (Matthew 6: 7-13) and is intended to facilitate Deity worship by assigning Dynamic Will to an external God, or Source. The second is from the Akashic Records and is offered as a reminder of the Sovereign Nature of the Human Soul.

Our Father,
who art in Heaven,
Hallowed be thy Name.
Thy Kingdom come.
Thy will be done,
on Earth, as it is in Heaven.
Give us this day our daily bread;
and forgive us our debts,
as we also have forgiven our debtors;
And lead us not into temptation,
but deliver us from evil.
(Added at a later date)
For Thine is the Kingdom,
and the Power,
and the Glory,
Forever, Amen.

The following is the same prayer as it was offered up to Creation by those who followed the Law of One in Atlantis, and then later in Egypt by those who followed the Pharaoh Akhenaton:

I AM the Mother/Father Creator
Hallowed is the name, I AM.
I AM the Kingdom come,
I AM will being done.
I AM on Earth, even as
I AM in all Kingdoms.
I AM this day giving life to all Creation, even as
I AM all Creation giving life to me.
I AM this day releasing all duality, even as
I AM all duality releasing me.
I AM the Sovereign witness of the unfolding Now.
I AM the Power, and
I AM the Glory, from
Everlasting, unto Everlasting. All this
I AM.

From the micro point of view, will power is little more than us narrowing our focus to achieve an outcome. From the macro point of view, Dynamic Will, as the outward expression of Love as Knowing, is the force moving through all of Creation. It is what holds manifest Creation together. Here we are speaking of the "*I AM, that I AM,*" that spoke to Moses in Exodus 3: 14

Is this the Will of God? Or is this the force in Nature?

Actually, this is more like a substance than a force. This Creator substance permeates everything. This Unknowable Substance responds to our Unity, our Wholeness. When thoughts and feelings are separated we experience the desire to <u>do</u> something to fill the gap. The farther we are from the contentment found in Unity, the greater the distance between thoughts and feelings. As the gap between thought and feeling widens we become obsessed with filling that space with something eternal. This is our need for religions. Where thoughts and feelings combine there is a Wholeness, a Unity within our being. In Unity our desire is transformed into urge. Urge is the Will of God Creator. A great deal of information is offered through an urge. Our urges happen from deep within and connect us to the Conscious Physical Universe. The more established this connection, the more our urges influence this Creator Substance.

What about free will?

Dynamic Will is a Universal Law and issues forth from the individual who has allowed the "Love expressing as Knowing" to express through him. You "will" to live in a contracted response to the events of your life, always trying to figure out how it is that you manage to make the wrong choices over and over again, OR, you <u>WILL</u> to live your life in an expanded response, in gratitude for each moment of understanding and Grace, allowing the fabric of Creation to supply the choices and fill in the details. Take whichever path you Will. The term free will is important to those individuals who feel powerless and at the mercy of others. Dynamic Will is the medium of our self-expression, our preferred currency of exchange.

And there is more to the question you ask. How is it that we can use the mechanism of the dynamic energy called Will to effect the desired changes in our lives?

The energy center located in the fifth chakra becomes dynamic in our affairs when the micro concept of duality is given over to Unified Truth. When you act as one being instead of several, when you are the same to all of Creation, when you have integrated thought with feeling, male with female, sorrow with joy, the Mastery with the Mystery, then the dynamic Will of the "I AM" Sovereign Being expresses as the Will of God Creator.

Here is a way of becoming more dynamic: be very mindful of every word that follows the I am declaration. I am happy, I am sad. I am angry, I am peaceful. We say things like, "I'm dying for a cool glass of water," or, "I am such a fool." What a waste of good energy. You will live out each "I AM" declaration. Why? The subconscious swings into action on each and every word. It is through the subconscious that we attract manifest matter with thoughts, excited by emotional energy, that are spoken into the ethers. This is the performance, the spoken word.

If you bear false witness, inner conflict is present. Tell the truth as you know it. Speak without inner conflict. The Master teacher Jesus said, "*Not what goes into the mouth defiles a man, but what comes out of the mouth, this defiles a man.*" (Matthew 15: 11)

If you wish to influence physical reality with the command of your voice then learn to discipline your spoken words. This is an art as opposed to a science, so you will find no equations informing you as to what word matches what influencing form. Here are some basic steps to using Dynamic Will: learn how to breathe a full yogic breath. Breathe deep into the body, then release the breath evenly as you speak. Find your true voice. That is to say, speak through your facial mask. When you are doing this properly you will feel a rattle, a vibration in and around your nose and mouth. Speak from this knowing and all that you ask will be realized.

Surround yourself with evenly experienced stimuli. The sensory organs tune the mind to certain thought frequencies. Thoughts have form and evoke energy in the physical body which is felt as an emotionally driven urge. Bringing thought and feeling together while speaking has a very powerful effect upon substance. Speak from a full response. Watch your words. Words charged with emotional energy when spoken manifest faster than those uttered without passion behind them. In all your exchanges with others be gentle and soft spoken. Words shouted in anger tear at the fabric of the Etheric body – yours and the one reviled. Believe in your words. Empower them with the vision of what is possible for yourself and others. Idle chatter is a waste of a great resource.

What exactly do you mean when you say bring thought and feeling together? Isn't it always together?

Unfortunately it is not always Unified. We often have a thought and then later feelings about the thought. We are trained this way. Most of us live our lives with our thoughts one place and the feelings another. We are taught to avoid having 'wrong' thoughts and to repress certain feelings. Thought and feeling coming together in full response expresses as an urge in the physical body. Urges defy control. No control, no success. No success, no validation. Example: most children, left to their own devices do very well connecting thought with feeling. Imagine a young boy playing in the sand. He is unaware you are watching. He is completely in the moment. Thoughts and feelings are one; thoughts and feelings are pouring out of him as he plays. His mouth creates the sounds that are playing across his imagination. His hands and arms work with the rest of his body to complete the picture. He is fully at play. You watch. A sense of pleasure passes over you as the child loses more of himself to play. You move or cough.

Suddenly he is aware of you. He acknowledges your presence by making sure that he's playing in the manner you prefer. His mind searches to make sure he's playing properly. He wants to please. His thoughts begin to separate from feelings. His passion seems to melt in the presence of so much intellect. Frustration replaces spontaneity. He acts out this new mood upon his toys. He can no longer fully play when observed by those who have the power to approve or disapprove.

Having our thoughts and feelings together in the moment creates authentic behavior and is rewarded in our culture only when we are a "star." The greatest opportunity to enjoy the experience of thought and feeling intertwined is through intimate relationships. Ironically, for most it's even unsafe to fully be themselves with the ones they love the most. This is the level of Dynamic Will expressing as Love that deprives. Unfortunately, instead of playing like children they act like their approving or disapproving parents did and end up missing the passion and intimacy available in the moment. Deep, passionate relationships are very rare. Most relationships today reflect the same type of frustration demonstrated by our child in the story. The critic and approver is present in both individuals.

When you bring thought and feeling together in a moment, you create the mystic's mind. And to the degree that you can stay in Unified Mind, Conscious Awareness, you will respond with greater clarity to the events of your life. In Unified Mind we create the AH HAs. AH HAs are a reflection of your willingness to respond with total intellect, total heart; body, mind, and Spirit. In this state nothing else exists except the Magical.

Many would say it is difficult to achieve Unified Mind, because of the critical voice of the parent whether internal or external. I would agree with this statement if it were not for the fact that we are Spiritual Beings embodied in flesh. We are not animal forms trying to achieve spiritual awareness. If you would like others to stop being critical of you, then you must stop being critical of others. Stop your critical mindset. The greatest wrong against another being is attempting to change them into your idea of perfection. Stop that voice by realizing it has no value. It has never been your friend, or helper. Never.

What about being with other people who are overly critical, like my mother?

If you take their critical remarks as a true commentary about who you are, then avoid their company. If you realize that their critical voice is telling you something about them, then you're so much the better for their company. Also, try to imagine what it must be like to be inside their being with this constant criticism of the world. Have compassion for their state of mind, for their insanity. Adopting their way of seeing reality would be senseless. Have your own point of view. The point here is to give up the case you have against yourself and allow enlightenment to blossom within you. Then you become the Witness of Creation. The Witness is unable to be critical.

Magic & Miracles

If we are only response, and have little to say in the makeup of this reality, how do you explain real magic?

Each of us carries the potential to be a sovereign expression of Selfless Self. In this state we are Ultimate Cause. This is how Magic happens: the basis of ritual magic is the desire to influence substance by directly applying Dynamic Will to the illusion. Pure response is Unified thought and feeling. Dynamic Will is focused pure response.

At some point in the process of evolving spiritually we drop the concept of intention and begin to realize there is one Dynamic Will in Creation. This Will is often experienced as the Great Substance surrounding and penetrating all of life. This Substance responds to our deepest desires when we as Sovereign Beings command this One Will and allow it to be the agency of our self-expression. It is when we stop trying to use this Substance to control others that we find our true relationship with this One Will. It is our sole purpose to make everything anew in each moment.

When we pattern certain thoughts and feelings into a ritual, or performance, with the sole purpose of altering existing patterns of illusion, we effect the Collective agreement surrounding the presentation of matter within the boundaries of this dimensional reality. Here we alter the lag time that is normally present between thought/feeling and manifested form. This is the basis of ritual magic, and we are simply rearraigning what is already here.

In ritual magic it is important to work in concert with the vertical Earth energies. That is to say, those energies expressing as a Source to your performance. If you doubt your position with relationship to these Source energies you will stop the flow of the vertical Earth forces. This is a form of betrayal: you not honoring your Sovereignty. If you are willing to betray yourself, it stands to reason you will betray others. If you betray the trust of Mother Nature, and the dimension of unseen beings that are guardian to her treasures, you might be in for a rather rude awakening. Study the concepts of magic before you perform. It is not enough to have good intentions in these matters. It will cost you if a mistake is made.

Can we perform high magic? Yes, we can dynamically effect our world in very magical ways. Do we have to become enlightened to do this? No. Does it require expanding our Consciousness to the point of being willing to live the rest of our existence as one of our Creations? Yes. Does all the efforting of learning the rituals, and boundaries of the magical realms lead to effortlessness manifestation? In a manner of speaking. Our hard work will eventually lead to less effort. But, as I once overheard Poonjaji, a teacher in Lucknow, India, tell one of his students, "Only effortlessness leads to effortlessness."

Is magic creating something out of thought?

Magic could mean altering the appearance of some already existing form. In the days before Christianity, there were many who could alter the outward appearance of animate and inanimate objects. The Witch or Sorcerer usually learned her or his alchemical craft through a long apprentice program that was guided by a very street-smart Mystic. Usually this program was an unlearning of social consciousness and an expanding of individuated Consciousness to include the unseen realms of fairies, brownies, gnomes and trolls, the realms of Pan. Because the disposition of a Witch or Sorcerer was often considered surly and disregarding of villagers, their lives were often at peril, so they learned a very important trick called, "glamouring", or "shape shifting."

If threatened by an enemy, a sorcerer would alter his or her physical appearance to elude physical harm. This "spell," or "glamour" would only last for several minutes, because it did not alter or interfere with any genetic coding. If the Magician "shape shifted," it could take days to return back to the original genetic form, because of the altered DNA of his or her physical body. I find it interesting that the word glamour survived the middle ages and retained its meaning – to alter the natural appearance of ones features.

What about miracles?

In our present condition, we rely heavily on the external world, the exoteric, the known, the provable, the doing, the world of thought, the concepts of Mastery, and dominion over the elements. When someone comes along who is living from the internal world, the esoteric, the unknown, the allowing, the being, the world of feeling, the concepts of Mystery, and liberating the elements, we see this as supernatural and label the presentation as miraculous. What is miraculous? A force in nature that delights our senses; something beyond our ordinary range of understanding; an unexpected happening?

Miracles exist only in realms that have very defined boundaries of Consciousness and Matter. This world of ours is extremely bound to dimensional definitions. It is the preferred method of inquiry to label, then place our discoveries into boxes. We then stack those boxes, one on top of the other and side by side, into the appropriate categories. After a while we have forgotten what's inside the boxes, mainly because it looks like we just have a collection of boxes. And with the majority, the mainstream, instead of knowing what's in each box, it's more important to have enough boxes in the right categories.

Miracles happen when we momentarily escape the illusion of this world of stereotyped expectations and step out of our boxes.

We as Creators

I know you believe we are not creators on this side of enlightenment, but, isn't the ability to imagine, to creatively envision a future a form of creating?

When we are only Cause, existing in the awe of Being, then we are Creators. When we are uninterested in the outcomes, when we have our existence in each moment, instead of looking back to see how we did, we are Creators. God as Creator is unaware of us as its Creation. God expresses in each NOW moment. When we live in the eternal NOW, God as Creator is aware of us. God as Creator is unconcerned with where Creation is going, or how Creation will turn out. There is only the moment. No hopes or dreams, no responsibility or blame. Just NOW. When we allow the NOW, we are Creating. Until the absolute NOW, we have no choice but to follow an invisible plan.

It is possible to bring your Awareness to such a point as to live just ahead of each future moment; a split second ahead of each unfolding layer of Creation. This is the mystic's experience. Here you are in the midst of Creation, watching as God Creator weaves the Mystery. This precognitive existence is thrilling to say the least. It's like watching brilliant actors in a great play, one you've seen a hundred times before and never tire of; or listening to your favorite composer being interpreted by the very best symphony orchestra. In the mystical experience we are the playwrights, the actors, the composers, the musicians, and the interpreters. We are as much a part of the unfolding layers of God Creator, as the Creator is itself. On this side of enlightenment we forget this life or death, good or bad, right or wrong drama is <u>just</u> a play.

God as Creator is so completely in the creative process that God is even unaware of itself. Creator has us to provide it with that range of experience. We do the watching, sniffing, tasting, hearing and touching. We give birth to all the concepts, religions, and philosophies to organize our inquiry of this dimensional reality. We are Awareness and, as such, are the senses of God Creator in this realm. It is when we assume the role of Witness that we fulfill our purpose and become passersby. Once we are passersby, we are on the way to becoming Creators.

It is said that we can move mountains with focused thought. Many would say moving mountains is an act of creation.

Manifest substance can be manipulated or altered when an individual has awaken from the dream of doubt. Doubt, the original sin, only serves to scatter our ability to focus pure thought forms. Pure, non-dualistic thoughts have forms which radiate energy. (Gratitude and Selflessness are perfect examples of this type of thought form.) These uncompromised forms act as the building blocks for matter. They are the base equation, the distributive principle of Creation. One of the ways this radiant energy can be experienced by Human Consciousness is as the current of sound being generated by matter. As we learn to attune our Awareness to this vibration and alter the oscillation of this "sound current," we change the outward appearance of matter. We are altering the structure, the organization of substance, and there is nothing being added to Creation. We are manipulating what is already there, we are not creating.

Okay. Say what you're teaching is true. What creates all that exists in the world?

The world and all that is within originated from an unknowable Source we call God or Creator. This unfortunately explains very little. Maybe this will help: let's expand for a moment on the role of Human Consciousness in this realm. Our presence in this dimension gives it its reality. It is true that Consciousness existed in the minerals, plants and animals of the Earth prior to our arrival, and it is our response, our perceptions of manifested form and its Consciousness that bring the recognition of life into this world. We are the trailing Awareness of the leading edge of Creation; we are the senses of the Creator. As such, we bring the understanding of God Creator into this world. This world, and all within, then knows its True Seed, God Creator, Originating Source.

Example: without us a tree only knows itself as a series of sensations. As the senses of God Creator, we are able to recognize the tree through the place within our Being expressing itself as the tree. The tree is deeply connected to us through the place within itself expressing itself as us, and knows of its external form through <u>our</u> observations of it. As the tree observes itself through us, God as Creator experiences the tree. As we fully attune to the tree we experience ourselves in the timelessness of non-sentient Consciousness. We are the link between the Creator and the Creation. This is our main purpose for being here – to be this link of appreciation and gratitude.

Our response to this world, this dimension, this realm of being, is the witness that brings multilevel Awareness into this reality. We are the portal through which the Creator enters this Realm. Without us, this world is a continual series of mindless sensations, each unaware of the other. We link the sensations of this world together. Through us the sensations of this world blend to form a Collective expression. We bring Light and Witness into this dimension. We are the mind of this dimension, the masculine aspect. Substance, matter, is the body, the feminine aspect.

What creates all the circumstances of this world?

The Collective We. Micro view: <u>our</u> response to events generates outcomes, which in turn, provokes circumstances. Macro view: there is one unknown in the moment of the birth of this reality. All substance, with its many possibilities and probabilities is known. The only unknown is our response to what is known. Response is once again the pivotal force.

In our present unenlightened state we are outcome oriented, obsessed with physical pleasure and comfort. This is why we are unable to really bring about lasting change in our internal and external conflicts. Until we shift our Consciousness from effect to Cause, from outcome to Response, we will continue to attract some rather harsh circumstances for ourselves.

Cause and Effect

Cause and Effect exist to help guide us through this realm of duality. The more we encounter cause and effect the greater our understanding of the relationship between opposites. This understanding smooths out our journey giving us a fullness of heart and mind. This fullness of experience and absolute confidence leads to profound understanding and gratitude. When we fully understand the nature of our existence, our gratitude opens our Awareness to the interconnectedness that exists between <u>all</u> events and responses. Here we know Consciousness and energy as one in the eternal NOW. This knowing expands our response to the events. The greater the range of response the more interconnected we are, the more we live in gratitude and Grace. If we want more fullness in life, to exist as Cause, we should seek Gratitude as the foundation of our lives.

Grace

The more experienced we become the greater our range of response. The greater the response, the greater the outcomes and the greater the circumstances beyond the event. Here we come to Grace through gratitude. This is where enlightenment is possible.

What do you mean by grace? Are you using "grace" as a Christian would?

Grace is the condition of mind/body just prior to <u>the</u> moment of enlightenment. Grace is the state of mind/body that allows perfect Communion with the one Will of Creation. Here the little self is given over to the larger Self, and inner conflict and judgment dissolve into the formless. This condition removes doubt because the individual is no longer self-antagonistic. It is important to note that the state of Grace is achievable through all the worlds' religions.

Does karma cease to exist as we enter this state of grace?

Excellent. Karma exists as a form of balance. Grace is Unity. Unity implies one form. If there is one form, karma and the need for balance melts into the void. Until we become enlightened we live in a world of delicate balances.

Karma

What do the Records say about the creation of karma.

The concept of karma only exists for those who live in conflict. Conflict exists when you knowingly perform in a manner that is in direct opposition to your core, your inner self, your authenticity. Karma, in light of our True Spiritual nature, is an illusion. To believe in it is to forget who you are.

Then most of us create karma everyday.

Yes, we have been taught to go against ourselves, our true nature, which is authentic response. It is more in keeping with our True Selves to give without consideration of ourselves. This is to be selfless. It is our basic nature to trust and to be fully open to all possibilities. We have an enormous range of tolerance and flexibility. We are extremely adaptable. Our ability to find resolution is legendary throughout the Conscious Physical Universe. We gravitate to Wholeness and Unity. We are amazing Beings.

The answer seems obvious. Our moment of awakening comes when we tire of having to balance this with that. So how do we stay in the work place, relate with our families, or be in this world and end the game of karma?

The answer is not as obvious as you might think. This is a very difficult problem. One that has been knocked around for many generations and will continue to be a concern until all duality ceases to exist.

First we must end our prejudice. This, unfortunately, can be difficult, because our prejudice lives so deep within us and the Collective Mind. Here is one way: if we have something against another person we must look for evidence that would support the opposite view. Disprove our position. Invalidate our beliefs about them. Do this with all prejudice. Live without a position, a personal point of view for a short period of time. Say a week. In other words, go on vacation from your need to be right. This will allow your innermost knowing about this world to surface.

Next, map your core beliefs, those ideas that form the foundation of who you are in this realm. These core ideas are the source of your prejudices. We humans have seven core beliefs that shape the total outward expression of our inner selves. These seven beliefs correspond with the seven chakras of the physical body, and deal with the dualities found within Human Consciousness: procreativity and sexuality, attraction and aversion, power and influence, acceptance and rejection, will and dominance, vision and control, wisdom and intellect. Our expressed levels of Consciousness change as we integrate the dynamics of each core belief. It is through our deeds, our performance, and our completion of life themes in each incarnation, that we integrate the wisdom found in each event and our core beliefs evolve allowing us a greater range of response.

Changing a core belief can be a hellish task if you try to go it alone. Find someone who is supportive of your ideas for change, a counselor, mentor or very sensitive friend. Enlisting family members is <u>not</u> an effective idea. They will have an investment in keeping you locked within your beliefs. Unless they are very aware of where the change is going they will feel threatened. They might even feel that if you are changing you will want them to change as well.

Core beliefs are our living philosophy, and as such, organize our inquiry of this world. Changing a core belief will enlarge your response to this world and therefore alter your investigation. Focus on expanding instead of eliminating certain beliefs. Be gentle with yourself.

Does each individual work with the same beliefs?

Ultimately, yes, and in their own fashion. We are each one cell within a Collective Mind, and we are equal in our diversity only. Our abilities vary as to the degree of knowing we possess and our quality of effort.

Is there any other way to achieve balance other than through the concept of karma?

Many believe karma is opposing forces – for every action there is an opposite and equal reaction. This is not a macro Truth, or even a micro law, but an idea gone amuck. Karma is generated by inner conflict. Do something against your core identity and you will seek balance through an equally energetic act. An act of evil isn't balanced by an act of kindness, any more than an act of kindness means an act of evil is imminent.

The middle road contains the best seats in the house. This is the narrow way spoken of by so many past teachers, Buddha in particular. Desire balance without being repulsed by opposites. If you wish to elevate karma you must lose the notion that karma exists as the balancing of opposing ideas. Non-aversion, non-attachment.

Something else: if you perform a task knowing it is a true task, executed to the best of your ability and finished to the letter of your agreement, then you have your existence outside the concept of karma. If an act is against your core, or you are performing in half measures, karma exists within your mind to bring you to fullness. When we do not give our full being to each moment we experience ourselves as being out of balance. The concept of karma exists to help bring us fully into each moment.

What about a code of ethics?

No one needs an imposed code of ethics to live by. Contrary to popular belief, we humans, by and large, are cooperative, peace loving beings. Laws to legislate morality or ethics are useless. If an individual wants to exist outside cultural laws they will. Karma is a result of inner conflict and is hardly brought on by the breaking of some code of conduct set out by a group, neighborhood, township, municipality, city, county, region, state, country, Collective Mind, realm, world, dimensional reality, or State-of-Consciousness, unless of course, the outlaw feels they are doing something wrong. As soon as they are in conflict, karma enters the picture.

This is an observable condition in the Akasha: individuals find a place within the Collective Mind, then incarnate over and over again in that niche. That is not to say, "Once a criminal, always a criminal." And prisons are hardly new experiences for most criminals. There are the innocent, those effected by accidents of fate, in our correctional institutions. This is karma the Collective Mind will have to balance.

This is a little scary. The first thing that comes to mind when I hear this is a state of anarchy where the physically brutal rule.

Yes, and not so surprisingly, this is the first thing that comes to most everyone's mind, because this is in fact how it is. Nations are forged, expanded, then protected through acts of violence. Imagine a global society that lives in harmony and communion with itself; without laws to govern how the members should relate to each other, or their environment. Imagine a world where everyone knows everything. Imagine a world that allows for diversity. There are worlds in Creation such as this. If we were to go there as Humans we would weep for the joy of liberation from the bonds of power and control that govern us here on this planet. Listen to John Lennon's song, "*Imagine.*" He was very mystical.

Are influencing factors from past lives considered karmic, or are they just bleed over from parallel selves?

It depends on the texture of the energy involved in the influence. Here is a case history with both.

An individual came for an Akashic reading, saying," I don't know why I'm here. My friend told me to come." I suggested we do a general reading.

I asked for her full birth name and date; her mother's birth name and her father's. I sat for a moment, focusing on my breath. As I repeated her birth name to myself, I was immediately shown her most recent past lifetime. Pictures of her being abducted and placed in the hold of a three masted schooner appeared above her right shoulder. It appeared to be in the middle eighteen hundreds. She fought her captors until one of them knocked her unconscious. Once on the boat she was taken downstairs, disrobed and thrown onto a pile of hay. She was going to be the sexual entertainment for this cruise. I described as many of the environmental details as was possible – colors, smells, size of the room, the swaying back and forth of the ship, etc.

She started crying. I waited until she stopped and asked if she wanted to continue and if knowing all the details seemed important to her. She nodded yes to both.

I continued. As the days wore on, she became sick from the physical abuse, dampness and poor nutrition. In her delirium she began hitting at her captors. They then tied her arms to the bulk head, but she continued her assaults by kicking her assailants. They proceeded to nail her feet to the floor. As a result she was left to lie in her own bodily waste. Her will to live diminished greatly. I explained that what was happening to her in those moments amounted to emotional, mental and physical annihilation. She said that the pictures explained everything. She then began sobbing again. I continued when she stopped.

There was a man on the boat who wasn't participating, and one night when everyone else lay in a drunken stupor, he untied her, removed the nails and threw her overboard. I read the young man's intent. It wasn't selfless; he was a religious man who was greatly disturbed by the screaming and mental images he saw of her naked below in the cell. He was also thinking of her humiliation. With the last of her strength she cursed him as he carried her upstairs and across the deck. The pictures ended. I asked her how this information explained events in her present lifetime.

"This explains everything," she said. She had married a couple of months earlier and they were unable to consummate their marriage. Every time they went to make love, her legs cramped, her feet curled up, and her wrists burned to the point that she wanted to scream. As a child she had had a repeating dream that she was being crucified like Jesus. For as long as she could remember she could not use public toilets. The smells would make her feel feverish and claustrophobic. I asked her husband's name. As soon as I heard it, I was shown the face of the man who had thrown her overboard.

We ended the session with some ideas of how to clear the memory of this experience from her Etheric body. About a month later she called and said they were finally able to make love, and that all the symptoms were gone. Six months later they were divorced. They had come together to release the curses she had given voice to as he threw her overboard. She and her former husband remain friends and have both sought past life counseling.

The bleed over in this case was the childhood dreams and phobias and of course the marriage to her husband. The unfinished business, or karma, was the healing of the curses.

Did she choose that event? Was it a lesson she wanted to learn?

Yes. Macro – every event is known from the very beginning by each Christ Soul.

Micro – what could possibly be learned from such a horrific event? The results of the lesson might take tens of lifetimes to unfold. So what value is it to the young lady who was minding her own business. It is easy for those who achieve macro Awareness to see the eventuality of where all the "lessons" are heading. To those in the experience it's difficult to understand how anyone could even imply that someone would choose such a harsh reality for themselves. Here is where compassion is very important. When you first enter the Records the tendency will be to dismiss every event as belonging to the big picture. After all, when you are in the Akasha, you are in macro Awareness. I caution against this approach. It is important to remember that macro Awareness is of little value to those existing outside of macro Awareness.

On the micro side of enlightenment <u>true</u> accidents of fate happen.

I'll explain as best I know how: in the micro experience events can happen to an individual that are in addition to the original plan. As part of every reading, I asked my guides to show if the events being presented are karmic or originating. In the example of the young lady and the ship, her fate at the hands of the sailors was in fact originating and accidental to the influences of past and futures lives. This was a random act that was in addition to her Soul's known journey; she was in the wrong place, at the right time. What she ultimately does with the information gained through this experience will shape the <u>balance</u> of her response to creation and can therefore be considered karmic. In the moment of her abduction she felt completely and utterly abandoned by God. Prior to being abducted she had been on a mission of mercy to an elderly lady who lived by the water front. The path she had chosen to return home was the safest known way. Her abductors knew of her plans and had laid in wait. The three individuals involved, as well as those on the ship who later took advantage of the situation, have all paid dearly for their act against an innocent being. They knew what they were doing was wrong, but where the Spirit is knowing, the flesh is ignorant. This is karma, inner conflict that arises as a result of self betrayal. It is their judgment against themselves that has sought to balance the scales of duality. Her curse against the young man brought about internal and external conflict that had to be healed.

Internal and external conflict from past or futures lives, in the form of vendettas influences us greatly. And there are the greater wills of the lesser gods at work as well – the lesser gods as the forces of nature and cosmic harmonics. It is important to know of the many factors influencing us in Creation. There is so much for us to be aware of on the road to regaining our Sanity, that the very act of staying fully present can consume our journey.

As I've previously pointed out, it can be argued that all events are known by those observing from <u>full macro</u> Awareness. While in the Collective Mind we are hardly operating from full macro Awareness. As micro minds go, accidents can happen. Earth is designed to accommodate approximately 550,000,000 human beings. With 6,000,000,000 humans inhabiting the planet it is becoming more and more difficult to avoid accidents of fate.

On this side of enlightenment we are well advised to keep our wits about us.

Earlier you said that the only unknown in creation is our response. How can you explain cosmic accidents in light of that statement? Everything here is a series of checks and balances. Right? I mean, how can something happen to you that isn't karmic in some way. Maybe she's paying back something from a lifetime in another system away from earth.

All manifestations are known to the highest levels of Awareness. Even response, which is considered unknowable to the micro and macro minds, is known at the Trinity Soul level.

As has been stated before: each one of us is composed of many selves, from the Highest to the lowest, each acting independently, yet in full cooperation with the others. We adopt the macro view when we successfully integrate, Unify, these many selves back into one expressed being. The Over-Soul, witnessing through the Higher Self, is the platform from which we view Creation with macro Awareness. At this level WE are aware of each of our incarnate selves simultaneously. We can know all past, present and future events by witnessing from this Over-Soul position. Response still remains a mystery until the Trinity Soul level.

As for balancing conflict from a system other than the Earth, we do not permanently leave a system without being in perfect alignment with the lessons of that sojourn. There is the occasional incarnation on other worlds to obtain certain pieces of information that will be helpful to our process of integrating data from this world. But for the most part, we will choose to stay within a system until all conflict is resolved. If the system we are currently residing in is destroyed prior to achieving Unity, we will find another system equal in every way to the one destroyed.

Here is an example: the Akashic Records show that this solar system has been inhabited by Human Consciousness for some 206,000,000 years. There have been Consciousness Beings associated with Earth, in one form or another, for over 100,000,000 years. The Earth has been supporting physical human life for approximately 56,000,000 years, but only in physical forms as we now know them for 4.5 million years. The satellite planet Maldec, once situated in an elliptical orbit around Jupiter, was the first to see physical human forms in this system. Maldec is now the asteroid belt that orbits the Sun between Mars and Jupiter and is comprised of some four hundred planetoids. Those beings who lived on Maldec who had not finished with their incarnations here in this system moved into the etheric body of Earth just prior to Maldec's final destruction. The hydrogen explosion that tore apart Maldec destroyed the atmosphere around Mars, almost throwing it out of orbit. The only thing that saved Mars was the foresight of several of its leaders. They knew what the final outcome would be on Maldec – complete destruction. Because of their close orbits they constructed two artificial satellites, moons, to stabilize the orbit of Mars when it was impacted by the blast from Maldec. Because no one had ever experienced a true hydrogen explosion they had no way of knowing their atmosphere would be destroyed. They had only estimated a compression wave that would alter their orbit around the Sun. Those whose physical forms perished on Mars also chose Earth as a place to complete their missions when their world was ruined. Maldec, Mars and Earth were identical in every way except one; Maldec was consumed with the concepts of power. In contrast, Mars expressed honor, and Earth is expressing compassion.

Those who did not complete their lessons on Maldec have been incarnating on Earth for the last two thousand years, but in greater numbers for the last five hundred years. Even the most casual observer can see the effect these souls are having on the Collective Mind. *Other Tongues, Other Flesh,* by George Hunt Williamson is the perfect reference book on this subject.

Are these Over-Soul, Higher-Self aspects you're talking about really our future lives?

No. The Over-Soul is a Consciousness position within the Collective Mind. Analogy: each of us has a conductor, if you will, to orchestrate and blend the many sounds of each lifetime into a comprehensible movement. The Higher-self knows the instruments, the score, and each musician. Every once in a while a musician's response to his instrument, to the venue, or even to the piece that's been selected to be played, is less than what is possible for the whole sound of the orchestra. Here the conductor lends his experience and inspiration by directing his full attention to the artist who is out of time, or hitting a flat note. On this side of enlightenment we call this Over-Soul mentoring a God experience.

I'd like to go over the cosmic accident one more time. Does this concept have anything to do with other selves – parallel selves?

Yes, in a very different way than you might think. Let's say you suffered from Multiple Personality Disorder, MPD. You are invited to a party with co-workers, go, and the next day at the office people are relating events to you of the previous evening and you have no idea what they're talking about. As a matter of fact what they're describing is more like the dream you had last night than the events of the previous evening. You feel confused. The lapses of memory and reports from friends and family of your different behaviors continue. Gradually your world seems unfamiliar. Things are becoming confusing; there are the times you find yourself standing in front of the mirror dressed in someone else's clothing; or you wake up in the back of a cab heading for God knows where. What's happening?

Your main personality, the one that has your personal historical memory as you know it, is becoming aware of other personalities with their own sets of memories. As a result, you become frightened and spend the next several months with a therapist who's specialized in MPD.

Here you make discoveries about the many identities that co-exist within you, each with its own point of reference. This is very scary, because for some reason they all want to lead in your reality. As more personalities emerge, you begin to realize that many of the lessons of <u>your</u> past have been more about some of the other personalities than about you. As a course of therapy, you, as the dominate personality, agree to let the others have a well defined share of your world while you diligently unravel the mystery of your fragmented self. You wade through the maze of your childhood memories discovering confusing beliefs, mixed messages, emotional abuses and physical traumas that were stuffed instead of confronted. Suddenly you realize that some of your past moods were really the other aspects of yourself trying to communicate their discomfort at what, you, as the dominant reality, were going through. The more you stuffed, the more determined they were to communicate their discomfort and the more powerful they became. Here is where the split began – your fear of confronting those who seemed more powerful than you.

Through careful work, you are now able to confront your feelings, absolve past issues and use the "lessons" of the other personalities as a means of integrating the pieces. This is pretty much how "you" appear to your Over-Soul or Higher Self – a fragment personality; a part of the overall self tired of certain discomforts and pains, who's trying to communicate in the best way it knows how, to the other aspects of itself. Many of what we call our life's lessons may indeed belong to a parallel self who's communicating through us to the Higher-Self.

Wow! Another place to lay the blame – parallel selves. And just when I'm giving up that need. Rats. Was the lady on the ship going to die at that point in her journey toward self-realization, no matter where she was?

No. Her death was a response to being captive and seemingly powerless. She saw little else in her future except death. How could she ever be the same after what had befallen her? How could she live beyond the shame of those grievous insults? She must have felt abandoned by all to whom she had ever prayed. She fought with all her might and received no assistance from anyone, physical or ethereal. She was utterly alone. To her, death was the only answer. And, we could live indefinitely in these bodies if we understood death to be a response, instead of an immutable event lurking out in the future.

To simply dismiss this past life experience as a chosen lesson would be an over simplification of the greater Truth. In working with individuals through the Akashic Records it is lacking to just offer images from past or future lives without helping the client to integrate the full meaning of their past and future life influences. It is more in keeping with the position of Seer to enlighten those who come for an Akashic reading as opposed to just exposing fragments of the past. A very important aspect of the woman's reading was the information that this was an accident of fate, so she could fully understand how the systems of sovereignty and karma work. This knowledge helped her to stop blaming others for her harsh reality. If you are unable to offer wisdom, and a path to liberation from past life influences, then the information you give in a reading will be of little value.

The Truth of her situation brings to light the knowing that, contrary to popular belief, there are anomalies in the sovereignty and karma systems. Because of this it is very important to be Self-Realized at this particular point in time. You are more likely to experience an accident of fate at this stage in human development than at any other in the history of the planet. There are many reasons for this, the least of which is the Earth's dense human population.

Again, macro – every event is consciously known; micro – only fragments of current life personal history are consciously known. Have individuals other than this lady had similar events thrust upon them? Yes. Have all of those individuals died in the process of the ordeal? No. This young woman's response was only one of many possible responses. It's true I've never personally viewed this type of scenario before in the Records, but I know it has happened to others. Nothing in this dimension happens in isolation. Nothing is considered singular under the sun.

Is anyone safe from these types of accidents of fate?

You, expressing as Ultimate Cause, Selfless Self, are the only escape from accidents of fate. Once you express as Ultimate Cause, Selfless Self, you create each moment in the moment.

Also: there are enlightened Masters who knowingly place themselves in harm's way, which in a sense Creates an accident of fate. They might make this choice to help a devotee who is faced with an unusually difficult karmic lesson, or they may simply desire to effect a certain change within a portion of the Collective Mind.

Is there a way of reversing karma?

Yes, through resolution. Some religions believe that being good is all that is needed.

Good deeds alone cannot wash away your unresolved past, or inner conflicts. If your attitude has been destructive and you reverse your condition through helping others, then good deeds could seem to be at the heart of your salvation. But you have actually changed internally and now wish to demonstrate that change to the external world. Without the internal change no good deed would be possible. Understanding and gratitude are the foundations to resolution.

From the macro: we reappear in this world only to resolve matters that remain incomplete. If you ever get a chance to be with an enlightened Master you might notice a certain expression on his face that seems to constantly ask, "What are you worried about?" For some it feels as though they are being taunted with the answer to a question they haven't even become aware of as yet. Or the Master might just come right out with it and ask, "Don't you get it? There's nothing to worry about." When you are unenlightened there's nothing to do but live out your plan, your destiny. There's nothing to worry about because you are choiceless. The Master might continue by saying, "The choices you made were always the choices you were going to make. As a matter of fact, choice is really choosing itself." When you're enlightened there is nothing to worry about because you are through with the concept of events and the concerns of choices.

This is the cosmic joke from the macro point of view: the only moment you ever will have is NOW. Time is simultaneous. All other moments are living themselves out right NOW. While it is true that you as Over-Soul have many incarnations, each influencing the other, you as individuated self will only live this one time. This is <u>your</u> time. Now is all you have. The other moments and lifetimes belong to themselves. When your body dies, the you you have become in this time and space will never be seen again. Death, then rebirth, will transmute your personality and you will never be made manifest again. At his death, Jesus knew it was within his ability to transmute the sins of the world. (Note: see John 1: 29 and Romans 5: 8) He understood that in the passage between this world and the next is where we are meant to release our misunderstandings. There is where our karma is transmuted. But most remain afraid of death and lose the opportunity to release this lifetime's inner conflict because they remain unconscious at the time of death.

This macro joke is difficult to comprehend when viewed from the micro mindset. Especially for those who find their salvation in the concept that they have more than one lifetime to work things out. The NOW is all you have. Make the most of it.

Based on who I am right now I have to assume I have leftover events. Probably a lot. Where are leftover events placed in subsequent lifetimes?

The object of the linear time incarnation game is to experience all events of a lifetime. If we should fall short, those events we were unable to experience in our current lifetime are scheduled into the next lifetime. When this happens, we have the events already scheduled in the next incarnation, <u>and</u> the leftover events from the previous life to move our Consciousness through. Many individuals carry events from lifetime to lifetime, never quite getting everything done. This is one form of karma – unfinished business.

Let's detail a life with a beginning, a middle, and an end. Imagine a long horizontal line representing your life force energy. This line does not represent time, it represents energy. Imagine short intersecting lines every so often that represent immutable, unchangeable events.

Prior to incarnating, we have determined these events and their order to insure our eventual Self-Realization.

Each event contains the possibility for fully awakening from the dream. Remember, you want to experience these events. Let's say from the first slap on the tukus over at the beginning, you become reactive and the ensuing use of your life force energy is negatively directed. The more physical, emotional, or mental slaps you have, the more reactive you become. Suddenly you've had just about all the slaps you can endure and use your remaining life force to actively protest your fate by becoming terminally ill. "That'll show 'em. They won't have me to kick around any more." All the energy available for this life experience is now expended. You run out of energy, and drop the physical body prior to finishing all your scheduled events.

We are at the effect of our response to the immutable events until we fully express each response. We fully express our response when we are authentically in the NOW. The more past responses we keep alive in the NOW, the more life energy we use. The more energy we use keeping the past alive in the NOW, the shorter our time in these physical forms. I have heard the argument that we have a greater chance of awakening when unfinished events of one lifetime are moved into the next incarnation, because there are more events to encounter. The more events, the greater the odds of awakening. Nice try. We only need one lifetime to Master this realm.

Let's go back to our imaginary life line. What if, instead of dying at a point in the middle of your journey, you become enlightened? What happens to all the unfinished leftover events? They come crashing into the moment, the NOW. An explosion of being expresses through you, and you no longer have immutable events. You Be. Now you can Create. For the first time since your initial entry into this system you get to truly Create. There is no schedule to follow. Your physical, emotional and mental bodies are in harmony, Unified in Self-Realization. There are no limitations.

Linear Time

I'd like to move to a different subject. Is time linear in the Akashic Records or does it reveal everything as happening simultaneously?

As has been stated, there are always two points of observation; macro and micro. Time is observable as being linear in nature when you are searching for specific moments, such as past or future life influences. It is experienced as simultaneous when asking questions about Soul groups, blocks of time or inter-dimensional worlds. This is because your first experience of the Akasha will be in the concept of time that is the most familiar and known to you. Then you will progress to time concepts that allow you the most efficient use of your energy while in the Records. We need only be familiar with the concept of simultaneous existence to access the Records.

The following understanding is important to reading and accurately interpreting the Records: time as a linear measure is used only by the Collective Human Mind as it relates to the cellular portion of that Mind, the human physical body. The Collective Animal Mind, Collective Plant Mind and the Collective Mineral Mind are unaware of the concept of linear time because they have their Consciousness in simultaneous realities.

Brace yourself. Just as you thought we'd moved away from the subject of response, here we are again. It seems response is at the bottom of the whole time perception thing. And it is.

Linear time is experienced as our Conscious Awareness responds to the events of the physical universe. The concept of time only exists because we respond. A simple example: we have a job which is far from alignment with our bliss. It's 9:00 in the morning, an hour goes by, it's 9:01; we work another hour, it's 9:02. That's one response. Another response, we love our work, it's 9 am, the next thing we know some one's asking us to lunch.

The distance between events is determined by our response to the events. The more expansive our response – the less time distance between events.

Remember this when viewing future records: response creates the illusion of time. How can there be 'time' if something is in the future and we have yet to respond to it? The energy of immutable events broadcasts out along the pathway of an individual in multi-dimensional waves of energy. These impressions of future events are presented in symbolic images that are based on the individuals' current perceptions and response patterns. In trying to determine the timing of future events simply look to the past for similar patterns of response to get the most accurate interpretations. This is a little tricky. As you can imagine, bringing forward an idea of time based upon similar past events and responses will lead to inaccuracies. There are many factors involved, the least of which is the fact that the individual you are reading for has expanded their view of creation since the past event/response. What to do?

Ask the Records to disclose any information from past life experiences that are similar in defining characteristics – age, sex, thought and emotional patterns, circumstances, etc. The more similarities from past lives, the greater your chance of accurately guessing the timing of future events. Very few interpreters of the Akasha get absolute interpretations of time. This usually improves with practise. Be patient.

Here is another important point – time predictions for individuals have a greater chance for accuracy than for groups. The more individuals involved, the greater the chance for influencing factors and the greater the chance for misinterpreting timing. This ability will improve with experience. Be at ease with yourself for missed timing in your predictions. I generally place all events within a given window of opportunity, unless a direct time is given to me by one of my guides. For example: a gentleman wanted to know when his life partner was going to die from aids. I was having a little difficulty interpreting the images I was being shown in the Records, so I asked my guides for help. Instead of the usual immediate response my guides seemed to just leave. I explained to the client that we would have to come back to that question because the answer was not coming through the normal channels. He immediately took that as a negative. I think I would have too. We continued with the reading, then suddenly I was given the date of October 17th at 11:37. The client was stunned by the details. He would have been happy to know within a week, or a month. His lover died on October the 17th at 11:35. He explained how happy he had been to know the exact time. Everyone was there at his passing. They were all thankful to have had the opportunity to be with him at his transition.

When viewing historical events in the Records you will see that the concept of linear time became very important about 13,000 years ago as Atlatia (Atlantis) began to self-destruct. The Records show that those individuals of Atlatia who followed the Law of One[2] moved westward into the high wilderness we call North America and the Caribbean to continue their focus on multidimensional creativity; while those who followed the Sons of Belial[3] moved eastward with the concept of linear self-expressed time. Those who followed the Law of One continued a simultaneous, multidimensional experience of Earth communion through Creativity. The followers of Belial invented laws designed to control the order of Creation by enacting linear time as the dominate measure of one's worth and contribution. Little evidence of astronomical observation exists in North America where the Law of One followers migrated. Wherever the Sons of Belial gathered they erected monuments to their time god. We have only to look at early Druid, Greek, Roman, Mid-eastern and Egyptian cultures to get an idea of their relationship with time.

The Lemurians were the only other civilization that had the efficient use of time as a measure of value. They believed that efficiency of efforts, in relationship to the amount of time passed, equaled truth. If it wasn't efficient, it wasn't truth. The Lemurians migrated to the areas we call Mexico, Central America, and western South America when their world was flooded due to the partial melting of the ice caps when the poles shifted, some 24,000 years ago. There they continued their worship of time through their calendars and observatories. The Hawaiians and Polynesians are also descendants of the Lemurians but through the thousands of years since the Unification of Lemuria these peoples have adopted different measures of value that have replaced efficiency of efforts.

Linear time truly is a construct of the mind. In the beginning everything was known. Nothing needed to be added or Created in addition to what was in that beginning moment. This is simultaneous time – past, present, future expressed as one. The Records show this to be the ultimate Truth – the ultimate Big Picture.

Simultaneous Time

I was first introduced to the concept of simultaneous time through the Seth Materials. Even though I don't need it to get into the records, would you take a moment to paint a simple mental picture of simultaneous time?

Simple? Hmmm. Let me express my view of micro linear, and macro simultaneous time together. Imagine Creation as a big blue ball of yarn. The external end, the one easily seen, is the beginning of your journey. Inside the ball is another end representing the finish. You are conscious of the beginning and want to know the end. As you unravel the yarn you are able to see where the line repeatedly touches itself. It is at these intersections where the single thread rests against itself that incarnations, or events happen. The ball of yarn is multidimensional, simultaneous time. The single string is linear. If you were to mark where each overlay happens, you would have a map of events as they relate to that ball of yarn. You might call the distance between those marks, a perception of time. Without response Creation is a ball of yarn expressing as simultaneous time. Unravel the ball and you have linear time. Mark where the string overlaps and you have a calendar.

What is awareness of time?

Awareness is generated when we investigate Dimensional Reality (response) and hold those findings as a linear progression through simultaneous time. It is the senses of the cellular mind, and the comparative response to stimuli that creates the illusion of linear time. If Awareness of linear time is an exercise of comparisons, then we can drop the illusion of progressive time by halting comparisons. As a child our comparisons are projected forward in time. After puberty our comparisons become increasingly past oriented.

Let's go back to our ball of yarn. When we unravel the ball of yarn the comparison of distance between points of overlay is the measure of time. When we first start to unravel the ball it takes longer to complete a revolution. The number of intersection overlays is many, so our comprehension of time at the beginning is given its definition by the size of our ball of yarn. The more we unravel the ball the less time it takes to get around the circumference. Our understanding of time is one thing in the beginning. Another in the middle. And yet another towards the end. Many of us are at the end of our blue balls of yarn in terms of incarnations and are experiencing time as being greatly compressed.

When viewing the Records it is advisable to focus Awareness as it relates to the Collective Mind in progressive linear aspects of time. Trying to focus Consciousness on both simultaneous and linear time would be conflicting to say the least. Because most individuals find it difficult to fully appreciate the concept of simultaneous time, it would be confusing to only use present tense terms when reading from the Records. How would clients focus their Awareness? How would they know if something had happened or was going to happen? In this case, the communication of information is more important than fully understanding and using the concepts of simultaneous time.

Progressive Reincarnation?

Do we always incarnate in a linear fashion through lifetimes?

Let's take a moment to remember what the Akasha is: the system of the Akashic Records works as a network of interacting points of view. In the Records, each manifest Human Soul expression is referred to as a Destiny Path. Each Destiny Path is connected to every other Destiny Path through a network of energy. This Etheric network of intersecting lines of energy connecting each individuated expression is the repository for all Human events and the ensuing individual and Collective Response, or in other words, the Akasha. This network includes every individuated expression from the Eau-Aum Ta-Rah to the Geh-Hen-Ah underworlds. Within each of us is the All of the network of the Akasha.

We, as Christ Soul projections, through the Over-Soul expression, select <u>all</u> destiny paths <u>prior</u> to the <u>first</u> incarnation. These event filled pathways are in every way compatible with our True Nature, our Soul, and reflect the measure of our understanding of Creation. Each path, or lifetime, is progressive in values of wisdom. We evolve Consciousness in multi-dimensional channels, as opposed to linear time. The experiences you need in your next incarnation to fully integrate the wisdom gained in this lifetime can be found in a setting that takes you 'back' in time. In other words, many individuals who are drawn to past periods, might well be headed there, instead of coming from there.

I will use this example because it is an extreme model of such a case. A gentleman came to me for a reading several years ago. As I shook his hand I immediately thought to ask him if he felt out of time, out of touch with the culture he was living in, but didn't.

His next lifetime jumped out at me as I entered his Book of Life. It was to begin in New England, at the beginning of the 1700s. After sharing the images of what I had seen, he seemed more than delighted. He explained how he had always been interested in Colonial America and had made it his life's study. He had even worked summers on Lake Champlain in upstate New York when he was in school so that he could be in New England. His acceptance of the idea of moving backward in time to his next incarnation was amazing. When I went on to share that in many past lives he was a linguist, and in his future life was to act as liaison between the Iroquois Nation and the white settlers, he began to cry. The Records showed him in his next life as the interpreter of the Iroquois Laws and one of the individuals responsible for the shaping of the Constitution of the United States of America. He shared that his main interest, and the area of his expertise, was the formation of the Constitution.

I explained he was here in this time/space gathering the foreknowledge that would help him in his efforts "back" then. I also explained that given his lifelong study of the Constitution, he was bound to lead a precognitive life in New England, moving from one déjà vu experience to the other.

Without warning he began to recite the Constitution, line for line. He seemed disturbed momentarily, then quickly returned to "normal". He explained how difficult it was for him to witness what the lawmakers in Washington had, and were doing to the original ideas of the Constitution with their amendments. He sat very still for about fifteen minutes then announced his decision to go back in time and find some way to prevent "them" from indenturing the sovereign citizens of the individual commonwealths that make up the United States of America.

We discussed his obsession for some time. Several things surfaced regarding behaviors: he was dreaming about his next incarnation almost every evening. His waking world was being fragmented by images from what he saw as the past. The more obsessed he became, the more he wanted to be completely alone. The more alone time he spent, the less "real" he felt in this time/space.

It was clear that his lifelong preoccupation with the subject of Colonial New England was given a burst of energy from our working together. We had two more sessions, during which more of the details concerning his next incarnation were discovered, such as, his occupation would be that of a printer; his wife would be the daughter of a wealthy English merchant who imported cloth and tea to the Port of Boston; his oldest child would die from wounds received from the very first shot fired against the Colonists in New York City; he would be initiated into the Masonic Order at the age of thirty-six and would later receive its highest degree; he would invent a drying system for lithographic prints; he would work with the entity, Saint Germain, the guardian sponsor of the Constitution; Benjamin Franklin would be his mentor and longtime friend; he would become one of the new government's first Senators.

It was during these sessions that he revealed his secret obsessions with Saint Germain,

Benjamin Franklin, the Masons, and wanting to be a Senator. Interestingly, his father of this lifetime owned a printing shop that my client worked in every summer learning the trade. He never got to see that dream fulfilled because his father died his senior year in high school and the family closed the business.

I have since been told by the mutual friend who introduced us that he is now living in New England. Our mutual friend was angry at the outcome of his reading because she felt the revelation of him as one of the framers of the Constitution exaggerated his obsessive/compulsive behaviors. Without breaching his confidentiality, I explained that it truly showed him as helping to prepare the way for the Constitution and that his "obsession" was future memories. Since then she has shown me a picture he sent. The smile on his face said it all. He had found where he belonged and was preparing for his next great adventure. He had gotten a job with the local Chamber of Commerce and was fully dressed in the clothing of his next incarnation.

It seems to me that the reading did cause him to become more obsessed with his interest in the past. How did it benefit him to have the knowledge that he was one of the framers of the Constitution?

The readings explained so much of who he was in current time. He had always been labeled as "different" by his family and friends. With the information from the reading he was finally able to understand himself. He gave up the fear of becoming "crazy," and the "unknown urges" that seemed to be governing his life were at least partially explained.

Being able to know the immutable events that will shape the balance of a current life is critical to the moment of enlightenment. Being able to remember incomplete responses to past life events that are influencing current experiences, helps to release fears of the unknown. Once an individual understands the nature of time – that it is simultaneous, instead of being linearly progressive – then the fears of 'what's to come' melt away. Once we have released these fears we automatically expand our response to upcoming events in current time by opening to the next greater possibility. This happens when we fully understand why we are here and what we are to do with our gifts.

In the case of this gentleman, he had always thought he was born to the wrong time. All his life he had felt out of place. He had also wondered about his preoccupation with the past and had secretly decided himself to be a little crazy. The knowledge he was to actually play a major role in the very event that was haunting him, was very freeing. He could finally understand his unrelenting drive toward the writing of the constitution. It had been confusing to think that he was moving away from the event because it appeared to be in the past. To know that time and incarnations are simultaneously progressive brought him enormous joy. To finally know why he felt so ashamed of our current government freed him emotionally.

To his friend, our mutual friend, he seemed worse, more driven than ever. To many who would meet him, he might seem eccentric or mentally off. To anyone asking about the Constitution he would appear to be an expert.

Another thing: what my client had been taught about time was making him crazy. He knew something was wrong with the order of things, and no one was there to help him sort it out. When he suddenly understood the nature of time, his fears diminished, allowing him the awareness of his authentic self. This authentic self, his true nature, is unconcerned with the opinions of others, so he was therefore able to drop his social obligations and allow his genius to emerge. As we expand and enlarge our response to the social order, we become acutely aware of the most direct path to the enlightened state and avoid many of the unnecessary negative response patterns brought on through our fears of 'what if,' and 'if only.' This happens because we are no longer fixed on external validation. We are at long last, self-validating; genius to those who understand, eccentric to others.

Aren't we all here to make a contribution to each other? It would seem your client's contribution was to be made in a different time, and that by him not being fully present, here and now, he was not living up to his fullest potential within this current life expression.

From the macro: time being simultaneous, we are all constantly contributing to the Whole of Consciousness. It is impossible to determine the contribution to the Whole by looking at just one lifetime, just as it is impossible to describe a star by looking at one wave of light particles. From the micro: we might see this individual as being elsewhere, and ineffective in the moment. Our judgment of him would lock us into a narrow range of response, giving us a rather small view of his contributions. From the macro: Jeshua Ben Joseph said, "*Truly, I say to you, as you did it to one of the least of these my bretheren, you did it to me..*" (Matthew 25: 40) This is a very powerful knowing.

If he had decided to undergo therapy to clear his obsession with the past, would that have altered his next lifetime?

No. The immutable events of the "past", as we who are obsessed with "this" time/space see them, would still have unfolded. There might have been slight variations, and those would be unnoticeable to the uninitiated. My client would still play his role in "past" events no matter how much therapy was employed to correct his seeming current life mental illness. From what I have seen from other past life readings, he more than likely would feel ill prepared, or at the very least uncertain in his next life role if he would have allowed himself to be "normalized" to this current time/space understanding of Creation. With the way things are shaping up now, he will be charged with the certainty of his task and his confidence will bolster the courage of the others, and even act as a catalyst for those attending the Constitutional Convention held in May 1787 at Philadelphia. The Records also show this individual as important to Jefferson's contribution to the drafting of the Declaration of Independence, some eleven years before the framing of the Constitution.

So by society judging him insane, and attempting to alter him to this time and space, our history could have changed.

As a Nation and a newly forming sub-set of the Collective Mind, we would have still declared our intention to break away from England as is recorded in history books, and my client might have had a personal crisis of Spirit due to his feelings of being ill prepared for the role he played in the task of separating from England. This was/is/will be an immense feat of will by those who designed the secession from England, and an even greater feat of will by those who were willing to live its consequences. If my client was made to feel his obsession in this current life was wrong and was willfully encouraged, by those who knew what was "best" for him, to have other interests, the stress of being ill prepared for that adventure might have been too much, causing an early death in that life. This early death would have cut short his opportunity to experience himself as "pure response" to the other chosen immutable events of that current life. These unresolved events would have him wanting to reincarnate. Reincarnation is hardly what Creation is all about. Liberation from the cycles of birth, then death, is the point of being here. We only need one incarnation to achieve that state of Being. We keep coming back to finish our business.

This leads me to believe that our lives might not be experienced concurrently in a progressive manner?

In the analogy of the amusement park offered earlier it was stated that there is an order to the rides. To this we can say our incarnations are progressive. If we were to look at historical dates we might find our incarnations running in a random pattern as opposed to a linear calendar expression. From the macro: the order of our incarnations self selects based upon our range of response. This self selection is in perfect alignment with our Soul's purpose for being in this manifest world.

When you do a reading for a client you might find his next incarnation begins in 1043 and ends in 1066 as William of Normandy invades the English coast. Trying to explain this to the average individual seeking guidance through an Akashic reading can prove to be of little value. It is difficult enough to comprehend concepts such as; choosing each event prior to incarnating, or the ever confusing – living synchronous lifetimes, let alone introducing the idea that we incarnate to experience instead of progressing through time in a time logical orderly manner. This concept is too far beyond the average individual's interest and will not be needed in order for the individual to live their life's purpose in this time/ space.

The concept of simultaneous time is so confusing. And now this. So historical sequence is of little value when looking into the records?

Exactly. Approach the records as though they were finished documents. That is to say, nothing is left to be done; past lives, current life and future lives. Witness the symbols from a place of Wholeness and all events will be revealed in a progressive manner. Example: an individual who reads this book sees it as a finished document, all the pages are assembled in the correct order so the reader can easily progress through the subject being presented. I can tell you from the position of writer this was far from the reality of what happened. This manuscript had an editor. A paragraph was taken from here, a sentence put there. Here an edit, there an edit. And if I were to look for the actual beginning of the manuscript, I might be shown a moment in time some several years ago – the scribbling of a note on a napkin. Yet I remember the exact moment when I sat down to organize these transcribed notes into a book. In my belief that was the beginning moment.

Most of us have become accustomed to thinking of lifetimes in the same manner as we consider the moments of our current lives – past, present and future. After all, we have a personal history to prove our linear existence. It is difficult to apply a concept such as nonlinear progressive Awareness to the subject of synchronous time because we have no real point of reference for either nonlinear progressive Awareness or synchronous time. Neither one really means anything to the majority of Seekers. Most accept these concepts because they seem grand or right, or simply feel accurate. And who has the time to consider all the possibilities.

Let's continue with our example of this manuscript: you, on the other hand are sitting through one of the sessions that will help make up the content of this book. You will have a different experience when reading the finished product; there will be a different level of Awareness on your part. You participated. Yours will be more multi-dimensional. The individual who was absent from the workshop will have less feeling than you. You will remember the room, some of your fellow attendees, and the gracious manner in which I facilitated the group. And it might even seem that a piece of you is co-existing with the now reading and the then participating. While reading through the parts of the book you were not present for, your response will be decidedly different.

Is knowing this going to help me sort out the details of someone's reading?

Yes. It is important to be exposed to more expanded concepts of time as a defining aspect of our reality. These greater understandings will unlock your knowing.

Also, when interpreting the Records you will need to know why it is easy to interpret certain time periods and why it's almost impossible to understand others. If you've had a lifetime during a period that's showing up for a client the images will seem easy to understand. If a client's records give information about a culture or period of time that you have never experienced directly, your interpretations might be less accurate and lacking in depth. It is important to depict as accurately as possible the information being given. If you find yourself in a past life reading and the details seem difficult to comprehend, ask the Records to present images that correspond directly with current lifetime elements.

What to do if you are unable to comprehend what is being represented in the Records? Always ask for the information to be given in a manner you can easily understand with your current state of mind. If you find too much is being offered to you at once, ask that the information be slowed. If you are receiving data in unfamiliar terms, what do you do?

Ask for it in a manner that I can readily understand.

Life Force Energy Versus Time

You talk in terms of life force not time when you speak of how long a person will be in any given lifetime. Can you explain what you mean by the term "life force" and how it is used up?

Time, linear or otherwise, has never been considered a universal, multi-dimensional unit of measure. The rest of Consciousness in Creation measures existence in units of energy. You bring a certain amount of Life force energy with you to each lifetime that you in turn mix with the Life force of the planet. This energy, whether yours or the planet's, is called chi in oriental cultures, or prana in the Vedic system. Interestingly, in Oriental languages, the term chi is found in many of their everyday words. We have failed to developed a main stream term in Abrahamic cultures for the concept of chi because our main focus is on time. The closest we get to understanding the idea of chi energy in main stream western culture is through the advancement of the martial arts, which of course have their origins in the East. There are many fine works on chi energy and related subjects. I'll give a brief summary of chi as it relates to the physical envelope we call our bodies:

Within each of us is an unseen inner-body that is identical in shape and size to the physical body, and is made up of an energetic grid that can be measured in electrical terms by science. This grid body has an outer surface much like our skin and inner centers of energy, called chakras, that could very well be described as organs. The inner-body is attached to the physical through energy channels, called nadis, that correspond with our nervous systems. As we breathe, the inner-body gathers prana, or chi energy, from the ethers as its nourishment, and feeds the physical body a portion of this energy through its connections with the nervous systems. The physical body responds by converting foods into subtle forms of energy that the inner-body uses to maintain its connection to the physical body. Without prana being passed from the inner to the physical body, and the counter action of the subtle energies passing from the physical to the inner-body, our physical bodies would, of course, die.

Just as the physical body, the inner-body is subject to wear and tear, the health of the physical body is subject to the proper balance of certain chemicals that are made up of substances friendly to the body environment. The inner-body's health is subject to the proper use of the subtle energies found in prana and certain food stuffs. If you put substances in the physical body that damage the connection with the inner-body, both bodies suffer stress and dis-ease. Substances that overly stimulate the nervous system are particularly bad for these delicate connecting points. In short, if the physical body is well taken care of, then the inner-body will be healthy, and vice-a-versa.

Life force energy is used in two ways. Chi is used to connect the physical and inner bodies to each other. It is also used when we respond with our senses. We live longer if we do not disturb the delicate connection between the physical and inner bodies through the use of stimulants and depressants. We conserve chi when we expand our response to life and live naturally without fear.

Dimensional Universes

What does the Akasha say about dimensional universes?

Dimensional is a term used to describe the essential factors or elements found within a given realm of Consciousness.

First-dimensional existence consists of a straight line, which is in fact a continuation of points. In some places this line is solid, while in others it is broken as discontinuous lines. If you were to view the inhabitants of this world you would soon realize that the only difference between them is the length of their segment. If two or more inhabitants are of exactly the same length, then it would be impossible to tell them apart.

Length and width are characteristic of the second-dimensional reality. Instead of just a line, here we have a surface or plane. Here the inhabitants are defined in terms of surface area. Imagine a puzzle made up of pieces that have an endless variety of shapes but lack depth. All the pieces fit together and are different only in terms of surface area.

Third-dimensional worlds consists of length, width and height, and progressive time and space. Here the inhabitants have a defining shape and things of like configuration share the same concept of time and space. Mineral beings, single and multi-celled biological plant or animal beings, all have their differing experiences of space, even though they may exist in the same time sequence. This is untrue for fourth-dimensional beings.

The fourth-dimensional factor is the element of communication expressed in measures of multi-dimensional space and simultaneous time. For the inhabitants of this realm time and space are experienced as a stretching between the elements of length, width, height and perception. Here Conscious beings from different time periods can share the same apparent space. This is the dimension where clairvoyance, clairaudience, and dejà vu experiences find their source. This is the realm of true Creative Self-Expression. Here the mystics play.

The fifth-dimensional realm consists of length, width, height, time and Spiritual Awareness. An observer of this dimension is at once aware of the level of Spiritual Awareness of each individual, compares the shapes as defined by length, width and height, as well as checks the time to distinguish beings from each other. In this dimension there are no secrets, everything is known to all inhabitants. This is the realm of Unified understanding. Duality no longer exists. The fifth dimension is that of Ultimate Cause.

The sixth dimension includes the elements of the first five as well as the element of Knowledge of God as Creator. This is the realm of Divine Wisdom and Compassion.

In the seventh dimension, altruism is introduced to the first six elements. The main concern in this dimension is Love and Service. This is the realm where Love gives without expectation or bias. This is the beginning of Christ Consciousness expressing in Human form.

In the eighth-dimensional realm, mercy is added. To express without Knowing of Self. This is the dominion of Selfless Self. This is the realm of Infinite, Inexhaustible Love as Existence.

The ninth dimension is substantially unlimited if compared to terrestrial or other planetary activities within our solar system. Most of the fundamental deities of world religions source from this realm.

In the tenth dimension there are three groupings of Consciousness; Grand Sun Consciousness, Moon Consciousness, and Earth Consciousness. The Grand Sun governs the active Will, the Moon Consciousness governs emotion and Earth Consciousness governs physical manifestation. These three levels insure the balance and integrity of our Spiritual/Human existence.

The eleventh dimension provides Spiritual guidance to all inhabitants of the first ten dimensions and maps our mission, or purpose for being. This is home for the twelve archangels.

There are twenty-two dimensional realities beyond this point. Little can be offered in terms of communication about these dimensional realms. Words would truly fail.

The Levels of Love

I am aware through other teachings that there are eleven dimensions that serve as realms of expression for Human Consciousness. Do the Records indicate how those in the eleventh dimension got there?

Yes. Love expressing as Existence at the eighth dimensional reality is the doorway into the eleventh dimensional Universe.

Part of the reason for our being here is to experience the core of the Collective Soul as it responds to the limitation boundaries of Earth Consciousness and its illusory presentation of matter to Human Consciousness. The Collective Soul is layered with ever expanding multi-dimensional forms which can best be described as feelings of Unlimited Love. As we explore this Soul, we move Consciousness through the levels of Love from instinctual Love, to Love that deprives, to Love that loves, to Love that forgives, to Love that nurtures, to Love that gives, to Love as Wisdom, to Love as unlimited Self Expression, to Love as Existence, and finally to Love as the personification of Creator.

Another interpretation of the term, Love, is Love as the Dynamic Singular Will forming Consciousness within Creation. Love by this definition is the unseen substance that permeates all matter. Still another definition has Love as the very Agency of our existence and one last definition has Love as the comforting Holy Spirit. When asked, each area of response within the Records shows one area of agreement relating to the subject of Love – little is known about Love beyond Love as Existence.

There are many teachers in this Earthly realm who are profoundly qualified in this subject. When you are ready they will appear.

What do you mean by instinctual love? What distinctions are you using to differentiate love?

"Instinctual love" requires no special effort and is driven solely by the Law of Attraction. Usually those of a grouping, i.e., family, town, city, area, region, ethnic grouping, country, world, solar system, galaxy, universe, etc., will be in instinctual love.

"Love that deprives," is a self centered, manipulative force. We learn this Love as we embrace the illusion that we have to do something to get something, and that being right equals being Loved. The word "no" is often the trigger for the experience of deprivation. Also, this is the feeling of powerlessness experienced when one steps out of their instinctual grouping. Within our group we are understood; outside the group we have to explain ourselves.

"Love that loves" is based on Love toward an object for which one has a natural concern. "Love thy neighbor, as thy self." This is the love that bestows goodwill upon the recipient. Even though this is one of the most common forms of love, it is difficult to fully achieve.

"Love that forgives" as in the phrase, "Love thy enemy." This requires a great deal of tolerance and is extremely rare in Human Consciousness. This is a Love of intelligence and reason.

The "Love that nurtures" eventually is achieved by everyone. This is a love of great compassion. Here Human Consciousness expresses its true nature.

"Love that gives" without expectation. This is well beyond the understanding of most humans. The score card has been dropped in favor of being a Source for those in the illusion of need. This is the Selfless Self.

"Love as Wisdom" is the joining of the heart and head. At this level the need to be right has all but disappeared, and thought is in perfect communion with feeling. This level is seldom reached by the unenlightened.

"Love as Unlimited Self-Expression." This is you expressing as a full sovereign Being, manipulating the illusions of this world through the power found within their limitations.

"Love as existence," and "Love as the personification of Creator God" speak for themselves.

Where is the collective mind on this scale?

To use these definitions as a scale of judgment as to where you or the Collective are in the progression toward Self-Realization would be an inappropriate use of this information. The levels of Love outlined are all expressing here on the planet or we would be unaware of them. And, there are more than likely other levels elsewhere. Here are some milestones from the Abrahamic religions: Solomon was a demonstration of Love as Wisdom; Moses expressed Love as the personification of Creator God; Jeshua Ben Joseph (Jesus) was expressing Love as Forgiveness and Love as Existence. And these from other cultures: Buddha demonstrated Love as Existence and Love as the personification of Creator God; Quan Yin was the expression of the Love that Nurtures and Love as Existence; Confucius demonstrated Love as Wisdom; Mohammed exampled Love as the personification of Creator God. There have been many others from all the world's cultures and religions who have achieved these levels of Love. One hundred forty four thousand to be exact. History, as it is chronicled by mankind, has missed the journeys of most of these individuals.

Probable Selves, Parallel Universes

I'm highly interested in probable selves and parallel universes. Are past lifetimes our probable selves, or do we have probable selves in each life time?

Yes to both. For every performance there is a series of probable performances. Some of these occur in time/space dimensions that could be viewed as past or future lives, others occur in true parallel universes. Are some more real than others? Hardly.

Unfortunately, if you look for these "other" parallel or probable selves in the Records you will be disappointed. The records of your probable and parallel selves belong to other Collective Minds, which have their own experience of the Akashic Records. The subject of probable selves and parallel universes can only be speculative from where we view Creation. I do know other selves exist in this dimension, mainly because I intuit their influence at what must be our mutual intersections. This is only an occasional experience. A wonderful book by Fred Allen Wolf, entitled, "*Parallel Universes*," covers the subject quite well. Another fine work is that of Michael Talbot's, "*Holographic Universe*." These two gentlemen have a wonderful take on reality and the subjects of probable and parallel selves.

Walk-Ins

This may seem like a silly question, but does everyone have an Akashic record?

Yes, every moment in every life, in every system is recorded. Everyone has a Book of Life in the Akashic Records. Even walk-ins.

How'd you know I was thinking of walk-ins?"

Call me psychic.

How do you access someone's records who's only just walked in, who has never been human before?

Excellent question. It is difficult to identify a walk-in. Here is the main reason: the first information you receive from the Records will be of the individual who was born to the body. This is solely because most walk-ins are unaware of the fact that they are walk-ins and continue to operate out of the context of the original owner – given name, family name, personal history of the cellular mind, beliefs, behaviors, etc. So when you use their Earthly name to access the Records, you get the original file. If you are truly reading for a walk-in, you will begin to spontaneously receive information that is other worldly, i.e., unusual settings and landscapes, unusual thought groupings, data that is difficult to readily understand, etc. When this happens I ask the Records for the Soul name of the individual sitting in front of me. If the Soul name resonates with the given name of the individual I'm reading, I know this is not a walk-in, but the original owner. If there is no match, well, here is where it can get exciting. To get information fresh from another system is very stimulating. Remember to ask for the information in symbols you readily understand.

It is important to know that most individuals who have been told, or believe themselves to be walk-ins, feel so because they have other world incarnations as their most recent past incarnation. Even though these individuals are not walk-ins, reading for such an individual is fascinating and very informative. Usually these individuals are to make earth shattering contributions to the Collective Mind. These are individuals who bring change through expressing genius. These are the innovators.

Please know that there are genuine walk-ins who are here to contribute at a very high level, and there are those who have walked in simply to balance an inner conflict originating in this dimension.

An interesting thought just crossed my mind. Much of the technical advancements that have happened over the last ten to twenty years are being influenced by individuals who have recently had past lives in other systems.

Very accurate thought. I've come across many who have brought with them an invention or two from other worlds.

Aliens

So, we are being influenced by aliens after all. Is this why the entertainment industry has taken such a futuristic bent.

In part. Are we being prepared for "close encounters?" Yes, beginning with the movie, *"The Day the Earth Stood Still."*

Timing is everything to these beings. They must become known at just the right moment, or their coming out to the general public will send too great a shock wave through the Collective Mind. Imagine the reaction of western religious leaders, or our world's power brokering governments. What if the aliens wanted to tell the general populous the Truth about Creation?

The visitors from other worlds are primarily here to witness the mass awakening of Human Consciousness in this dimension during the Twelve Days of Light.[4] They are not here to aid us in any way, or to interfere with our progress. They are simply here to observe.

Sounds pretty far out there. I would like to think that we are obtaining new technologies because we have evolved to the point of understanding our world; that we have earned where we are and we have managed it on our own.

Yes. We, as the Consciousness of Creation, are all advancing in the many dimensions and realities with the help of each other. These outside alien influences have advanced our physical evolution greatly. When you look into the Records you will see that we are different from those of other systems only in the shapes of our bodies and some bodily functions. Here on Earth we started out as one race. Through genetic engineering alien intelligence brought about the different races. This allowed us the experience of blending our obvious external differences. Interestingly, our physical bodies are genetically linked to the same Source as those who visit us from other worlds and genetically interfered with our physical forms to help us in our Collective journey.

I recently had a new client on the west coast who went to a healer to have her kundalini more completely awakened. My client related that she had been studying several of Muktananda's books when she spontaneously received shakti from His Spirit. While her symptoms were far less than what they could have been for such an experience, they were energetic and classic kundalini type performances. She wanted more.

The healer was very up front with my client when she described that she had received instructions for the work she was performing while in the depths of a nervous breakdown. The client was also told by the healer that she channeled ninety-one beings from a distant star system and that they would be working on her Etheric body to open all seven chakras on each of the seven levels of existence. The healer said that this work would happen in two sessions.

Immediately after the first session my client began to feel the presence of alien forms around her. She could feel them working in her body. The healer said they were installing an Etheric grid that would help my client shift to a higher dimension. My client said she did not want this and asked that they immediately stop what they were doing. They didn't. They would work on her whenever she was alone. She could feel energy runs, clicking sounds and thumping sensations, and streams of cool energy blowing through, or out of her physical body. She couldn't sleep or rest. In short, they were driving her nuts.

My client went to several "sensitives" seeking relief from the alien intrusions. One told her we are Sovereign Beings and if they were not stopping at her request, it was because she had an agreement at "some level" that allowed them to continue.

She was very agitated and very tired of the whole mess by the time she arrived for our time together. I checked the Records to see if she had any agreements and there were none. The next step was to find a way to communicate directly with these alien forms. That night I went out-of-body and stayed within her etheric field. When they showed up to continue their work, I presented myself as an individual Consciousness who was interested in their work. In no way did I confront them on behalf of my client, I was in their eyes an observer, not an antagonist. They were very cooperative and revealed that they were from the star system Cirrus and that I could refer to them as Zaee-Tah-Vah. After our initial exchange I had enough information to be able to intrude into their Akashic system. There I found a series of symbols that when placed within the subconscious mind of my client would trigger a deep repulsion response in their subconscious minds. I wrote the coded messages in the symbols of their language on a piece of paper and gave it to my client with instructions of how to use it. She called the next day and related how that night she felt them dismantling the inner grid and leaving. She was finally able to rest.

We will remain in touch to monitor her progress. This was fascinating for me and horrifying for her.

†Σ†

Footnotes:

[1] Read the Arthurian trilogy penned by Mary Stewart. The titles were, *The Crystal Cave, These Hollow Hills, & The Last Enchantment.* Her final book on the subject was titled, *That Wicked Day*. These are wonderfully told and surprisingly in accord with the accounts held within the Akashic Records of the life of King Arthur, Merlin and ensemble.

[2] These individuals did not have one leader, they shared leadership with each Soul group. Their main desire was to exist in perpetual harmony with Nature.

[3] Belial is one of the Elders who stayed with Human Consciousness after the break up of Lemuria and who later ruled for 16,000 years in Atlatia. Later this individual was known as Thoth in Egypt. After Egypt, Belial advanced to the level of Time Lord and is now an Eternal Being. He is mentioned in the works of Edgar Cayce.

[4] The Twelve Days of Light will be chronicled as the beginning of the New Age, the Age of Enlightenment, and the thousand years of peace. While in the Records ask for data signaling the Age of Unified Collective Mind. Further information available from author through publisher.

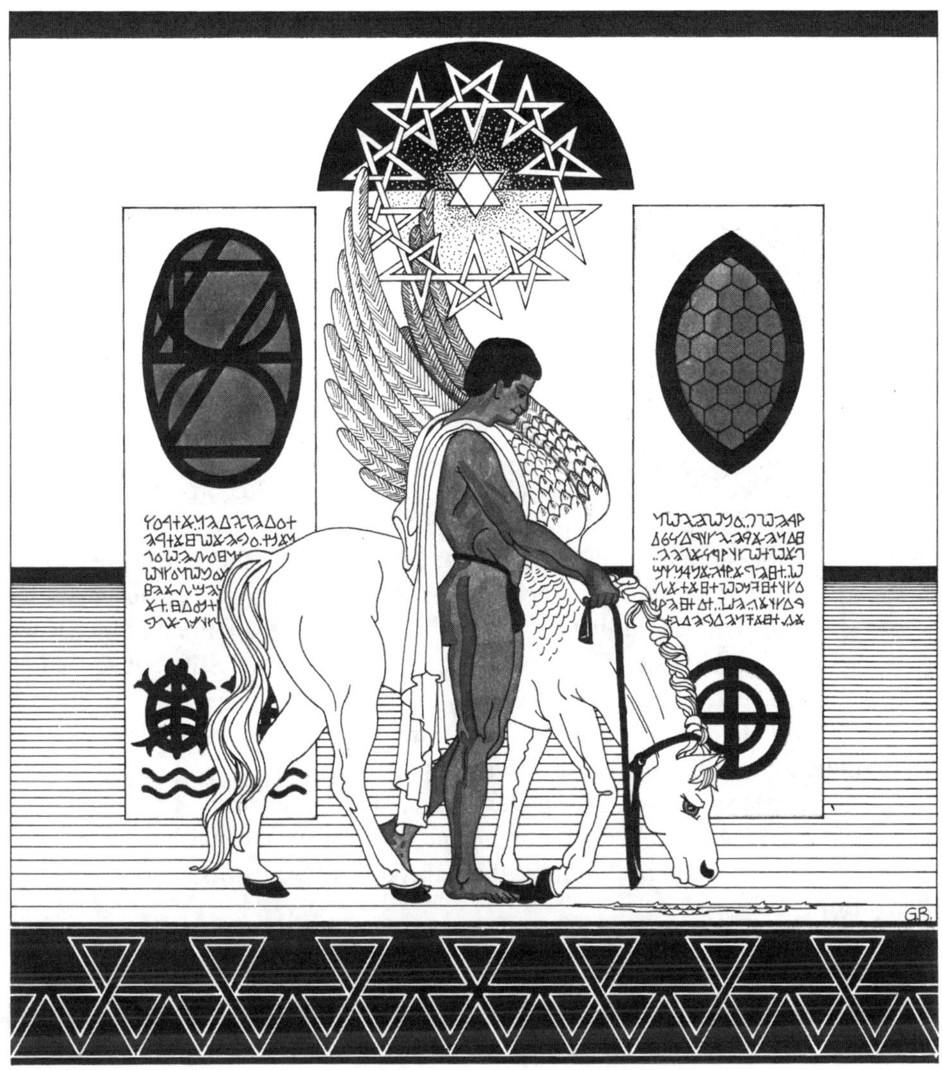

The Process

Taking the Most Direct Route

In the following pages you will find a variety of techniques designed to help you gain entry into the Records. The techniques offered are a very simple means by which to enter the Records. There is no need to make this difficult. As in all spiritual endeavors it is very important to allow the experience to unfold. Pushing yourself will not get you there any sooner, nor will it take you to a deeper level. Relaxation is a key. We live in a culture that believes stress is important to succeed, so some will find the relaxation aspect of this work more difficult than others. Relax at your pace. No one personality type finds accessing the

Akasha easier than the others. It is really a matter of the willingness to know greater boundaries of yourself. Focus your intention. In the Records intention and outcome are the same.

The technique for entering your Book of Life, or for accessing the Akashic Records is basically the same; both contain the same steps. Remember these steps are a process to get you there, and once you have entered the Records, whether through your Book of Life or the Akasha, you may eliminate the process. If you run into difficulty after eliminating these steps, go back to the process until your confidence returns.

The breathing, relaxation and meditation techniques on the proceeding pages are meant to be used in a certain sequence:

Preparation:

- Clear your mental and emotional bodies by focusing intention toward Unity. Attune your mind to thoughts and feelings of wholeness.
    - i) Decide on the information wanted from the Records.
    - ii) Write an outline for each visit that includes a list of questions. It is easier at first if you focus your attention either in the past, present or future. After you gain experience it becomes easier to mix tenses during each visit.
    - iii) Write an outline before each visit and keep a journal of the answers after each visit. The answers from one session will stimulate questions for the next. Notice if there are any questions that you repeatedly forget to ask with each visit. These might be areas where you are blocking.
- Alternate nostril, or 7-1-7 breathing pattern.
    - i) Be sure to start the pattern with a deep exhalation.
    - ii) Imagine the breath flowing into your body at the back of the neck where the head and neck join, and out through your nostrils.

Relaxation:

- Give recognition to the physical structure.
    - i) Create a very soothing environment.
    - ii) Support the body under the knees, lower back, and under the neck.
    - iii) Cover the body in an appropriate blanket. The body can become chilled while in the Records.
- Use a relaxation technique that progressively relaxes the body.
    - i) Give yourself permission to relax.
    - ii) Relaxation techniques using the breath do not replace the alternate nostril pattern of breathing.

Scripting:

- A structured inward journey directs Consciousness to the appropriate areas within the Collective Mind.
    - i) Use the appropriate meditation script. If you want to go to the Akashic Records use one of those scripts. Do not mix the elements from the Akashic scripts with the Book of Life scripts.
    - ii) Creating your own script using the key elements from the meditations can be very interesting.

iii) No music in the background of your meditations. If you feel you absolutely need something in the background then use a constant repetitive theme such as a constant drum rhythm. No peaks or valleys.

Once you have found your perfect formula of relaxation to meditation, stick with it. Also, picking the most appropriate time and place based upon your life style is very important to the success of the techniques offered in this work. Your approach must make sense to your present circumstances and be practical in terms of fitting into your everyday schedule. If you are unduly distracted during your practice time the results will be unsatisfactory. If this undertaking places an unnecessary burden on your time or energy, you will abandon it. Those who give up usually do so because they feel they are giving more to the work than it is giving back in experience. Unfortunately for the bulk of us, this is the case in the beginning. Be reasonable about how long this will take. Most individuals who are intent get into the Records after just a few weeks of practice. This is important – if measurable results do not present themselves within a specific time frame, stop your practice sessions for a short period of time, then resume when your interest is drawn back to the Records.

A side note before we move on: there are no eating, sleeping, or life-style habits that can keep you from entering the Records. That's right, you can eat meat, drink alcohol, and smoke cigarettes while drinking a wonderful cup of expresso. However, having balance is important to the depth at which we will be able to relax and focus our intention. In all Spiritual endeavors, if we are out of balance it will show up quickly. Look at your diet, sleep, and exercise. If something feels as though it is controlling you, it needs changing. Introduce the change gradually. There is nothing to be gained in haste. Changes made quickly seldom last.

– Alternate Nostril Breathing Pattern –

We naturally alternate nostrils throughout the course of a twenty-four hour period. Our nostrils are designed to alternate the direction and volume of the pranic energy attached to the molecules of oxygen. This is necessary to maintain the proper balance of the subtle life force energies that give vitality to the physical, emotional, mental and Spiritual bodies. In his book, *Psychic Breathing*, Robert Crookhall goes into the details of this age old study. Without a strong understanding of the importance of the breath and its relationship with prana, little is possible in Spiritual studies.

The wonderful teachings of pranayama, the study of influencing the movement of pranic energy through the vital centers of the body, goes back several thousands of years and is central to the study of yoga. The work of B. K. S. Iyengar, a renowned Master of hatha yoga, brings profound understanding to this subject. His book entitled, *Light on Pranayama*, offers subtle insights into the workings of these vital forces. This book is a very important reference document and a fine addition to any metaphysical library.

Technique:

Body Posture: Always sit comfortably with your spinal column erect and lifted. When sitting on the floor a small pillow, or two, can make the difference if your hamstring muscles or hips are tight. It is important not to use the back of a chair for support. Keep your back straight by adjusting your hips. Do not rest your head against the back of the chair. Using the arm of the chair to support your right arm will put you into the wrong posture. Imagine the crown of your head being attached to a string hanging down from the ceiling that is gently pulling you upward. Your chin will naturally tilt slightly downward as you imagine the lift.

Hand Posture: The last two fingers of the right hand control the flow of oxygen into and out of the left nostril, while the thumb of the right hand controls the inhalation and exhalation of the right nostril.

The Breath: This breath is not a balanced breath and should not be done for extreme lengths of time. For the average person ten to fifteen minutes is enough. If you feel any nausea or dizziness while doing this breath, stop for a moment, then continue replacing the exhalation through the mouth with exhaling through the left nostril. This breath is designed to awaken the spiritual centers at the back of the brain that allow for greater vision.

Always begin this breath with three conscious exhalations through both nostrils. Expand the diaphragm as you breathe deeply into your belly through your nostrils, then contract the diaphragm as you exhale through both nostrils. Repeat two more times.

- Close your left nostril and breathe in through right nostril.
- Close both nostrils and breath out through your mouth.
- Open your left nostril and inhale.
- Close your left nostril at the top of your inhalation, open your right nostril and exhale.

– Repeat –

- Keeping your left nostril closed, inhale through the right nostril.
- Close both nostrils and exhale through your mouth.
- Keep the right nostril closed. Open the left nostril and inhale.
- Close the left nostril, open the right and exhale.

– Repeat –

- In through the right.
- Out through the mouth.
- In through the left.
- Out through the right.

There is another element to be added once you are confident with the pattern. Imagine that your lungs are now located at the top of your neck. Inhale (through nostrils) as though you were breathing in through the back of your neck exactly where it joins with your head. Feel the energy of each breath moving in through the neck at the base of the skull. Exhale as you normally would, through your mouth or nose. This element is as important as the pattern of breathing itself. This helps to awaken the visual centers located at the back of the brain and also excites the third eye of the Etheric body.

At first this will seem like a lot to do. My suggestion would be to focus on the breathing pattern itself for several days, then add the last element. If you are unaccustomed to doing these types of exercises it may seem odd at first. Stick with it, the reward is sweet.

Sometimes it is difficult to breath through one nostril or the other. Clearing the nose with tissue or a saline solution is recommended. If nothing seems to help try spreading the nostril open by gently pulling the skin of the check next to the nostril sideways away from the opening. This will widen the airway by pulling the skin on the inside of the nostril away from the turbinaters located in the nose.

If you lose your place and are unable to remember whether you are breathing in through the left, out through the right, or otherwise – stop for a moment, collect yourself, then begin again. It is very easy for every day thoughts to drop in unexpectedly. Be kind when this happens. Simply remind yourself it is time to do your breathing and continue.

– 7 • 1 • 7 Breathing Pattern –

This next exercise is for those who are truly unable to do the alternate nostril pattern. This is not the preferred breathing pattern to enliven the visual centers.

Lay down with your knees and neck supported. It is important that your body is as comfortable as possible. No mouth breathing. Inhale and exhale through your nostrils. Do this exercise slowly and deeply. With your imagination, select only the finest quality of oxygen. See it suspended in the air in front of you as tiny points of Light. Imagine that your navel is able to inhale the oxygen up into your lungs. While breathing in through your nostrils, pretend you are slowly drawing oxygen into your body through your navel for a count of seven, hold for a count of one and exhale through your nostrils for a count of seven. Hold for a count of one, inhale, 2, 3, 4, 5, 6, 7, hold for a count of one, exhale 2, 3, 4, 5, 6, 7, hold for a count of one, inhale, 2, 3, 4, 5, 6, 7, hold, exhale 2, 3, 4, 5, 6, 7, repeat this pattern for a total of twenty-two repetitions.

– Pause for a Moment –

Again with your imagination, select only the finest quality of oxygen. See it suspended in the air in front of you as tiny points of Light. Imagine an opening in your cheek bones just below each eye that is able to inhale the oxygen. Instead of sending the oxygen down into your lungs send it to the very center of your brain. While breathing in through your nostrils, imagine slowly drawing oxygen into your body through the openings below your eyes for a count of seven, hold for a count of one and exhale through your nostrils for a count of seven. Hold for a count of one, inhale, 2, 3, 4, 5, 6, 7, hold, exhale 2, 3, 4, 5, 6, 7, hold, inhale, 2, 3, 4, 5, 6, 7, hold, exhale 2, 3, 4, 5, 6, 7, repeat this pattern for a total of twenty-two repetitions.

– Pause for a Moment – Repeat the Cycle –

Repeat this pattern of alternating cycles of twenty-two breaths for at least thirty minutes. Remember to inhale through your navel up into your lungs. As you hold for the count of one, imagine your lungs glowing bright with Light. As you release, imagine all the impurities leaving your system on the expelled gases. Imagine the same process when you inhale through the openings in your cheeks and send the prana to the center of your brain. This pattern will achieve the same end results as the alternate nostril technique.

The Alchemy of Relaxation

It is important to be as relaxed as possible when using these techniques. Distractions will halt the movement of your Consciousness toward the preconscious areas of the Collective Mind. The problem here is that when most individuals deeply relax they go unconscious. Being completely relaxed while maintaining full Conscious Awareness is difficult. For many this will feel as though they have entered that dream like space just before sleep. Remain alert as you enter this area of Consciousness. This is where the journey into the Records begins.

There are a few things you might consider before starting the relaxation process.

One: as you begin to fully relax your body you might notice certain muscle groups, especially those around the eyes, twitching or jerking. This twitching, and sometimes jerking, is very natural to the deep relaxation process. Let it happen even if it is distracting to the point of taking you out of the experience. Trying to control these sudden movements will be more distracting than the movements themselves.

Two: if you are lying on the floor make sure a pillow is placed behind the knees and under the neck and head. The point here is to be as comfortable as possible. Cover your body with an appropriate blanket.

Three: as your body begins to profoundly relax, your bladder will want to empty. Drinking fifteen to twenty minutes prior to starting your relaxation is not a good idea. You will be interrupted.

Four: if you must have music in the background keep it very light and as nondescript as possible. Be careful with your selection. Any sudden shifts in tempo or pitch will act as an irritant. A constant drumming is the best.

Five: doing this work in the same place, at the same time each day will actually train your body to relax. After a few days you will notice your body beginning to relax as your appointed time approaches, or if you should walk into the area where you are doing this work.

Just relaxing, in and of itself, can be so enjoyable. And who can deny it, we could all use a little more power lounging time. Our culture, with its, "what have you done for me lately" undercurrent gives us the message that it is not okay to fully relax. There are so many ways to achieve deep relaxation. Here are just a few. If you have others that have proven to work well for you, incorporate them into this work. The point is to enter a deep state of relaxation. The following scripts could be recorded, or memorized, whichever suits your personality. Each guided meditation in the next two sections has a relaxation technique at the beginning. If the one being offered is not the one that works for you, replace it. The relaxation techniques suggested do not have to be used as scripted. You can substitute other relaxation techniques.

– Relaxation Technique Script #1 –

Take a moment to focus on your breathing. Do this technique in a slow, deliberate pattern.

Breathe deeply into your belly. Connect the inhalation to the exhalation. In other words, no pauses or holding the breath between inhalation and exhalation. Holding the breath stimulates the body. Become very aware of the moment when the inhalation touches the exhalation. Again, breathe deeply, moving your lower abdomen out as far as possible, then move the inhalation upward filling out the middle ribs, then up into your chest. At the top of the inhalation shrug your shoulders and inhale the last few inches. Repeat this breathing pattern for at least five minutes.

– 1 minute Pause –

Allow your breathing pattern to return to normal. Notice any sensations your physical body might be experiencing before going onto the next part of the exercise. Remember it is easier to follow the suggestions being offered, than it is to resist them.

– Slight Pause (10 seconds) –

Direct your attention to the muscles and tendons of your toes. With your imagination visualize each toe, from your little toe, to your big toe. Ask the muscles and tendons of each toe to completely relax. Imagine you can feel each toe relaxing, softening. Feel the skin of each toe softening. Relax your toes completely.

– Slight Pause –

Now allow the relaxation from the bottoms of your toes to spread to the skin on the balls of your feet. Allow the skin of the arches of your feet to feel the relaxation spreading out from your toes. Completely relax. Feel the skin of your heels softening, relaxing.

Every inch of the skin on the bottoms of your feet is completely and wonderfully relaxed. So soft. So relaxed.

– Slight Pause –

Move the feelings of relaxation through your feet, from the bottoms to the tops of the arches. Allow the muscles and bones of your feet to fully relax. Feel your feet softening. Relax completely. Completely relax. Your feet are so relaxed. So relaxed.

– Slight Pause –

Invite the feelings of relaxation from your feet up into your ankles. Feel the joints soften. The tendons are softening, relaxing. Feel each ankle completely relax. Allow the relaxation to become warmth. Allow the warm comfortable sensations to spread over your feet and ankles. Your are completely relaxed, feeling wonderfully warm in your feet and ankles.

– Slight Pause –

Move the warmth in your feet and ankles up into the calves of each leg. Allow the relaxation to soften the muscles of your calves. Feel the warmth of relaxation spreading from the bottoms of your toes, through your feet, into your ankles, up into your calves.

– Slight Pause –

Spread the warmth from the bottoms of your toes, through your feet, into your ankles and calves, and up into your knees. Feel each knee flexible and strong. Now feel the backs of your knees begin to soften. Feel the skin relaxing. Softening. Allow the joints deep inside each knee to fully relax. Completely relax your knees. Command the muscles and tendons to fully relax. Feel the warmth of relaxation in your knees. Move the warmth up into your thighs.

– Slight Pause –

There are many muscle layers in each thigh. It is important to relax each thigh completely. Allow the warmth from your toes to move upward along the bones of each thigh. Imagine a warm sensation surrounding each bone. Feel the warmth deep in each thigh. Allow the warmth to spread up along each bone into each hip. Radiate the warmth of the thigh bones outward into the muscles and tendons. Feel the deep muscles sag against the bone as they soften with relaxation. Radiate the warmth out to the skin. Feel the warmth pushing out through the pores of the skin. Allow all the muscles of each thigh to soften with relaxation. Move the warmth of relaxation from your toes up into your hips.

– Slight Pause –

Allow the deep muscles of the hips and buttocks to soften. Feel your hip sockets relax their hold on the tips of the thigh bones. Allow your hips to spread open. Release the tension in your buttocks. Feel the warmth of relaxation spreading through your hips into your buttocks. Every layer of muscle tissue in your buttocks is completely relaxed. So completely relaxed. Relax completely.

– Slight Pause –

Allow the warmth to spread into your genitals and lower belly. Feel your anal sphincter muscles relax. Relax and soften the muscles in and around your genitals. Feel the warmth of relaxation spreading upward through your lower belly from your hips. Soften your stomach muscles. Allow your colon to relax. Allow your small intestines to relax. Ask that the warmth from the tips of your toes move up through your body and into each organ in your belly, bringing relaxation and warmth. Each organ is completely relaxed and warm. Feel the warmth spread upward into your stomach.

– Slight Pause –

Bring the warmth up from your toes, through your hips and lower belly, into your stomach. The warmth of relaxation is becoming a wonderful bright yellow glow that fills your solar plexus as your stomach softens. Your stomach is now completely relaxed. Allow your stomach to glow with warmth. Spread that glow out to the ribs and the muscles between each rib. Your ribs are completely relaxed.

– Slight Pause –

Spread the yellow Light up into your chest, and into your heart and lungs. Allow your heart and lungs to relax and soften. Completely relax. Feel the bones, muscles and organs of your upper body soften in the glow of this bright yellow Light. Feel your upper body relax. Completely relax.

– Slight Pause –

Spread the bright yellow glow of relaxation into your shoulders. Feel your shoulders completely relax as the glow moves from your chest into your shoulders. Allow the warm glow of relaxation to spread down from your shoulders into your upper arms. Relax your upper arms. Feel the warmth spreading into your forearms. Your forearms are wonderfully relaxed. Allow the relaxation to spread into your hands and fingers. Your shoulders, arms, hands and fingers are completely relaxed. Feel the warmth spreading from your fingertips, back into your forearms and upper arms, and shoulders. Your fingers, hands, arms, and shoulders are glowing with the warmth of relaxation.

– Slight Pause –

Allow the warmth to spread from your shoulders into your throat. Feel the soft tissues of your throat relaxing. Feel the muscles and tendons of your neck softening in the yellow glow of light coming from your chest. Completely relax your throat and neck. Completely relax. Your conscious mind is alert.

– Slight Pause –

Move the glow of yellow Light up into your face. Allow the muscles of your face to completely relax. Feel the muscles of your jaw soften with relaxation. The muscles around your mouth soften. The muscles under your eyes soften. The muscles in your eye sockets soften. Soften your eyes. Move the warm feelings of relaxation up into your forehead. Feel the muscles above your eyes soften. Relax your forehead. Completely relax. Feel the warm glow of Light from your chest spreading to the top of your head. Feel your scalp softening in the glow of relaxation. Allow your conscious mind to be completely alert.

– Slight Pause –

Allow the yellow glow of Light covering your scalp to sink down into your brain. Feel your brain soften with relaxation. Allow your brain to sag against the base of your skull. Allow your brain to soften, to relax. Completely relax. Move the warmth of relaxation from your brain into the brain stem, and down into your spinal column. Allow the warmth of relaxation to spread down your spinal column into your lower back, buttocks, and into your legs, feet and toes. You are wonderfully alert.

– Slight Pause –

Feel a wave of warmth moving from your toes upward through your body into your brain, then down your spinal column, through your buttocks, into your legs, feet and toes. Allow the warmth of relaxation to spread from your toes back upward to your brain, then back again to your toes.

– Slight Pause –

With each wave of warmth you move deeper and deeper into relaxation. A thousand times more relaxed than ever before. Allow your conscious mind to remain alert.

– End –

– Relaxation Technique Script #2 –

Tense all the muscles of your lower body, toes to buttocks, at the same time. Hold the tension for a count of five, four, three, two, one. Release. Command the muscles and tendons of your lower body to relax. Repeat...tense all the muscles of your lower body, toes to buttocks, at the same time. Hold the tension for a count of five, four, three, two, one. Release. Repeat...tense all the muscles of your lower body, toes to buttocks several times, at the same time. Hold the final tension for a count of five, four, three, two, one. Release. Relax. Alert.

– Pause (5 seconds) –

Tense all the muscles of your upper body, buttocks to scalp, at the same time. Hold the tension for a count of five, four, three, two, one. Release. Command the muscles and tendons of your upper body to relax. Repeat...tense all the muscles of your upper body, buttocks to scalp, at the same time. Hold the tension for a count of five, four, three, two, one. Release. Command the muscles and tendons of your upper body to relax. Repeat...tense all the muscles of your upper body, buttocks to scalp, at the same time. Hold the tension for a count of five, four, three, two, one. Release. Command the muscles and tendons of your upper body to relax. You are alert.

– Pause –

Tense all your muscles, lower and upper body, at the same time. Hold the tension for a count of five, four, three, two, one. Release. Command the muscles and tendons of your entire body to relax. Repeat...tense all your muscles, lower and upper body, at the same time. Hold the tension for a count of five, four, three, two, one. Release. Command the muscles and tendons of your entire body to relax. Repeat...tense all your muscles, lower and upper body, at the same time. Hold the tension for a count of five, four, three, two, one. Release. Command the muscles and tendons of your entire body to relax.

– Pause –

Relax. Completely relax. Notice any sensations that may be present in your physical body. Send healing thoughts, thoughts of relaxation and warmth to any area of your body that may still seem tense. Mentally massage any tension from your body. Take your time.

– Pause –

Focus your attention on your breath, breathing slowly and deeply. Fill the bottoms of the lungs first, then the middle, then the top. Slowly exhale from the bottom of your lungs first, then the middle, then the top. With your next inhalation, imagine selecting only the finest molecules of oxygen to breathe into your body. Suspended in front of you are only the purest molecules of oxygen. See them as tiny points of Light. Inhale. Allow those points of light to come into your nostrils, down the air passageways and into the lungs. Feel the warm glow of Light coming from each molecule of oxygen. Allow the Light to fully relax your throat and expand your lungs. As you exhale, imagine releasing any impurities from your body on your breath. Repeat the cycle.

– Continue breathing in this fashion for 15 minutes –

– Relaxation Technique Script #3 –

Get comfortable. Gently move your body until it finds exactly the most comfortable position. Take three deep breaths, letting out a deep sigh at the end of each exhalation. Allow your body to completely relax.

With your imagination, envision a beautiful fall colored tree directly in front of you. The leaves are brilliant with color. This is the most colorful tree you have ever seen. It is a perfect fall day – the sky is clear, the sun is bright, the temperature of the breeze declares the end of summer. Look up to the top of the tree. The gentle breeze is tugging at the leaves hanging at the uppermost branches. Watch as a beautiful leaf breaks free and starts its journey toward the earth.

Watch as the leaf floats back and forth...back and forth...on the breeze, making its way to its winter resting place. It has served the tree very well through the spring and summer, and now it will rest. It floats so easily on the cool currents of the breeze. Back and forth...back and forth. Watch as it touches the earth. Deep waves of relaxation spread through your body as you watch the leaf settle to the ground.

– Pause (5 seconds) –

The sun is warm, the wind is cool, you are perfectly bundled in your favorite fall clothes. It is so pleasant watching this beautiful tree. The tree is so beautiful.

Look up again to the top of the tree. Another leaf is breaking free, and gently, back and forth...back and forth it begins its journey to earth. The leaf is moving very slowly downward. Very slowly. Back and forth on the cool breeze. Back and forth. Watch as it joins the other leaves already on the ground. A great wave of relaxation moves through your body as the leaf touches the earth. Feel your body completely relax. Relaxing. Completely relaxing. You are relaxed and very alert.

– Pause –

Look up again to the top of the tree. You will watch one more leaf at the top of the tree as it breaks free, falling gently back and forth...back and forth on the cool breeze. Back and forth, back and forth. Watch as it makes its way to the earth below. It is time to relax. Completely relax. As the leaf touches the earth, command your body to completely relax. Allow your consciousness to be very alert.

End –

Relaxation of the physical body is extremely important to the process of accessing the Records. In order to get into your Book of Life, or the Akasha, you must be able to consciously let go of the physical body and remain fully aware while entering the theta level of consciousness. You will only enter this experience if your physical body feels safe and cared for. This is difficult if you are distracted physically. As you begin the process of relaxation mentally or verbally affirm, "Any sounds, smells or movements that are important to the safety of my physical body will immediately bring me to full physical Consciousness." This assures the physical body that you are not abandoning it in favor of a larger playground.

If you are an over achieving type 'A' personality and none of these techniques work, take heart, all is not lost. There are many books available on the subject of relaxation. Try as many different techniques as are necessary to bring yourself to the point of Conscious Theta Awareness.

Imagination

The Power of the Mind

Many great thinkers have offered much on the subject of imagination. Here is what one noted thinker had to say: *"The fairest thing we can experience is the mysterious. It is the fundamental emotion which stands at the cradle of true art and science. He who knows it not and can no longer feel amazement is as good as dead, a snuffed out candle."* Albert Einstein also said, *"Imagination is superior to intellect."* I am glad he made that statement. I like Einstein. His hair, and the sparkle in his eyes bring joy to most everyone.

Imagination is the doorway leading into the mysterious dimensions Einstein knew so well. Without imagination we would not have visual and performing arts, music, architecture, science, language, or even God. Without imagination we would still think the earth flat, and the center of the Universe.

Think of the courage it has taken for visionary men and women throughout the centuries to share their imaginings. The forward thinkers of every age would marvel at the technology of our every day modern world. And now that we have wrestled with atoms and sent probes toward what we think is Galactic Central Point, we are left with the greatest frontier – Individual and Collective Consciousness.

It is very difficult to isolate that part of our Consciousness we term imagination, primarily because the ability to imagine is critical to <u>every</u> aspect of Awareness. Scientists have recently discovered that not only is imagination vital to envisioning what is possible in this world, it is also vital in our abilities to function from moment to moment. Several studies have been done with children who were blind from birth and later had their sight fully restored. To the amazement of those performing the miracle of sight, the children were still unable to see in a normal fashion. The children saw a flat world, one lacking perceptions of height, width and depth. Objects that they could describe with touch were unrecognizable by sight, even after repeated attempts. Other studies show that our ability to imagine develops early, and if during this development period a child is unable to discern movement, shape and color value relationships, the child will be unable to "see" if sight is later restored.

Imagination is the power of the mind and without our ability to imagine, little is possible in daily life. Imagination is fundamental to success. In today's business world a healthy imagination is a must if an individual is to succeed. All businessmen and women forecast out of the ability to envision what is possible for their service or product as it relates to the market place. If you wish to play sports beyond the basic skills, you must be able to use your imagination and play an inner game. If you are unable to play the inner game, top levels of play will elude you. Actors and entertainers imagine themselves in the roles they take. It is interesting that the individuals we call "stars" are those who use imagination to the fullest.

Unfortunately, the average individual is talked out of imagination at a very early age, particularly in western cultures. How many times have you heard someone say, "That's not real. It's just your imagination." As children we are taught to draw a line between what is real and what is considered imaginary. The irony of this is, we draw the line between what is real and imaginary with, you guessed it, our imaginations.

The use of imagination is central to the techniques offered in this work. In this work we are entering the mysterious. It is impossible to get there through logical means. Example: if we take our logical minds into the mysterious realms of simultaneous existence the absurdity of it all would overwhelm us, leaving us with an, "Alice in Wonderland," type of experience. It is therefore important to enter the Records with the awe and amazement of a child, without an investment in the outcome. The shift from imagination to actual experience comes when you approach the Book of Life, and the Akashic Records, as a witness with no need to be right about the correctness of the information being offered, just the wonder that the experience is possible.

Meditation Techniques

Effectively Using the Process

One of the most effective ways to use the following meditations is to create an audio tape of your voice reading the script. Rehearse the script a few times. Use a slow and easy pace. The more familiar you are with the script the smoother and more confidant your presentation will be. This added confidence will transfer onto the tape and help you in your inward journey. When you hear a professionally done meditation tape, you can bet there were many rehearsals and takes. Very few individuals get it right the first time. If a recording you have made seems to disturb you in any way, such as a mispronounced word, or a stammered phrase, re-record the meditation.

By all means experiment with the guided image suggestions. If an image other than the one suggested in the script repeats itself to you during your practice of the technique, re-record your tape with your element replacing the one suggested in the script. This is your inner journey, personalize it with your images. If the images you receive are nowhere near the suggestions offered, then go with the script. Example: if the script suggests the image of a lake and you are seeing trees, go with the image of the lake in your recording. If you have difficulty visualizing or connecting in a sensory way with the suggested images, just holding the thought of it will suffice until you allow yourself to fully visualize the details of the suggested symbols. If you simply have never been able to visualize while being guided through a meditation, I recommend creating a "real" world experience of each symbolic element, then recall those experiences for the meditation. Sounds elaborate, and it works.

The human mind is such a wonderful playground. There is no other place like it in all of Creation. It is positioned at the axis of several dimensional universes. All we need do to experience these other dimensional realms is allow our Awareness of those "other" places to become dominant within our mind. The most difficult aspect to this type of exploration is the fear of losing our way back to this dimension. We will always return if we go there consciously.

Many people have gone into probable realities as a result of trauma to the biochemistry of the body. The form of trauma could be severe physical injuries that have the body producing an abundance of endorphins to counteract the pain, or just plain mind altering substances intentionally ingested to bring about an altered state. We do not need to alter the chemistry of the brain to open the doorways to these other dimensions. Allow yourself to consciously enter these other realities by opening to the possibility that you are truly more than meets our present state of Awareness. It is that simple.

With the power of your mind, your imagination, allow yourself to feel, hear, see, smell and touch all the suggestions being offered in these meditations. Have fun with the images. Find greater and greater dimensions in which to allow yourself to play. Enlarge your sand box. If you find yourself unable to visualize after giving yourself permission to do so, then know that holding the thought of the suggestion being offered is just as effective as an internal image. You do not have to be able to visualize to have this experience. Believe in yourself. This is a key ingredient.

A side note. At any time during the Akashic Records meditations you may ask that your Spiritual Guides be present with you. You do not have to be on a first name basis with your guides, or even be aware of the guides who help you through each day. Your guides may or may not appear in the Records when helping. They may simply inspire certain thoughts or urges. There is also an Akashic Master who resides within the Records. You may call upon the help of this being in translating symbolic information. There are no magical words, or special thoughts. Your intention to be helped is all you need. Many who ask for help do so only after they have become frustrated by the lack of results coming from their own efforts. Asking for help in the beginning of your process is more effective than asking once you are in the Records.

After each meditation there is a listing of the key elements found within each guided journey. The brief descriptions of the key elements are just that, brief descriptions. These elements are very symbolic to Human Consciousness and it could take several volumes to cover their complete meanings. Once you have gained access to your Book of Life or the Akashic Records and feel confident in your ability, you may want to bypass the process of the meditation. A trigger element can be used to enter the Records. Focusing your concentration on one or more of these key trigger elements will allow you immediate entry.

The first three guided meditations are for entry into your Book of Life. These meditations are feminine in nature and utilize earth symbols to move Consciousness through the mind. While it is not necessary to enter your Book of Life before entering the Akashic Records, it is helpful to the Akashic experience to have connected with the deep inner place afforded by these meditations. Individuals who go into the Akashic Records first report that they feel substantially more grounded after experiencing their Book of Life.

The Akashic Records have a masculine orientation and can seem very heady when compared to the heart felt spaces of the Book of Life. While the symbols used in the Akashic meditations have earth origins they are used outside of their natural context. This can make for a surrealistic meditation experience.

The most important thing to remember about these relaxation techniques and guided meditations is this: allow your imagination to transport you into the experience. Trust in your imagination. Be as natural with it as a child. The only way we eventually experience anything in this world is when we can imagine ourselves in the experience. Without your imagination you would be unable to make anything out of the details your senses are reporting.

One thing to keep in mind: individual memory is very selective and the Records are impartial. There are no sides to be taken in the Records. We all have any number of ways to excuse ourselves from certain realities and to stuff feelings of shame and guilt. The good news – you'll find the Records to be blame and guilt free. This new impartial slant on the past will change your ability to respond to Creation. Once you're back in the "real" world you will have a different view of your role in your personal history.

Some aspects of these guided journeys will be more appealing than others and therefore easier to visualize or hold. One of the reasons you might find yourself drifting off into "Never Never Land" is because the images being offered are simply unappealing. Drifting off indicates boredom or distraction, and not that you are unable to function in meditative environments. Always remember to be gentle with yourself and to leave the critical voice out of your visualization experiences.

During the guided journeys, many individuals have reported feeling a concentration of warmth spreading through their skulls from the base upward. This is common. The point of each meditation is to focus energy at the base of the brain in such a manner as to open the channels that allow Consciousness to witness Creation as both simultaneous and linear. In this condition you escape the boundaries of logic and select where it is you want to concentrate your attention; past, present or future. In this multi-dimensional experience several regions of the brain are excited simultaneously. It is this added energy flow of Consciousness that helps to create the feelings of warmth spreading through the brain.

As in all other Spiritual practices it remains important to enjoy these exercises, realizing that once they have taken you the distance, you will no longer need them. These are tools. Nothing more, nothing less. Once you have obtained entry into your Book of Life or the Akashic Records all you need do is imagine yourself there.

Book of Life Meditation Scripts:

Introduction

These meditations make up a system designed to guide you to your Book of Life. An individual's Book of Life is viewed through the preconscious mind, so a high level of relaxation and focused intention is needed to achieve the best results. Because so many of us have difficulty fully engaging our imaginations, these meditations are designed to be effective even with those who believe that imagination is less real than sensory experience, or have determined themselves unable to visualize.

In the beginning of new endeavors we first explore our safe zones and boundaries. As we progress, feelings of confidence begin to dominate our experience and our efforts are rewarded. Remember these meditations are just vehicles. Once you have experienced your Book of Life, all you need do is focus your thoughts on any one of the key elements within the meditation to gain entry to your records. These guided journeys are only needed in the beginning. Treat them as though they were a treasure map – find the treasure, discard the map.

Give yourself permission to fully use your imagination. Notice any uneasiness present in your body or mind. Mentally "massage" those areas, allowing a sense of well being into your experience. Assure yourself that it is okay to access your Book of Life with the intention of using it for yourself and others as a guide to living a purposeful life.

Each of the following scripts begin with a short relaxation technique. You may want to add more, or change this section of the script.

–Script Number One–

Meditation: The Eternal Flame

Relax. Allow yourself to fully relax. Focus on your breath. Imagine your breath entering and exiting at the back of the neck where the neck and head join.

Inhale, 2, 3, 4, 5, 6, 7. Hold. Exhale, 2, 3, 4, 5, 6, 7. Hold.
Inhale, 2, 3, 4, 5, 6, 7. Hold. Exhale, 2, 3, 4, 5, 6, 7. Hold.
Inhale, 2, 3, 4, 5, 6, 7. Hold. Exhale, 2, 3, 4, 5, 6, 7. Hold.
Repeat this pattern for a total of twenty-two times.

– Slight Pause (30 seconds) –

Relax. Allow your breathing to return to normal. Focus your attention on your solar-plexus. Imagine a ball of bright yellow light floating above your stomach. Allow the light to get brighter and brighter. Slowly reach out with both hands and pull the ball of light into your solar plexus, into your stomach. Feel the glow spreading throughout your body. Feel your body completely relaxing as the light spreads down to the bottom of your toes – then up to the top of your head. Relax. Completely relax. Allow your body to soften.

– Slight Pause –

Feel your brain soften as the light touches the top of your head. Your brain was like a tight fist. It is now like an open palm. Soft. Gentle. Receiving. Giving. Allow your brain to relax, to soften. Feel it sagging against the back of your skull. Allow your brain to gently relax.

– Slight Pause –

Feel the base of your brain soften. Feel the muscles around your spinal column soften. Relax. Relax.

– Slight Pause –

The words of this guided meditation will help form the details of a beautiful pathway stretching out in front of you. Experience the pathway. Give yourself permission to feel the pathway beneath your feet. The different textures of earth. Sand. Gravel. Rocks. See the pathway. The green plants. Colorful flowers. The shapes along the path change as you continue. Look up to the sky. White clouds play in the currents of light air.

Allow the fragrances of the trees, flowers, and earth to fill your nose. The smells along your pathway excite a deep inner memory of long ago peaceful moments. The sounds of birds singing, and the rustling of trees fill your ears as you continue along the path. This is your pathway. See it continuing out in front of you. Everything is just as you want it to be. The textures, the colors, the shapes, the smells, the sounds are perfectly balanced. Continue walking along your familiar setting. Relax as you walk.

– Slight Pause –

Now the pathway begins to incline, gently rising in front of you. The further you walk, the steeper the path becomes. You can feel your legs working more vigorously now to carry you along. Your arms are swinging back and forth as you lean forward to match the angle of the path. Everything else disappears as you focus all of your attention on the path. The pathway is getting steeper and steeper. Your legs, buttocks, back, shoulders and arms are joyfully working to move you forward and upward. Look up. There ahead of you is the opening to a cave. It is just a little further ahead now. The path is almost done. There. The cave is right in front of you now.

– Slight Pause –

What a wonderful cave, an ancient cave. The opening is about a foot taller than your head and just slightly wider than your outstretched arms. You can feel a soft cool breeze coming from somewhere deep in the earth. Smell the air of the cave. It's so clean and fresh. Just stand for a moment. Be very still. Feel the cave pulling at you, urging you inward. Before you enter the cave, turn around and look up at the sun. Allow the rays of the sun to penetrate deep into your eyes. Feel the intensity of the sun. Allow the brightness of the sunlight to take away your sight. You are momentarily blind, unable to see.

– Slight Pause –

Even though the sun has taken your sight, turn around and begin your descent into the cave. Your feet know the way. Slowly. Move slowly. Your feet easily find the descending path. Smell the cave. Listen to the sounds of water trickling down the walls. Reach out and touch the smooth walls.

The sun's brightness is leaving your eyes now. You can faintly see the details inside the cave. The path is narrow with many different stones lining its way. Feel your body weight shift slightly backward as you follow the path further downward. More details reveal themselves as a wonderful light shines toward you from somewhere up ahead. The path ahead turns slightly to the left. Follow the path. The path straightens once again and up ahead is a beautiful glow of light. The walls and ceiling of the cave begin to move farther apart, suddenly opening into a cathedral like room. The pathway ends at the top of twenty-two descending steps.

– Slight Pause –

There are two flights of eleven steps with a landing separating them. Across the room is an altar. There on the altar is the flame of a candle. Constant. Eternal. Beautiful. It looks like a solitary star hanging in black space.

Stop for a moment. Take a deep breath. Soften your mind. Slowly move down the stairs towards the altar. Count each step as you make your way downward. 22, 21, 20, 19, 18, 17, 16, 15, 14, 13, 12, and pause for a moment on the landing. Look around. Behind you. To each side. Upward. Take a deep breath. Now focus on the altar and the candle's flame. Slowly begin going downward. 11, 10, 9, 8, 7, 6, 5, 4, 3, 2, 1. Behind the altar is a dark shining vertical surface. It is as smooth and flawless as a mirror's surface. Notice nothing reflects in this mirror. Even the light from the candle is absent in the mirror's surface. This mirror is perfectly black. The mirror is very deep.

To each side of the glowing candle is another candle. One on the right. One on the left. It is time to light the candle on your left. Lift the candle and light it in the flame of the center candle. Hold the left candle out in front of you at eye level. Look past the flame into the liquid darkness of the mirror. Allow your vision to soften. From deep inside ask a question concerning your most recent past life. See the answer forming as a small image deep in the mirror's surface. Allow the images of the answer to get bigger and bigger. Allow the details to fill the surface of the mirror. Allow the answer to be voiced inside your thoughts.

– Long Pause (2 minutes)–

Allow the images of the past to fade away. Put out the flame of the candle between your fingers, and place it back on the altar. Turn around and face the twenty-two steps. The ceiling above you is very high, and vaulted. Hanging on the back wall opposite the altar and mirror are several tapestries. Wonderfully woven carpets. Breathe deeply while you remember the images from the past that were just revealed in the mirror and in your thoughts. Allow yourself to relax as you look around the room. Take a deep inhalation, then exhale.

– Slight Pause –

Turn back to the altar. Take the candle from the other side of the center candle and light it in the flame. Hold it at eye level. Look past the flame into the deep surface of the mirror.

Soften your focus. Ask a question about your near future. Allow images of near future events to appear before you in the center of the mirror. Imagine them as very tiny, then allow them to become larger and larger. Ask that the answers to your questions be given in a manner you will be most able to understand.

– Long Pause –

Allow the images of the future to fade away. Put out the flame of the candle between your fingers and put it back on the altar. Take a deep breath and remember all that has just been revealed to you about your future. Turn around and face the stairs. Look around the room once again. Notice if there are any changes.

– Slight Pause –

Turn back around and face the altar. Reach out and pick up the center candle with both hands. Hold it out at arms length, look past the flame into the black mirror. Ask to be shown anything that may be blocking your ascent into enlightenment. Allow the answer to form in the mirror and in your thoughts.

– Pause (1 minute)–

Ask if there is any karmic lesson influencing your present incarnation.

– Pause –

Ask to be shown how to best clear any karmic lesson.

– Pause –

Put the candle back on the altar. Allow the flame to burn brightly. Take a deep breath. Remember what has just been revealed. Turn and ascend the steps. Count them as you move upward; 1, 2, 3, 4, 5, 6, 7, 8, 9, 10, 11. Pause and look around. Look behind you, to each side and above you. Then proceed upward; 12, 13, 14, 15, 16, 17, 18, 19, 20, 21, 22. The walls and ceiling begin to narrow as you move up into the narrowing of the cave. Feel yourself leaning forward into the steep upward path. The walls glisten with moisture. The smell is rich and earthy. Allow yourself to move upward through the cave.

The bright sunlight pouring in from the outside opening of the cave makes it hard to see. Keep your eyes wide open. Allow the sunlight to penetrate deep inside your eyes. Allow the sunlight to take your sight away. Allow your feet to find their place. Trust. You know the way.

A warm breeze wraps itself around you as you step from the mouth of the cave. Your weight shifts backward as you move blindly forward on the path that leads to your physical body. Remember all that was revealed to you in the cave. Remember the center candle and its flame.

The further you move along the pathway, the more you become aware of your physical body. Awaken to your physical reality. Move your inner body. Wiggle your toes. Open your eyes. Relax your physical body.

– End –

Key Elements: (The elements in bold type are trigger elements.)

Upward leading pathway • Blinding sun light • Cave • Downward leading path in the cave • Twenty-two descending steps • **Lighted candle** • Two unlit candles • **Altar** • **Black mirror** • Tapestries • Inner chamber

Explanation of Key Elements:

Upward leading pathway. The upward climb to the mouth of the cave is a symbolic invitation to the vertical earth energies of the lower body to travel upward and collect at the third eye, or sixth chakra.

Blinding sun light. When you turn around, look up at the sun and allow it to take your sight. This is the symbolic act of giving up your "real" world sight with its many judgments in favor of the one sighted mystical Awareness.

Cave. Represents the energy channels associated with moving Awareness into the Book of Life.

Downward leading path. Walking blindly into the cave is a great act of courage and trust, especially when the path is leading down hill. It is this trust of yourself that restores inner sight and allows you to see in your Book of Life. This path represents Consciousness moving toward the altar. The feeling of leaning backward as you descend into the cave is your control of the flow of energy into your Book of Life. This reinforces you as director of this experience.

The twenty-two steps. The steps leading downward are symbolic of your descent through the layers of mind to the inner teacher.

Two unlit candles. These represent your concept of past and future linear time.

The center candle. The center candle is the inner teacher, Higher Self, your Eternal Self that lives in the eternal NOW. It lights the inner chamber with a constant, unwavering light. The candles on the left and right, when lit, shine the light of knowledge in either direction along linear time lines bringing clarity to the dual nature of your worldly perceptions.

The altar. The altar symbolizes your inner most Self.

The black mirror. This is the opening to the Collective Mind.

The tapestries. The wall hangings above and behind you represent the civilizations you have attended and can be viewed in detail at any time. Simply stand with your back to the altar and focus all your attention on one of the tapestries. You may ask any questions about the incarnations within the civilization the tapestry represents. Allow the images to become three-dimensional and surround you as you stand there in the chamber. It is through asking questions of these tapestries that you will discover the many different connections you have to individuals in your current life.

The inner chamber. The cathedral like inner chamber represents your deep inner sanctuary. Here is where you are on even terms with Creation. You as impartial Witness. This is your Book of Life where every past moment is recorded as it happened, and every future event is registered as the highest probable experience. There are also immutable events that will reveal themselves as you gain confidence.

A side note: Many people when face to face with the image of a black mirror feel fear. This is understandable in light of Christianity. Christianity sought to control this Source of information. The black mirror in your Book of Life is symbolic of the internal axis within the mind upon which all sensory data is imprinted. When consciously directed upward through the body, the vertical earth energies stimulate these horizontally stored impressions, creating everything from heightened intuition to true clairvoyance.

As the mystic and Master Teacher Jesus said, "*You are the Light of this world*" (Matthew 5: 14). If you look into the Light you're going to find very little except reflections of Light. If you want to see beyond your current life's reflections, and into the multi-dimensional sensory impressions contained within the holographic fields of the Akasha, you'll need to look into the void, where there are no reflections.

Questions Concerning this Meditation

I found it a little difficult creating the upward path. Is it okay to have a little fun with the images?

Yes. Have fun, and if the images get too far off the suggested beaten path, use the images I am suggesting. As was stated, we move Consciousness through the mind with thought symbols. Certain symbols take you certain places.

What range of play are we talking about here?

The upward path through nature directs Conscious Awareness into the areas of mind that allow imaging to dominate. Once you have clearly connected with the images or thoughts of an external path, your Consciousness can then move into the deeper passageways of mind associated with the brain stem. We do this by symbolically entering the cave. If you were to image a man-made path, such as a sidewalk, the quality of your thoughts would be such as to keep you from entering the deeper layers of your mind. You would be more inclined toward current cultural associations, such as: sidewalk – street – automobile – work – home – family – responsibility – trapped – must get away – what happened to all my wonderful dreams of what I was going to do with my life? What happened to my life!? The next thing you know you're completely unaware of the fact that you are in an activity devoted to Spiritual studies, because your Consciousness is floating aimlessly through the layers of "what if" and "if-only" concerns located forward in the front of your mind.

I don't think I'm that out of touch. But I get your point.

That was not meant as a personal observation.

It is difficult to be a little distracted. You either are, or you are not. These guided images are important to the process. We want the dormant vertical earth energy at the base of the spine to join our Awareness, at the base of the brain. If your range of images or thoughts is too broad you will diffuse the energy by trying to decide which image to use. Also, it is highly significant that you want to alter the suggested images. This is a control issue.

One last thought – the part of you that feels it will cease to exist if you become enlightened – in other words, the ego – is going to become more and more assertive the closer you get to witnessing the Collective Mind. It will do this only because it feels threatened by your belief that <u>it</u> is the problem. Your ego is not the problem.

I'm sure you're aware that it was me who kept sneezing. It's amazing to think that even just the suggestion of looking into the sun can produce such a strong reaction. You said earlier that this is symbolic of transmuting my sight from an external to an internal orientation. Is my sudden fit of sneezing revealing an unconscious desire to keep my sight externally focused?

Yes. This ties into the ego again.

The ego is an important part of our <u>Whole</u> journey, and the belief that we must somehow rid ourselves of it in order to become awakened to the workings of the universe, is a form of madness. As a matter of fact, the ego can be of great service to us in our journey toward completion. Unfortunately, many of those who have studied Eastern Spiritual paths have come away with the notion that the ego must die if they are to attain Cosmic Awareness. This is, on the most part, incorrect. The ego, like all other structures within Creation, can never be destroyed. Energy is always energy. When Unified Mind is achieved, the ego is integrated into Collective Consciousness. In this state we experience existence as Love. While it is true that the ego is changed, it is also true that the ego still exists.

Actually, trying to eliminate the ego is in fact the ego's greatest catch-me-if-you-can game. Many become profoundly lost in this activity. At just the right moment, the ego integrates into the Whole. At that particular moment, you, as individuated Conscious Awareness, are no longer concerned.

I have never felt such a stirring as when I went into the cave. The smell was overwhelming. I could actually feel the temperature change. It was so real, I even opened my eyes to see if I was gone from this room. This has never happened before. Any comment as to why it was so intense?

Remember, we are moving our Consciousness into the very primitive areas of the cellular mind. In order to do that we must somehow replicate the state of mind that existed before collective civilized thought, what we call social consciousness.

In the past, a very long time ago, prior to vanity, our sense of sight was less dominant. In the primitive state, the ego existed as an urge to survive and didn't identify with any one given sense. This allowed for a greater range of multi-dimensional experiences. In this day and age the sense of sight is directly identified with the ego. In allowing the bright sunlight to take away your sight, you entered the cave with your socially dominant ego sense off line. This allowed for a greater experience.

My cave was very small and cramped. It didn't feel anything like hers. It felt wet and slippery, and the air was hard to breath. I must have an active imagination after all.

Personally, I'm excited about your images. These are excellent beginnings and show a quality of sensation that will support your Akashic adventures very nicely indeed. I notice you weren't afraid when in the cave. This is really very good news.

I wasn't afraid, but I didn't really get off on what was happening either. I would have liked hers better.

Yes. I like as little confrontation as possible myself. I have noticed, however, that when confrontational images are present in my meditations, or external world, much wisdom is about to dawn. But only if I remain awake. The mystically aligned mind is neither attracted to nor repulsed by the conditions of this, or Etheric dimensions. Noticing when we are repulsed or attracted serves to bring us back into the mystical mindset.

I began to slide very quickly through the cave as soon as my sight returned. It felt exciting, but also out of control. Then I went somewhere. I don't remember anything after seeing myself sliding toward the candle's flame.

The suggested sensation of leaning backward while moving in the cave is to keep this very thing from happening. The tendency here is for Consciousness to be like a horse that is turned toward the barn at the end of the day – the closer the horse gets, the faster it wants to trot.

Find a sloping pathway in your real world, close your eyes, then lean slightly backward as you move forward. This will help settle your energy when using this in meditation. What you have experienced is very common with this guided visualization.

This is also a statement of your tendency to go unconscious when you feel out of control. Here you have many colleagues. Notice where this is happening in your day-to-day life. Just the right amount of control is important if this is happening. You will have to experiment with exactly how much is needed. I previously have spoken of letting go of control (the known) in favor of the 'flow' (the unknown). Use a little control. Allow it to be present without making it wrong.

The steps kept changing form, then extended beyond the twenty-two. It looked as though they went on forever.

Remember energy flows through the mind in response to symbols. This could simply indicate your journey through the layers of mind needs more "time." Slow your descent by counting more slowly. From time to time you may find another set of steps appears at the bottom of those you have just descended. If a double set of steps repeats itself often this is a form of resistance. When this happens, simply focus on the symbol of the altar as you begin to descend the steps. Count only twenty-two steps. Ignore any additional steps. If the steps disappear as you are descending, continue counting. This is yet another form of resistance.

The candles to the left and right had different colored flames.

One will be blue, the other purple.

Yes, that's right.

The one on the right is purple. The one on the left blue.

Right.. But you didn't suggest those colors.

There are many details that will be the same for everyone. These are the universal symbols of the Collective Mind. Here is where the continuity of your Book of Life and the Akashic Records presents itself.

One individual insisted that if we were getting the same symbols, then we must be in exactly the same place. And if that was the truth, then we must be able to see each other while experiencing the Akasha.

The Akashic Records are viewed through your innermost self. You are witnessing the Collective Mind, so many of the symbols will be the same. And you are alone, save for your guides.

I lost track of how many steps there were, mainly because of what I saw on my altar. It was cluttered with odd looking pieces of pottery. I had to push them aside to get to my candles. Then when I would ask a question, they would rearrange themselves on the altar. It was very distracting.

Often objects spontaneously appear on the altar. It is important to remember to stay focused when descending the twenty-two steps. Keep your attention on the flame of the candle. There will be plenty of time for you to explore on your own after you've fully presented yourself to the Records.

I'm embarrassed to say, but my altar was more like a coffee table.

I have been fortunate to also teach this technique in Asia. There, the descriptions of the altars are quite different from ours in the West. The altars are low and the individuals kneel, or sit before them, however, descriptions of the mirrors are the same. If your altar becomes overly small it would do for you to visit a temple or cathedral to get a real world look at an altar.

I never follow exactly what is being said during guided meditations. The outside edge of my mirror was kind of free formed with alternating rough and smooth areas.

My role is to suggest an image. Your role is to fill in the details. It has often been reported that the mirror is framed in a window casing, or that it appears in what looks like a window in the cave wall. The black surface is important. The frame is up to you.

As far as you never following exactly what is being offered during guided meditations: putting your own signature upon the script is very important. This allows you to be creative. Leave your defiance in the dimension deserving of it – the world of your disappointments. It is difficult to fully relax if your are defiant or overly stubborn. Go with the natural flow of energy that leads Consciousness into the Records.

Okay, I'm in front of the mirror. I'm really excited. I didn't think I'd get that far, that soon. I ask a question, and zip-o. As a matter of fact the mirror got darker if that's possible.

Frustrating! It still happens to me. I'll be sitting with an individual, get all the information I need to access their Records, and it's like the teller machine that refuses to give me my money. I do a few of the tricks I've learned through my years of accessing the Records, and still nothing. That's when I open my eyes and tell the individual it will have to be another time.

Then they immediately think I am unable to read for them because something awful is about to happen, or that their life is so filled with negative karma that I am being repelled. I assure them this is something that happens for many different reasons, all of which are about me and not about them. And I've learned that trying to figure out why this happens only leads to more frustration. It happens a lot less often as I gain experience. In the beginning it was about one in five clients, now it's about one in thirty.

What does it mean if the images of your past aren't as vivid as the ones from your future?

You are probably more intent upon the future than the past. Were the past images blurred, or just lacking in vividness?

Now that you ask, I would have to say a little of both, actually.

The lack of clarity, of course, indicates a reluctance to view past events and your responses, whether of this lifetime or a past incarnation. And the same would be true if it had been the future images that were dimmed. Now, if the images of the past are seen through a gauze like veil, or are strongly lacking in detail to the point of only being outlines, this indicates a major inner conflict that is very likely effecting your physical, emotional, mental, Etheric and astral bodies and might be at the root of any dis-ease you might now be chronically dealing with.

How do I find the problem?

If you are viewing information on a particular subject, be it past or future, and this type of imaging occurs, stop your line of questioning, turn your back to the altar, relax a moment, then return to the altar. Pick up the center candle and ask that any past or future life blocks be revealed to you in a manner you can readily understand. Ask the Records to reveal any and all information, in this dimension or simultaneous parallel dimensions, related to this area of conflict. This is very important. This type of experience indicates that you have found a substantial block that is altering your core identity.

It was very difficult getting anything to appear once I was at the mirror. Suddenly I just found myself back here with my body. The obvious answer would be my fear of what might be shown in my Book of Life. Is the answer that obvious?

This might be easy for some to hear and difficult for others: the only reason anyone would have this experience would be out of a fear of what is in the Records. Our fear of humiliation, then physical suffering, and then ultimately dying is at the root of all fear. Please remember, even death itself is a response, instead of an event. Another very potent deterrent is anxiety over performance.

Most individuals who are able to understand the concepts of the Akasha, for the most part, desire an effortless life filled with meaningful contribution to others. One of the main reasons an individual would undertake this course of study is to improve upon the depth of his journey here by moving beyond fears of the unknown. This individual understands that if he were precognitive he would be able to respond at greater levels of Consciousness. This enhanced foresight allows for greater response and that, in turn, allows for greater outcomes. Greater outcomes ensure less effort. Less effort invites more peace. Peace leads to joy. Joy brings bliss. Bliss is Oneness. Being at One fills the Human Soul with a profound gratitude. This deep expression of gratitude is our natural state of Being.

This is why an individual would want to view the Records: to be aware and fully Conscious in the moment. Take courage. Be at ease. You are your response. The Creative substance of the universe is attracted to you as response. The more this is known in your core, the greater your response of gratitude. Gratitude leads to grace. Grace opens the door to the mystical realms of the fourth and fifth dimensions.

– Script Number Two –

Meditation – The Beehive

Relax. Allow yourself to fully relax. Feel a softening sensation happening in your brain. Feel your brain sagging toward the base of your skull. Allow your brain to soften. Soften. Completely relax.

– Pause –

Relax. Allow yourself to fully relax. Clear your throat.

– Slight Pause –

Let out a deep sigh. And another. And another.

– Slight Pause –

Clear your throat.

– Pause –

Relax. Whisper in your mind the sound, "LUM." (Slight pause equalling one deep breath.) Whisper in your mind the sound, "VUM." (Slight pause) Whisper in your mind the sound, "RUM." (Slight pause) Whisper in your mind the sound, "YUM." (Slight pause) Whisper in your mind the sound, "HUM." (Slight pause) Whisper in your mind the sound, "AUM."

– Pause –

In your mind whisper, "LUM." (Slight pause) In your mind whisper, "VUM." (Slight pause) In your mind whisper, "RUM." (Slight pause) In your mind whisper, "YUM." (Slight pause) In your mind whisper, "HUM." (Slight pause) In your mind whisper, "AUM."

– Pause –

Mentally whisper, "LUM." (Slight pause) Mentally whisper, "VUM." (Slight pause) Mentally whisper, "RUM." (Slight pause) Mentally whisper, "YUM." (Slight pause) Mentally whisper, "HUM." (Slight pause) Mentally whisper, "AUM."

Relax. Completely relax.

You are standing in an open field of waving grass. A warm steady breeze moves across the landscape. The air is fresh and clean. White puffy clouds dot the blue summer sky. In the distant shade of a large tree sits a white beehive. Begin walking toward the tree and the hive. The grass moves gently out of your way as you move toward your goal. There is a lot of activity around the tree and hive. Bees are busy collecting nectar for the winter. It is a wonderful day for the bees to be about their work. There is a different quality and attitude about these bees – a friendliness that you haven't experienced before. As you get closer, allow yourself to begin hearing the sounds of the bees. There is also the smell of honey in the air now. Their friendliness fills your body with joy. Feel the smile upon your face. The wonder of nature. These bees are just like you – they follow instinctual activities; they enjoy the comfort of relationships; they communicate their discoveries of life to each other and they seek to be of service to one another. This beehive is a metaphor for the Human experience.

The bees seem to be beckoning you. Allow yourself to feel their invitation. Allow yourself to get closer and closer to the hive. Hear the bees gathering around you, guiding you to the hive. The smell of honey is strong now. Bend down closer to the hive. The bees on the ledge in front of the opening of the hive are dancing in figure eights as you investigate the entrance to their home. Watch the bees coming and going. One lands at the opening of the hive and dances for a group of others. When it is finished telling of its discoveries, several of the listening bees take off in the same direction. Another bee lands at the hive and the dance is repeated.

Most of the bees have gone to collect more nectar. Bend even closer to the opening. Place your right hand against the outside of the hive. Feel the vibration coming from deep inside. Move your face so that you can look through the opening into the honeycomb. See the honeycomb shapes pressed against each other. There are thousands of them. Some closed, some open. With the power of your mind, focus your thoughts on the open cell to your left in the honeycomb and allow it to grow larger. Larger. Allow your Consciousness to leave your body and move toward the opening in the honeycomb. The sound of bees working fills your mind as you begin your journey along the inside of the hexagonal shape. The sound vibrates deep inside your chest. Allow the sound to get louder and louder, overwhelming the thoughts of where you are. All that exists now is the sound of the bees.

– Pause (15 seconds)–

At the very end of the hexagonal tube you are traveling through is a bright light, as brilliant as the sun. Consciously choose to move toward that light. The light is the center of this inner microcosm. Feel yourself being drawn forward on the beams of light, on the sparkles of light that are reaching out to you. Allow the light to penetrate your entire being. Feel yourself being drawn deeper and deeper into the warm comforting light.

The light is getting brighter and brighter. So bright the walls of the honeycomb completely disappear. Feel yourself expanding in the light. The brighter and brighter the light, the larger and larger you become. The light is so warm and so huge.

– Pause –

You are the light. Allow yourself to expand out to the very edge of the light. There is a boundary to the light. Move forward. Approach the outside edge of the light. There in the distance is the beginning of darkness. Continue forward. Allow yourself to go to the fuzzy edge of the light. Look out into the vastness from your edge. There is a depth beyond knowing. Allow the vastness to become darker and darker. There in front of you is the very center of the darkness. You can look deep into the center of this vast darkness because you are the Light. Ask your God or Goddess to allow the answers to your questions to take shape in the darkness of the void. Ask any question about your most recent past life. See the answer forming off in the distance. Allow the answers to become more and more real. Allow the answer to present itself in images readily known to you. Hear the interpretations of the images as your thoughts.

– Long Pause (1 minute)–

Allow the images to fade. Remember all that you have been shown and have heard.

– Pause –

Ask to be shown those events in your immediate future that are unchangeable. Allow the answer to form in the void. Hear the interpretation of the images as your thoughts.

– Long Pause (1 minute)–

Allow the images to fade. Remember all that you have been shown and have heard.

– Pause –

Ask any question concerning your health. Allow the images to form in the void. Hear the interpretation of the images as your thoughts.

– Long Pause –

Allow the images in the void to fade. Remember all that you have just experienced.

Bring your thoughts back to the very center, the brightest point of Light. Allow yourself to once again hear the sounds of the bees. Experience the incredible sound of the bees. Feel the vibration of the bees all around you. Feel yourself moving back into the honeycomb. Move along the hexagonal shape back toward the opening of the hive. Sunlight is pouring in from outside the hive. Allow the sunlight to penetrate deep into your eyes, momentarily blinding you. Feel yourself moving forward into the sunlight.

Allow your Consciousness to move back into your body. Feel yourself kneeling in front of the hive looking into the small opening. Stand and take a step backwards. Look at the tree and the sky. Turn, now follow your way back through the tall wavy grass.

– End –

Key Elements: **(The elements in bold type are trigger elements.)**

Field of wind blown grass • Large tree • Sheltered beehive • The bees • The smell of honey • **The sounds of the bees • Honeycomb • Blinding light • Black void**

Explanation of Key Elements:

Field of wind blown grass. The field of grass represents your conscious mind at rest. No one thought or subject is dominant. You are in a semi-trance state of mind.

Large tree. The tree sheltering the bee hive is the tree of life. This represents both the vertical Earth energies of the physical body (trunk), as well as the horizontal chakra energies of the Etheric body (branches).

Sheltered beehive This represents your physical body – in and of this world. This is where your Consciousness collects itself as awareness.

The bees. The bees represent the constant coming and going of thought with feeling. When a bee dances for you, it is comparable to when a thought flies in from the periphery and catches your attention.

The smell of honey. The smell of honey represents our gratitude for the experience of life. This symbolic sweetness is at the center of all Life on Earth.

The sounds of the bees. The sounds and vibrations of the bees represent the sound current. The sound current is the resulting vibration when Consciousness and energy collide to form the illusion of the manifest reality of the physical Universe.

Honeycomb. The image of the hive represents your brain with all its synapse connections creating neural passageways. Selecting, then traveling down one hexagonal route is you directing your Consciousness toward the Inner Teacher. The hexagonal shapes of the honeycomb represent the foundational forms of the Akasha where the information gathered by your senses is stored.

Blinding light. The light represents your Over-Soul, Higher Self. As you move your Awareness through the hexagonal portal toward the light, you allow your inner sight to become dominant.

Black void. The void, with its pure black center, represents the preconscious area within your mind. This action would be comparable to peering through a looking glass, only this surface is the mirror to your deep subconscious.

Questions Concerning this Meditation

Is it important to actually see the field of grass? I got so involved in feeling it that I had to play catch up and went directly into the Light in the beehive.

Feeling the grass is a wonderful experience. As a child I had daily opportunities to sit quietly in tall grass. On the days when the wind would blow, it was marvelous. It was like the grass was playing with me, urging me into movement. Seeing the images are valuable in helping you connect at a deeper level with symbolic meaning of the mind at rest. Imaging this will also help induce a mild semi-trance state.

Visit a field and imprint the image of waving grass in your mind. It will make a difference as you begin your release of physical body Consciousness.

The tree represents to me the very substance of consciousness. My tree spread out across the sky in all directions making it difficult to clearly see the sky. I knew if I tried I could see each individual leaf, and yet each leaf was a part of every other leaf. It was really the first time I could see such a detailed image. I knew I wasn't making up my tree or the waving grass. It was great. My question is, how do I not feel overwhelmed by the presence of the tree?

Excellent description of your tree. Knowing what all the images symbolize before you journey inward will give you a slight edge in overcoming this feeling of overwhelm. Be in awe of the images. There is a need to be in the awe. This feeling of awe is very accurate when we think of our relationship to Creation. After all, Creation is in awe of us.

Now, as meditator, you are both the Conscious Mind and the inner manifest form – cause and effect. You are the one who has evoked these forms and are therefore the Source of the experience, just as when you are in the dream realm. When you are in your dream body, you are all the details of the dream, and you are the Dreamer, the Source of the dream. Source is always the event and response. Be a little overwhelmed, and be at ease. Fear will interrupt the experience, joy will prolong it.

When you do this meditation on your own, take as much time as you want at the tree. Be in awe. The energy of awe is very healing. When I first saw the *Wizard of Oz*, I thought they were saying the *Wizard of Awes*. It made perfect sense to me, because everyone was in awe of his wizardry. It wasn't until I was in my teens that I was corrected.

My bee hive wasn't under the tree. When I touched the side it was hot from the sun beating down on it. Can it be out in the open, or do I need to shelter it like you said?

It's fine out in the open. Was the bee hive vibrating?

Yes, almost to where it was visibly shaking.

Excellent! Did you notice if it was hot inside the bee hive?

I don't recall. It might have been. It would only seem logical.

Logic applies to the outer worlds. Some individuals have experienced winter conditions in their hive, blizzards in fact. If it is too hot, take the time to image cool surroundings, conversely, if it is too cold, image warmth. Be kind and compassionate, the bees are the coming and going of thoughts. Be focused and driven by your intention, and at the same time be at ease as thoughts play across your mind.

I have a real hard time with bees. It's a family thing. We all hate bees.

Use one of the other meditations.

I was hoping to really hear the bees. (Pause) The sound current wasn't very clear to me, more like a baby mosquito than a bumble bee. I guess what I'm saying is that I thought it would be like a big sound if there were so many bees.

Many experience the sound current as a faint whirring that they have to listen very hard to even hear, while others complain of its intensity. The first time I encountered the sound current was in the boxing ring at the age of fourteen. I was living in a very small town in British Columbia, Canada, and during the winter months there was little to do except play pool, ice hockey, or join the Golden Gloves Boxing team. I tried all three and found boxing to be the lesser of the evils. My coach, a wonderful native North American, Johnny Dixon, had coached the team very well and we were all ready for our first legitimate bouts. As luck would have it, the young man I was to fight had been boxing for three years and had thirty-two amateur fights under his belt. Johnny reassured me I would do well against Stewart Goodfellow, because what I lacked in ring knowledge, I made up for in guts. (I took guts to mean, Spirit.)

As soon as the referee called us to the center of the ring to shake hands, I was overcome with this sound. I could see the referee's mouth moving, and all I could hear was this sound. The crowd was cheering, my father was shouting something from ring side, there was nothing but this sound. I went to my corner to wait for the bell. My coach gave me last minute instructions, all I heard was the sound.

I remember only parts of the actual fight – the moment when a flash of light knocked me to the canvas, and the moment I knocked Stewart to the canvas. The judges called it a split decision draw. We both won. I like win/win outcomes.

I was different after the fight. You might say I was preoccupied with this sound. The sound followed me for several months afterward. I played with the sound. What else could I do? I learned how to control its intensity, so at least I could hear the outside world when it was present. The most interesting piece of data about the sound was, there would be times when all thoughts would disappear into the sound. Suddenly twenty minutes would have gone by. I was profoundly aware of everything around me with no thoughts to disturb me. It was a big feeling, one I kept to myself.

It wasn't until later when I went to live with my grandmother, Rowena Wescott Bonnell, that I was given an explanation. No one, including Johnny, had been able to solve the mystery up till that point. Rowena gave me Paramahansa Yogananda's materials to study. She was one of his early students when he first came to Los Angeles.

To this day the sound is still like a train engine when I experience it. But that's my personal experience.

Just because it was small in volume doesn't mean it is less effective. Let it be what it wants to be. Big or small.

I love the smell of honey and have actually been to a tree hive out in the Colorado Rockies. So my hive was actually in the tree.

Excellent! I suggest the image of a white hive because many have seen them in the countryside. Also, domestic bees are often more gentle in temperament than those found in the wild, so it is a little easier for the imagination to accept the calm condition of the bees suggested in the meditation. By all means have the hive in the tree.

I really enjoyed this one. All of the elements seemed so real, and when I entered the honeycomb, it was like I was home. Everything, the sounds and smells, even the visual images were so familiar. Why was I so taken by this meditation?

I'm happy at your success.

Remember, the images are symbolic. You are in fact returning your Consciousness to areas of the mind that are very familiar. That is why you felt so at home. The images suggested in the meditation only serve to take you there. Eventually the images will drop away and you will be left with a truly multi-dimensional experience, one that defies explanation.

Be aware of any tendency to form attachments to the images. It is important that you witness the images and allow them to change as they want to. This is one of the secrets of this work: be at ease with whatever presents itself. Non-attachment, non-aversion.

The blackness in the center of the void was frightening. I have only learned to meditate on the Light. (Pause) It seems altogether odd, and inherently evil that I should look into this colorless void. Every teacher I know says to picture the Light, that Truth and Light are one and the same. Where there is Light, there is Wisdom. Can't I see the answers in the Light?

I understand your concern and can only offer the following: we are in a world of duality. Many of us were taught by our parents and teachers to believe in the conflict of Light versus Dark, Good versus Evil, Right versus Wrong, my God is bigger than your God, this idea is more right than that idea, etc., etc. Unfortunately, as children, we are all taught that evil lurks in the darkness of night, and this belief is reinforced in our adulthood every time we hear a story on the news about a helpless victim who has been overcome in the night by someone wishing to take their belongings, or their life. This is a sad truth in our violent world culture.

Why look into the void? That's where the answers are to be found. We are the Light of this dimensional reality. To get the answers we must look beyond our boundaries. If we are to know ourselves completely we must jump into the abyss, the colorless void. Our humanness would want the abyss to be a two jump deal with the guarantee of a landing place somewhere in the middle. The abyss is a one jump proposition.

An interesting side note: the science of physics states that Light, expressing in waves or particles, makes up only ten percent of all matter. Ninety percent of matter is dark matter, or the unseeable energy of the universe.

So when I get into the my Book of Life and the Akashic Records for the first time will I be able to interpret the images being revealed to me?

Because you have a language skill, you are able to read. You have acquired this skill over the years and would think nothing of opening a book at any place and begin reciting from the text. The more often you look into the Records, the more proficient you will become. The fact that you have already acquired languaging skills will make your task of learning the symbols of the Akasha that much easier because you are accustomed to reading data in symbol forms.

– Script Number Three –

Meditation: The Flower

Relax. Become aware of your breath. Select only the finest quality of oxygen as you inhale. See the molecules of oxygen as tiny points of light. Allow these points of light to fill your lungs with a soothing healing glow. As you exhale, send the light upward through your throat, into your brain. As the glow of the light touches your brain, your brain begins to soften. Your brain was like a tight fist, and is now becoming an open palm. Feel your brain relaxing, softening. Inhale, filling your lungs with brilliant sparkles of healing light. Your lungs are glowing. Exhale. Send the light upwards, through your throat and into your brain. Your brain is bathed in a soft glowing light. Allow your brain to soften. Feel it softening, sagging against the back of the skull. Allow the softening energy to spread down into the base of the brain where the neck and the head join. Feel the softness in the brain stem. Feel the back of the brain settling, softening, relaxing. Allow the soft feelings to move down your spinal column. Feel every muscle in your body soften as your spinal column glows in a column of wonderful healing Light.

– Pause –

With your imagination, envision a beautiful fall colored tree directly in front of you. The leaves are a brilliant yellow. Watch as a cool fall breeze plays with the leaves. Allow the gentle breeze to tug at the leaves hanging at the very top of the tree. Watch as a beautiful yellow leaf breaks free and starts its journey toward the earth.

Watch as the leaf floats back and forth...back and forth...on the breeze, making its way to its winter resting place. It has served the tree very well through the spring and summer, and now it will rest. It floats so easily on the cool currents. Back and forth...back and forth. Watch as it touches the earth. As the leaf touches the ground send the command through your physical body to relax. Deep waves of relaxation spread through your body as you watch the leaf settle to the ground. Look up again to the top of the tree. Another leaf is breaking free, and gently, back and forth, back and forth, it begins its journey to earth. This leaf is moving very slowly downward. Very slowly. Back and forth on the cool breeze. Back and forth. Watch as it joins the other leaves already on the ground. Another wave of relaxation moves through your body as the leaf touches the earth.

Look up again to the top of the tree. One last leaf at the top of the tree is breaking free, and falling gently back and forth, back and forth. Watch as the cool gentle breeze rocks it back and forth, back and forth. Gently downward it rides on the breeze. Back and forth, back and forth. As it touches the earth, command your body to completely relax.

– Pause –

Look forward. A wonderful tree lined lane with many different homes is reaching out invitingly before you. It appears to be somewhere and some time in the middle 1800's. No power lines. No paved streets. No music or glaring signs to distract you from your walk. Flat field stones line each side of the road serving as a walkway for those wishing a relaxing stroll. The yards and flower gardens along this street are well kept. The people living here feel a deep connection to their homes. Enjoy your stroll. Count each step as you continue along. Left. Right. Left. Right. Left. Right. Left. Right. Left. Right. Left. Right. Walk along. Walk along. There ahead on the left is an open gate leading to a backyard garden. The owner is very friendly and genuinely pleased when someone spontaneously comes in to admire the garden. Walk toward the garden gate.

The gate has a little squeak as you open to pass through. What a marvelous place this garden is with its many plants and stones. So much care has been given to this place. The owner must have a deep connection with the realms of the wonderful fairies, brownies, and gnomes that play amongst the plant and mineral Consciousness. If you soften your focus you can catch a glimpse of them as they go about their business.

– Pause (15 seconds) –

This is truly a magical place. Allow yourself to meander through the garden for a while. Explore the many colors and shapes – the leaves on the plants, the moss surfaced stones, twigs on the ground. Listen. The sound of running water coming from behind some small sculpted shrubs plays like music in your ears. Pull back the taller shrubs. A stream glides through the under growth. Follow the stream. Move past the lush green plants covered in beautiful flowers. Ah h h h! There in front of you is a wonderful pond. Lily pads with beautiful white and pink, and lavender flowers dot the liquid surface of the garden pond. Crystal clear water suspends brilliant orange and white goldfish above the sandy bottom of their home. Count them as they swim from shore to shore.

– Pause –

The sun dances across the water creating triangles of shimmering light. Each time the light catches your eyes, you can see more and more of the delightful beings that inhabit this garden. Fairies playing amongst the foliage. Brownies dancing around rocks. Dragonflies, with silvery gauze wings, pause in mid-flight as they dash from resting place to resting place. Small yellow and black bumble bees race from flower to flower gathering their nectar. Little green frogs jump and splash, making ringlets on the water's surface.

Watch as the sun moves its reflection across the tiny triangles of the pond's surface. Allow the day time in the garden to slip away toward dusk. Each time the sun reflects in your eyes you are able to see more and more of this magical place.

Water spiders, with crane like legs, dance upon the upward edge of the pond. The lyrics of invisible tree frogs and rusty old toads fill in the evening melody of crickets.

A wonderful sense of well being fills your body and mind as you continue watching the activities around the glistening pool. Everything seems to come together in the pond; those living beneath the waters edge, those on the water's surface, those reflected in its surface and those beyond the water.

Allow your attention to be directed to the lily pads and their flowers, over near the edge of the pond. Beads of water meander atop the dark green pads that frame the lily flowers. Move closer to the flower directly in front of you. Kneel and extend your finger tips to touch the soft, colorful petals. As you touch the flower it magically begins to grow. Allow the lily to continue to grow. Notice how the essence of the flower fills the air around you with the scent of lavender. Breathe in the fragrance. Fill yourself with the flower's gift. The smell gets stronger and the colors get brighter as the flower continues to grow.

The flower is very big now, large enough for you to climb. Step out onto one of the leaves of the lily pad. It stretches like a bridge from the shore to the flower itself. Your weight goes unnoticed by the lily pad as you pull yourself up to the flower's edge. Turn and look at the last of the late day's sun. Allow those shafts to pierce deep into your eyes. Turn back to the flower. Reach up, feel the flower's edge in your hands, pull down the lip of one of the petals. Climb blindly upward onto the petal. Allow yourself to slide to the center. Rest there in the quiet shelter of the flower. Hold your hands over your eyes. Feel your sight returning as you allow relaxation to spread throughout your body. You are relaxed, a thousand times more relaxed than ever before. Here you are completely open in your heart, trusting and allowing.

Your lily begins to close as the sun begins to move down behind the trees of the garden. The petals completely envelope you like a warm blanket on a chilly winter's night. Feel yourself being pulled downward as the last of the daylight leaves the beautiful world of the pond. Something is gently pulling you down to the heart of the plant. You are traveling through the stem toward the roots. It's a tight fit. Feel the stem's walls pressing against you as you make your way.

Collect your thoughts as you move further downward. Allow the tightness of the stem to press your deepest question into Conscious Awareness. Hold that question. Feel the question deep inside your body.

Suddenly, you are free of the stem's pressure, and find yourself in a large chamber. What a wonderful place this is, filled with all that you have ever known. Take a moment to look around. This place is just as magical as the garden and pond. There at the very center is a wonderful piece of antique furniture. Allow yourself to examine it. Slowly, carefully, examine what is in front of you.

Slight pause - 5 seconds

Behind the piece of furniture is a black mirror. Look deeply into the mirror. It appears to go on forever. And yet there in the very center, off in the distance, is something of interest. It appears to be a small, faint image. (Slight pause) It is the answer to your question. Allow it to come closer, to fill up the mirror. Watch as the answer gets bigger and bigger. Allow the details to become three-dimensional.

– Pause –

Notice how easily the images in the mirror answer your innermost question. Ask the same question, differently. Watch as the images change. Notice how your senses are responding to the images.

– Pause –

Remember what you have just experienced. Allow the images that formed the answer to your question to fade. (Slight pause) The mirror is empty now. Ask a different question.

– Pause –

Watch as a distant image begins to form in the mirror. Allow it to get closer. This is the answer to your question. Watch as it takes on more details and fills the mirror's surface.

– Pause –

Remember what you have just experienced. Allow the images that formed the answer to your question to fade. (Slight pause) The mirror is empty now. Ask a different question.

– Pause –

Watch as a distant image begins to form in the mirror. Allow it to get closer. This is the answer to your question. Watch as it takes on more details and fills the mirror's surface.

– Pause –

Remember what you have just experienced. Allow the images that formed the answer to your question to fade. (Slight pause) The mirror is empty now.

– Pause –

A gentle upward movement interrupts your concentration. You are now being delicately pulled upward, away from the mirror, out of the chamber at the base of the flower. You can feel the tightness of the stem pressing into you from the front, back and sides. Lift your arms upward as though you were about to dive into water. Streamline your body. Feel it becoming sleek and slim. Stretch upward.

A brilliant light shines directly above you. Allow yourself to stretch and, at the same time, feel yourself being pulled toward that light. Look upward. Allow the light to blind you. Feel it burning deep inside your eyes.

– Pause –

The upward movement has stopped. You are resting at the base of the flower's petals. Your sight has returned. Look around you. The petals have opened in response to the sun's morning light. Reach up and pull yourself from the center of the flower. Step out of the flower onto the lily pad. The flower returns to its normal size as your feet touch the shore. (Slight pause) Find the path that leads to the garden gate. (Slight pause) Pass through the gate. (Slight pause) Feel your physical body. Wiggle your toes. Wiggle your fingers. Join completely with your physical body.

– End –

Key Elements: **(The elements in bold type are trigger elements.)**

Victorian town setting • Garden gate • Path through the magical garden • Sound of running water • Pond • Reflected sunlight • Flower • **Lavender fragrance • Center of flower** • Flower's stem • Large underwater and underground chamber • **Antique piece of furniture • Black mirror**

Explanation of Key Elements:

Victorian town setting. The Victorian town setting is created to take you back to a time before the technological explosion. A time devoted to family and community where you are only aware of what is happening on a local level.

Garden gate. The squeaky garden gate is representative of the portal that exists between the parallel universes of the physical and Etheric realms. The squeak sound represents the slightly irritating energetic field that separates both Kingdoms.

Path through the magical garden. The meandering path represents a calm and innocent exploration of the wonders found within the garden. It is also the imaging of our journey into, and through, the preconscious aspect of the Etheric realms.

Sound of running water. This is a very reassuring sound to the physical body. The negative ions generated by small streams and brooks with their many falls and eddies enliven the cellular mind.

Pond. The pond is the emotional body. The surrounding garden is the mental body with all its many forms of Consciousness as imaged in the minerals, plants and animals. As you follow the stream to its resting place, you are moving along the currents of the emotional body. Where the stream empties into the pond is exactly the point within our beings where the emotional and mental bodies have their connection. This connection is very delicate in that self-degradation and external humiliation tears at its fibers, the stringlets that bond the emotional and mental bodies. When most of these stringlets have been damaged, the emotional and mental bodies lose the ability to relate creating a profound sense of confusion.

Reflected sunlight. Reflecting, sparkling sunlight resembles the nature of the Over-Soul's personality, the Higher Self of Human Consciousness. When you allow this light to blind you, to eclipse your own vision, you have allowed the higher aspect of your nature to "see," instead of the mundane sight of the physical world, filled with its many expectations and obliging illusions.

Flower. The flower represents that place where the physical and Etheric bodies first connect. This is often referred to as the Crown chakra. As we rest in the Crown, our understanding is transmuted to the highest level of Awareness.

Lavender fragrance. The lavender fragrance triggers a deep inner trust of all that exists within the garden. If you were to wear this fragrance as a perfume, you would notice a difference with regards to the trusting of others and their trusting you. This fragrance also excites the upper chakras mainly the sixth wheel or third eye.

Center of flower. The center of the flower is the perfect mind/body expression.

Flower's stem. The squeezing sensation of the flower's stem represents the narrow energy channels of the cellular brain. This narrowing sensation is, of course, only symbolic. Entry into the Book of Life is gained when we consciously move our Awareness into the primal cellular mind.

Large underwater and underground chamber. The large underwater and underground chamber is the seat of the Inner Teacher. All immutable events of the individual's current lifetime, as well as any past or future lifetime can be viewed from this inner place.

Antique piece of furniture. The antique piece of furniture represents the altar of the subconscious mind.

Black mirror. The black mirror is the portal to the subconscious, and that place within through which the Akasha can be viewed.

Questions Concerning this Meditation

Why can't I get past seeing cartoon images? With each meditation it's grown worse. The Victorian town was like the entrance to Disney World. Even the answers in the black mirror were one-dimensional. What am I doing wrong?

Nothing. There is nothing to do wrong. The most important thing to remember when doing this type of work is to relax into the visualization. At first simply allow whatever comes to come. I am unaware of the answer as to why this sort of imaging occurs, and this is fairly common. I have known many individuals who work very hard trying to eliminate one-dimensional images only to find them becoming more and more prevalent. Part of the problem is that they are working so hard.

One last thought – allowing yourself to be distracted by the one-dimensional images is your way of controlling the experience. Let the images take you. Give up your need to be right about how the images present themselves. To fight against something makes it real.

I have a strong aversion to the images of the Victorian period. Driving down a street lined with Victorian homes is very uncomfortable for me. I don't like organized gardens with artificial fish ponds. What would you suggest I do?

Use a different meditation. No one method works for everyone.

The garden gate was locked, so I climbed over the fence. I didn't hear any squeaking. And it was like I was watching myself climb instead of being there on the fence.

The next time you try this exercise imagine the lock opening, or have the key to the gate appear in your hand. This gate represents the strength of your intentions. If it is locked against you, check your intentions. Also, you may be trying to prove to yourself the strength of your conscious resolve of getting into the Book of Life by scaling the fence. Command the gate be open, and it will. Climbing over the gate or fence is much more work than is necessary. There is nothing to prove here.

I'm really into plants, especially trees. I didn't pay any attention to where I was putting my feet. In other words, I'm not sure if there was a path through my garden. But then I followed the stream, so I guess that's a path. Is it okay not to have a path?

As was stated earlier, the meandering path represents our innocent journey through the Etheric realms. It feels as though you are innocent enough in your view of creation, primarily because you were fine without having a distinct path, and were very willing to follow the path of the stream. Very natural.

Many times those individuals who are more intellectually oriented become concerned about where each path leads, or they create their inner gardens to look as though they were created by an overly anal type. No need to be retentive or expulsive. Allow the garden to create itself. Watch the mood of the garden path. If there are things in your way, or you notice the path disappearing from time to time, this could indicate some deeper emotional issue you haven't faced about obstacles.

I didn't hear a word you were saying until you said to imagine the sound of running water. Then I wasn't in a garden, I was in the Rim area of Arizona where I used to hike. I found the pond and the Lily, and even imagined it growing, or it was more like I was shrinking. So the rest of the time I was with you all the way. The only problem was that the piece of furniture was ultra-modern, not antique. I tried to change it, but it stayed the same. The mirror was like a window looking out into night. I really enjoyed the images that appeared in answer to my questions. So I guess I'm doing okay, right?

Just dandy, I'd say. It feels as though you have fully gotten the message to let it happen. Suddenly being able to "see" the suggestions being offered in the meditation is excellent. Allowing yourself to fully relax in the beginning is vital to the experience. You simply jumped into Conscious Awareness from an unconscious state with the suggestion of running water. This image must be very exciting for you.

Yes. I'm on a high when I'm there, even if it's just in my head.

The response of your physical body to the suggestion of the running water was what brought you back.

Most individuals have unconscious triggers that can alter an experience, whether it is a mundane, or an extraordinary event. These triggers are learned from an early age and can be anything from an unfamiliar word, confusing movements, a familiar fragrance, or the sounds from a favorite song. Example: you are enjoying a book and suddenly find yourself day dreaming instead of reading. You go back to a page you remember and start over. The same thing happens. There is a phrase out of place, a word misspelled, something is wrong with the text, or it might be a concept that challenges your personality. Another example: you are listening to your favorite song. Pictures of who you were with when you first heard the song crowd your mind. One word or phrase, or even a combination of the melody with the lyrics triggers you elsewhere. The next song on the CD begins and you suddenly find yourself back in current time and space.

Go with it. That is exactly why we have these activities in our lives – to trigger us into multi-dimensional experiences.

What does it mean if your pond is murky? I could see the outlines of the fish, but couldn't see any real colors.

The murkiness of the pond would indicate a lack of clarity regarding the relationship of your mental body with your emotional body. Perhaps you suffered at the hands of a harsh task master when little. If that is the case, it would be good to forgive anyone who might have harmed you when you were a child.

How do I do that?

Confront the parent involved. If the parent is in denial, then you must work it out yourself. Journal your feelings and thoughts. Sit quietly and remember what it was like to suffer so. Then bring a greater understanding into the suffering – your tormentors did not do the best they could, they blew it. They knew better. Their guilt has turned into denial. They are doomed to repeat this at another time and another place until they wake up. Feel the anger you associate with them, then let it go.

Will the image of a murky pond keep you from your Book of Life? No. Does it indicate that your interpretations of the images will be colored? Yes. Because you carry resentments and unresolved feelings, your interpretations will be tainted. Not horribly, but tainted none the less. More than likely the resulting distortions in your interpretations will be in your ability to determine timing of events accurately.

Is there any meaning to the fact that my pond had a lot of levels. Its sides had a lot of shelves where the fish would rest. It sounds odd, doesn't it?

Yes, it does sound odd. Is it odd? No.

Many people report special areas where the fish rest, or even hide. One individual had invisible partitions between the fish that didn't like each other; another had twenty-two small ponds located very close together. We had an open discussion in the workshop as to what this could possibly indicate. Each individual in the workshop had a distinctly different interpretation. These variations have special meaning to each individual's Consciousness. It would take many hours to dissect the psychology of each.

I thoroughly enjoyed the sunlight reflecting on the pond, but it made me feel sad. It took me back to a time when my father and I would sit by the water's edge and tell stories to each other. He died two years ago and I still miss him. Will my strong emotions about his death keep me from getting into my Book of Life?

My father has also passed away so I can get a measure of how you feel. A simple no is the answer. Your enormous feelings will give added depth to your journey. Watch your feelings of sorrow. Notice when you are actually wanting them instead of wanting feelings of joy. Sometimes we mourn out of a sense of wanting to keep the deceased alive. Did you think the sunlight was the trigger for your feelings of sorrow?

I didn't mean the sunlight per se, it was my relaxed state of mind and the mood of the meditation that cau...

Pay attention to what you are saying. You, as your physical, emotional, mental and Etheric bodies, can only be influenced by external happenings if you create those happenings to be highly significant to the present moment.

Go out into the wilderness and spend a night alone.

That would scare me to death. (Pause) How could that possibly help?

Better to be dead than only partially alive.

In the meditation, you have relaxed deeply, dropped your guard for a moment, and all your unresolved feelings of father have raced to the surface. Go out into the wilderness your father loved so much. Get away from the safety of your home. Spend a night alone with your father. Camp along the side of a lake. Watch the sun reflecting in the morning, midday and at dusk. Remember as much as you can about your father. Your love for him is eternal, from everlasting unto everlasting. That is really who your father was and is; your love for him. He was really nothing more than what you thought and felt him to be. Get away from your safety nets. Go visit him. He is waiting there for you.

The closing of the petals and the constriction while going down into the stem freaked me out. I've never been claustrophobic, but that really had me going. Do you think my over reaction is from some past life?

What a wonderful opportunity! You have found a missing piece of yourself.

Of course. Most strong, unexplainable, uncharacteristic reactions are an indication of unresolved emotions. The fact that you are unable to remember ever being claustrophobic in this current life experience would indicated past life, or even future life influences. However, this could also be from early early childhood, back in a time you have chosen to forget. Because we suffer from selective memories, it is difficult to be absolutely certain as to where the influences are coming from. The full answer to this question will be found in your Book of Life. This is an opportunity to ask the Records the origin of this sudden feeling. Remember to ask that the information be given in a manner that is easy to understand with your present personality.

How come the lavender smell was so strong? It almost burned my nose.

The fragrance of lavender is very important to inner work. Its presence in a meditation indicates the sixth and seventh chakras are responding to your thoughts and feelings. They are expanding. One teacher I had would place a drop of lavender oil on the wrist of his students to help open the pituitary and pineal glands. Another teacher used alternating lights of violet and purple. You can purchase the essential oil of lavender at any health food or metaphysical book store. Most art stores carry large pieces of colored film that make wonderful color effects when you shine a light through them.

I must have fallen asleep just before you mentioned the flower and fragrance. I remember the sunlight and I got to the roots, but no flower or fragrance. Is that an indication that my master gland was not responding or something?

It is true that the combination of the images of light and the scent of lavender are placed within the meditation to help facilitate the upper two energy wheels to spin at a higher rate of speed. Just because you zoned out for a minute only means you went unconscious at the mention of the Lily flower, pads, or the fragrance. This probably happens to you during the day as well. My feeling is that you were bored. If your master gland was unable to respond to your thoughts, you'd very soon be dead.

Try this: place some lavender at hand's reach and smell it just as the suggestion is offered in the visualization. This would get the ball rolling.

The flower's stem was very easy for me. I could reach out and touch the sides as I gently descended into the Earth. Should I feel a constriction when moving downward?

It helps to experience as many of the suggestions as possible. These symbols are important to directing Consciousness to specific areas of the Collective Mind. The constriction is an indication that your Consciousness is on the move. Allow the stem to narrow during your next journey, you might feel a sensation deep inside your brain, a warmth.

The underwater cavern was more like the church from my childhood. The stain glass windows were dark and the altar was smaller than I remembered, but this was the church my parents took us to every Sunday until I was twelve. Any comment?

I always have a comment. My comment would be it's nice to bring forward images from our childhood. This gives us the opportunity to visit with our inner child.

This internal chamber is the inner temple, the inner cathedral. This inner place is sanctuary. You will naturally add and subtract items from time to time. Do not be surprised if the church becomes something else.

My antique was ultra modern. Could it be that this is an altar from a future aspect?

Possibly a future antique perhaps? Micro point of view: I use the image of an antique to move your Consciousness deeper. Antique implies past. There is a depth to the past – it contains both the event and response. If you are getting ultra modern images they might be from a civilization that predates this Urantia period, such as Lemuria or Atlatia (Atlantis). Images from Atlatia are modern beyond our current design concepts. Allow your images to continue, and ask your Book of Life for their origin.

Macro point of view: all lifetimes are simultaneous. That's why you allow spontaneous images to continue. Past or future, it really doesn't matter. The images are there to take you deeper.

I must have had a lifetime during Louis, the Fourteenth. My altar surprised me and almost stopped my experience. I currently believe that less is more. What happened?

The configuration of the altar will constantly change. Some individuals have written with concern about this, asking if their daily mood could influence the design of the altar. Yes, your mood will effect the images of each meditation. Keep a journal that includes observations such as how you were feeling, the mood of your personal relationship, any changes in your work environment, sleeping patterns and dreams, etc. Because mood does come into play, this vital information will help you later in determining how mood alters your interpretation of the images presented in the Akashic Records. Keeping a journal of significant dreams will also be of great value in this work.

No images appeared in my mirror. I just sort of went blank. I kept asking my question over and over again. A big zero.

Did you have any strong urges or a series of unusual thoughts?

No. It was more like a transcendental experience. At one time I tried to make up an answer, but wasn't even successful with that.

Interesting. What was your intent at the beginning of the exercise?

To be successful, to read from my Book of Life.

How did you do with the images leading up to the mirror?

Very well. I was really enjoying myself. I'm very visual and your use of adjectives was exciting.

How was the mood of your meditation?

Well, now that you ask I'm suddenly aware that I'm very tired.

Are there any major changes happening in your life at this time?

Yes. At work – I competed for a new position this last year and finally won. At home – my fiancee and I are reviewing our relationship. We're both bored with our relationship patterns.

I believe resistance is keeping you from imaging the answer. It is also your resistance that's creating the tired mood. You have the ability, your intentions are clear, and being confronted with another item to balance at this moment is probably the last thing you need. Your plate is full.

Go into your Book of Life with the intention of just looking for raw data from past lives. By raw, I mean data that deals with past life influences to this lifetime that might be creating areas of denial. Create a non-judgmental frame of reference. Outline the many facets of your current personality by tracing their origins to past life influences.

What questions would I ask?

Simply ask to be shown the original moments when certain traits began. Example: you have the habit of sabotaging intimate relationships. Just when you are about to fully reveal yourself to your partner, you panic, feel vulnerable, then use the ploy of boredom to withhold. Ask your Book of Life when it was that you first learned to successfully use this ploy. The answer will astound and amaze you.

Why? This is all pretty amazing stuff. I am constantly flabbergasted by the intricacy of Creation. The notion that the past and future exist NOW, and that somehow we can access information in either direction along a dimensional illusion called a time line, is utterly baffling. And being able to visit other real world dimensional illusions called, "other time/space," truly smacks of the ultimate in science fiction.

And to be a little more self centered, I'm constantly perplexed at the source of my personality. Just when I think I've got a handle on who I am, another layer peels back, and it's like I'm meeting myself for the first time, again. One day, or so my teachers say, I will find myself at the last layer. What then?

†Σ†

Akashic Records Meditation Scripts

Introduction

Entry into the Akashic Records, which gives you access to all recorded data, not just your own, is gained when our focused attention is directed inward to the preconscious areas of the Collective Mind. This inward gaze is best achieved when our external world is at rest. Doing these meditations early in the morning between the hours of three and six will help greatly. The reason for this is the fact that the ether tide[1] is at its highest when the majority of individuals are in deep sleep. If these times are not available to you, then build on the energy of your inward journeys by doing them at the same time, and in the same place each day until you have achieved complete entry into the Records. Once you have the full experience of the Akasha you can gain entry at any time and in any place.

Remember to fully engage your imagination. Allow yourself to play with the images being suggested in the following meditations. Engage as many of your senses as possible. This will help later when you are actually in the Records. Just as in real life, you will only be able to use your senses while in the Records to the degree that you can imagine using them. As was earlier stated: these meditations are designed to be effective even with those who have the belief that the imagination is unreal, or have determined themselves unable to visualize. Each of the following scripts begins with a short relaxation technique. You may want to add more, or use your own relaxation technique instead of following the script.

– Script Number One –

Meditation: The Hall of Records

Relax. Focus on your breath. Feel your body expand and contract as you breathe. Select only the finest quality of oxygen molecules as you inhale. See those molecules of oxygen as tiny points of Light. Allow these points of Light to fill your lungs with a soothing wonderful healing glow. Exhale. Send the Light upward through your throat and into your brain. As the glow from the Light touches your brain, it begins to soften. Your brain was like a tight fist, now it is becoming an open palm. Inhale, filling your lungs with brilliant sparkles of healing light. Your lungs are glowing. Send the light upwards, through your throat and into your brain. Your brain is bathing in a soft glowing light. Allow your brain to soften. Feel it softening, sagging against the back of the skull. Feel your brain relaxing, softening. Allow the softening to spread down into the brain stem, at the base of the brain, where the head and neck join. Feel the softness in the brain stem. Feel the back of the brain settling, softening, relaxing. Relax. Allow yourself to fully relax.

Allow the softness of your brain to spread down your spinal column. Feel the warm glow from your brain flowing through each and every nerve. Your muscles respond with joy as they soften.

– Pause –

With your imagination, envision a beautiful fall colored tree directly in front of you. The leaves are a brilliant yellow. Watch as a cool fall breeze plays with the leaves. Allow the gentle breeze to tug at the leaves hanging at the very top of the tree. Watch as a beautiful yellow leaf breaks free and starts its journey toward the earth.

Watch as the leaf floats back and forth...back and forth...on the breeze, making its way to its winter resting place. It has served the tree very well through the spring and summer, and now it will rest. It floats so easily on the cool currents. Back and forth...back and forth. Watch as it touches the earth. As the leaf touches the ground send the command through your physical body to relax. Deep waves of relaxation spread through your body as you watch the leaf settle to the ground. Look up again to the top of the tree. Another leaf is breaking free, and gently, back and forth, back and forth, it begins its journey to earth. This leaf is moving very slowly downward. Very slowly. Back and forth on the cool breeze. Back and forth. Watch as it joins the other leaves already on the ground. Another wave of relaxation moves through your body as the leaf touches the earth.

Look up again to the top of the tree. One last leaf at the top of the tree is breaking free and falling gently back and forth, back and forth on the breeze Watch as the cool gentle breeze rocks it back and forth, back and forth. Gently downward it rides on the breeze. Back and forth, back and forth. As it touches the earth, command your body to completely relax.

– Pause –

Deep inside your nonphysical body is a wonderful light, a brilliant light. This light is always burning brightly, constantly. It is with you through all your lifetimes. This is your Source, the place deep inside where you are in communion with all of Creation. Just remembering your inner Light causes it to shine brighter and brighter. Just having the thought of your deep inner Source, allows it to fill your being to overflowing with a vibrant glow.

Imagine your physical body to be hollow. Allow your deep inner Light to fill your physical body, from the bottoms of your toes to the very top of your head. Feel the Light pushing against the inside of your skin. Open up the pores and allow this Light to fill the space around you.

A wonderful halo of Light surrounds your body. Extend this Light to fill your room. (Slight pause - 15 seconds) Your dwelling. (Slight pause) Your neighborhood. (Slight pause) Your city. (Slight pause) Your region. (Slight pause) Your state. (Slight pause) Your country. (Slight pause) This hemisphere. (Slight pause) The globe.

Allow your Source Light to surround the Earth. See the Earth spinning in the glow of your inner Light. The Light is a message to all life on earth from your inner Source. The message is of peace, goodwill, joy and perpetual balance to all. See the Earth suspended in space, spinning in the glow of your inner Light.

In just a moment you will turn around and begin a journey away from the Earth. Before you turn around take a moment to know that all Consciousness is aware of you – minerals, plants, animals, clouds, water, all animate and inanimate life recognizes you in this moment. Be in perfect communion. Feel your mutual gratification for each other.

Slowly turn around. There in front of you is a wonderful staircase lifting upward toward a majestic pair of lions – a male and female. There are thirty-three steps. Count the steps as you ascend toward the lions. 1, 2, 3, 4, 5, 6, 7, 8, 9, 10, 11, 12, 13, 14, 15, 16, 17. Pause for a moment. The lions are alive. You can hear and feel the vibration of their purr. Their eyes are watching your intention for visiting this place. Feel their acceptance of you. Hear their purring.

Behind the lions is a wonderful set of carved doors. Feel yourself being drawn toward the doors. Continue your climb... 18, 19, 20, 21, 22, 23, 24, 25, 26, 27, 28, 29, 30, 31, 32,

33. Quietly approach the lions. Their eyes are so clear, so beautiful. Allow your eyes to meet the eyes of the male lion. Feel the dignity and courage that flows between the two of you. Now look deeply into the female lion's eyes. Feel the honor and nurturing flowing between you and this wonderful animal. Step between the lions. Reach out and touch their fur. Their skin quickens to your touch.

Approach the doors. Allow them to open. The brightest Light you have ever encountered shafts its way deep inside your eyes as the doors begin to separate. Keep your eyes open. Allow this Light to blind you. Without looking down, focus all your attention at your feet. Your feet know the way through the Light. Move forward.

The intensity of the Light is lessening. Details of a splendid hall are taking form as you walk forward through the Light. Allow yourself to see the images taking shape in the Light. Imagine the statuary, the tapestries. The hall opens to a magnificent room. Look up toward the high ceiling. This is the grandest temple ever created by Collective Consciousness. Look around as you continue forward. More and more details take form. The floor is brilliant with so many colors and shapes. The walls are covered in wonderful paintings and stained glass windows. This is a grand place.

There in the very center of the cathedral-like room is a shaft of rose colored Light rising from floor to ceiling. Allow yourself to be drawn into the Light. Feel the Light swirling around your body. Smell the rose fragrance as it lifts around you. Allow the Light and the fragrance to lift you upward. Feel your feet separating from the multicolored floor. Lift. Look up in the shaft. A beautiful six pointed golden star with a lapis blue circle in the center is suspended at the top of the rose Light. Look down past your feet. A mosaic of the Collective Human Mind creates a living picture of Humanity on the floor of the room.

You are getting closer and closer to the ceiling now. The rose Light is pushing from below. The star at the ceiling is gently pushing against the top of your head. Allow yourself to be caught between the upward pushing force of the Light, and the resistance of the Star from above. Feel yourself being compressed between these two forces. Feel yourself getting smaller and smaller as the forces work against you.

Suddenly the resistance from above gives way as the blue center of the Star opens into an upper chamber. You are standing in a very comfortable room. The room is furnished with artifacts from past and future lives. A large black mirror hangs on the wall directly in front of you. This is a full length mirror. The frame is just as you imagined. A small table made from a very dark wood is just off to the right of the mirror's frame. A beautiful tapestry extends across the floor from the base of the mirror to your feet. Walk across the rug toward the mirror. Get closer to the reflecting surface.

As you get closer you see this is more than a mirror. It is the opening to a parallel dimension. Begin to see the details of the room on the other side of the mirror's surface. Directly on the other side, placed against the opposite surface of the mirror, is an altar with a very curious looking book resting upon its surface. Reach through the mirror and place both hands upon the book. Without warning you are suddenly on the other side of the mirror. You can now see the room in which you were just standing. There in the center of the floor is the golden Star with the blue circle, and the rug leading toward the mirror and you. Just off to your left is the small dark wood table.

Allow the images in the mirror to dissolve into a deep black surface that reflects or shows nothing. Open the cover of the book. Allow the pages to turn themselves to your current time and space. Reach out with your left hand and place it upon the right page. Reach out with your right hand and place it upon the left page. Look deep into the mirror and ask that the answers to your questions be formed in a manner you are able to readily understand. Ask any question about yourself or anyone else, and allow those answers to fill the black surface of the mirror.

– Long Pause (1 minute) –

Ask another question. See the answer forming in the far distant center of the mirror. Allow the answer to get closer. Closer. Allow the answer to fill the mirror's surface. Now allow the answer to extend beyond the mirror's surface. Allow the answer to surround you. Hear the answer. Smell the answer. See the answer. Taste the answer. Reach out and touch the answer.

– Long Pause –

Ask another question. See the answer forming in the far distant center of the mirror. Allow the answer to get closer. Closer. Allow the answer to fill the mirror's surface. Now allow the answer to extend beyond the mirror's surface. Allow the answer to surround you. Hear the answer. Smell the answer. See the answer. Taste the answer. Reach out and touch the answer.

– Long Pause –

Ask another question. See the answer forming in the far distant center of the mirror. Allow the answer to get closer. Closer. Allow the answer to fill the mirror's surface. Now allow the answer to extend beyond the mirror's surface. Allow the answer to surround you. Hear the answer. Smell the answer. See the answer. Taste the answer. Reach out and touch the answer.

– Long Pause –

Remove both hands from the book. Allow the image of the upper chamber to form once again in the mirror's surface. See the golden star at the very center of the room. Step through the mirror onto the tapestry that leads from the base of the mirror to the center of the upper chamber. Walk to the center of the room and stand on the blue center of the six pointed Star. Feel the rose colored light pulling at you from below. Feel your resistance to the pull. Allow the center of the Star to give way. Allow yourself to gently sink downward toward the floor. The great mosaic of the Collective Mind is stretched out below you now. Notice where the shaft of rose colored Light is taking you. Notice the shape and color of the tile at the very center of the shaft of Light. This is your place within the Collective Mind.

Feel the waves of certainty move from your toes to the top of your head as you get closer to the floor.

Touch your toes then the balls of your feet against the floor. Now your heels. Walk directly toward the doors. Your sight is taken once again as the intense Light greets you. Allow your feet to find the way. There, out in front of you, is the purr of the lions. Those great cats are sending their deep wonderful purr to assure you. Feel the vibration of their purr in your body. Allow yourself to see them. They are looking back at you through the Light. There is so much dignity and courage with the male; so much nurturing and compassion with the female. Reach out. Touch them. Feel them lean towards you, into your touch. Stop for a moment. Stand in their sound. They completely accept you as their own. You accept them equally.

Move down the steps. Count each step...33, 32, 31, 30, 29, 28, 27, 26, 25, 24, 23, 22, 21, 20, 19, 18. Pause to remember all that you discovered in the upper chamber. Continue. See the Earth suspended in space, spinning in your Light. 17, 16, 15, 14, 13, 12, 11, 10, 9, 8, 7, 6, 5, 4, 3, 2, 1...imagine yourself next to your physical body. See the glow coming from your body. Such a wonderful color. Move into your body. Become completely aware of your physical body. Wiggle your toes. Make a fist. Open your eyes.

– End –

Key Elements: (The elements in bold type are trigger elements.)

Inner Light • Earth spinning in your Light •Thirty-three ascending steps • Pair of lions • Purring sound • Pair of doors • Blinding Light • Large room • Shaft of rose colored Light • **Golden star • Pressure below and above • Upper chamber • Mirror • Book** • The mosaic

Explanation of the Key Elements:

Inner Light. The eternal inner glow is your Source, the seat of your Soul. Extending this Light out into the world is the natural expression of each Human and part of the reason for you being in this dimension.

Earth spinning in your Light. Allowing all manner of Consciousness to dwell within your Source Light is symbolic of your greater Awareness directing your thoughts away from bias and judgment. This allows you to be in perfect communion with the illusion of manifest matter.

Thirty-three ascending steps. To enter the Akashic Records we must move our Awareness upward and away from the centers in the brain where sensory data is processed. Our Awareness must be centered in the third eye of our Etheric body. The ascending stair case represents this process. The Master numbers, eleven, twenty-two and thirty-three are symbolic of the different levels of 'seeing' through the Etheric body's third eye.

Pair of lions. The lions at the top of the stairs are symbolic of our Highest animal nature. The American Indians call these inner animal pictures "power animals." These particular animals represent Dignity, Courage, Compassion and Nurturing. Also the clarity expressed in their eyes is a mirror of our own clarity while in the Records.

Purring sound. Their purring sound and vibration is symbolic of the sound current. This is the sound generated by the oscillation of atomic structures. As we move Conscious Awareness from the physical body into the Etheric body, we can encounter this phenomenon. Also, this sound is present in the mind during intense moments of concentration. Many individuals studying rigorous forms of meditation, experience this vibration while still fully in the body.

Pair of doors. As we move Conscious Awareness from the physical to the Etheric body we encounter the Doors to Eternal Knowledge, the Gates of Heaven, Saint Peter's gates perhaps. There have been many names given to this symbol throughout history.

Blinding Light. The Light at the doors represents the transition from validation oriented physical sight, where we only find what we are looking for, to Etheric sight where creation is presented as it is. Walking blindly forward establishes our commitment and brings forward our trust and belief in ourselves.

Large room. The large room of the temple, or cathedral, is the manifest form of the Akashic Records. This is the Great Hall of Records spoken of in many literary works over the last six thousand years. The more you experience this place, the more real it becomes.

Shaft of rose colored Light. The shaft of rose colored Light is symbolic of the stream of Christ Conscious energy that enters the Etheric body from the Over-Soul. The Source of this Light is the Elohim. This Light travels from the Christ body through the Celestial body, Mental body, Causal body, the three Astral bodies, the Etheric body, then pierces the outer Spiritual veil of the physical body. When you allow yourself to be lifted upward in this Light you are Ascending on the energy that gives you Life Everlasting in all dimensions.

Golden star. The Golden Star, with its lapis center, is the symbol of the eighth chakra of the Etheric body. This is the third eye of the Etheric body and serves that body much the same way the third eye of the physical body serves Human Consciousness in the physical realm – to see beyond the limitations imposed by conscious beliefs.

Pressure from below and above. The lifting sensation from below and the pressure from above represent the final experience of duality – the urge and the resistance – the homeostasis process of Spiritual evolution.

Upper chamber. The upper chamber is where Consciousness looks out into the vast realms beyond individuated Human Consciousness into the Collective Mind.

Mirror. The mirror is a symbolic image of that place within the Super Conscious Mind that allows you to see beyond the illusion of time and space. When you move through the mirror, you have become the witness to what is manifesting in the upper chamber.

Book. Each Soul has its own Book of Life where it records the events and responses of each incarnation. All the immutable events of every lifetime are written prior to your <u>first</u> incarnation. Your response is recorded as you focus Awareness within a given life expression.

The mosaic. The mosaic on the floor is the Collective Kodak moment; the picture, if you will, of Human Conscious at the exact moment you are viewing it. If you were to just hang, suspended above the floor, you would see that it is a living document, changing in each moment. This is the Mt. Olympus of early Greek mythology. This is where the Gods and Goddesses watched the progress of humankind.

Questions Concerning this Meditation

I had difficulty finding my Light within. The harder I tried, the farther behind with the meditation I got. Finally I just quit. How important is it to see that inner Light?

It is very important to remember and honor the place within you that is your Source. Please understand this is a process. This technique is designed to take you to your inner most witness with the least amount of effort. The point here is to simply remember the place within that is your Source. Working hard at imagining defeats the purpose. Relax into this experience.

Gently connecting with your deep inner Light has two effects: 1) The emergence of your Light into the Conscious Physical Universe as you invite a halo to form around your physical body has a very grounding effect upon your entire being. This action is felt in the seven bodies that make up the Human experience. 2) This light is at the very foundation of the meditation process used to get you to your upper chamber. As such it is the energy that fuels the experience. Without this connection you would become very tired, very fast while attempting to get into the Records.

Just your thoughts of this inner Source, this eternal Light, are enough in the beginning. The image of it will come as you gain familiarity and confidence.

The stairs were more like an escalator. Is it okay to have such modern images in Spiritual meditations?

You're spending too much time in the mall.

More important than following my exact suggestions is your willingness to be directed along an inner path. Allow the suggestions of the meditation to help guide you. You already know the way. The staircase can even be an elevator. One individual's only way to the lions was in a glass elevator. He simply watched at the top of the elevator panel while it counted the thirty-three floors. When the doors opened, he was standing in front of two wonderful animals.

His upward glance while counting the numbers is very appropriate here. The upward direction is really an important aspect to this part of the meditation. The upward concentration of energy in thirty-three equal measures is also important.

Why would someone be following me up the steps?

Many individuals experience the presence of their guides while visiting the Akashic Records. Actually, we are <u>never</u> alone while traveling in the dimensional realities beyond the Conscious Physical Universe. This is largely owing to our human concerns, and deep seated fears of the unknown. Also, these Spiritual escorts seek to bring deeper meaning to our journeys beyond physical space and time. You may call on these Beings directly, or you may find yourself in their company through your intention to be helped, or your fear of the unknown.

One individual who was using this technique would become annoyed at the presence of his guides. At first he thought they were eaves-dropping on his Akashic material. He had never encountered the concept of "guides" prior to doing this type of work. When he would confront them from this attitude, they would just smile, then disappear. I asked him to detail each step of his approach to the technique. He revealed that just before using the meditation he would ask God to guide his intentions. I explained, "There you are. You've extended an invitation." He decided that as far as he could tell, guides and God were two different things. Then he stated he would like to be alone in the Hall of Records. I suggested he guide his own intentions and not ask for direct help from God. I never heard back from him.

Guides are extremely allowing. Most have been Human as many times as those they are guiding. And those who have never been in a physical human form have studied the Human experience for a great many millennium. Allow your guides to help. It will advance your experience of the Akasha.

The lions you suggested were more like ugly Chinese dogs, the ones I've seen at the entrance to temples. I didn't hear any purring, so I'm guessing I didn't hear the sound current. Is it okay?

It is profoundly okay to have your own experience of this technique. Many individuals have never experienced the sound current and they use this technique every time they venture into the Records. Others report that all they need to do to get into the Records is to hear the sound current. Allow your way to unfold itself. All the elements of this technique have meaning, singularly and together. Each element could be your trigger at different times, or you may be one of those who only needs to have the intention to find yourself in the Records.

As far as the animals are concerned they do not have to be lions. They can be your idea of the highest animal consciousness. Many experience deer or bear. I use the image of lions because they seem to be a universal symbol. After all, we Humans do refer to them as the King of Beasts. If you use other animals let their natural sound represent the sound current.

I only had one door and it wasn't carved. Actually, I don't even think it was a door. It was more like a veil of fine cloth.

Each individual's doorway will be unique. They will sometimes change from meditation to meditation, leaving you to wonder if you are at the right address. The suggested images are there to stimulate thought energy, which in turn guides your Consciousness as it chooses the most direct path to your inner teacher. Be a witness. Allow your Consciousness the freedom to take you on the most direct path inward. Allow your symbolic images to change as you gain confidence in your journey inward.

Instead of Light blinding me at the door, I got darkness blinding me. It was hard to walk forward in the darkness. I had to do that a lot as a kid. My mother worked late and I had to stay at my aunt's until she got home. Then I had to walk across the field. This triggered some old fear.

Many people have experienced similar conditions in their meditations. When I suggest blindness, most individuals image darkness first, then replace the darkness with Light. Most of us envision darkness when we hear the word "blind." It only seems fair that you would extend this attitude into my suggestion of being blinded by the Light.

The image of the blinding Light is important to this work. It changes your way of imaging. Keep working with this element. The darkness is also more than likely a manifestation of your fear of the unknown. Allow that fear to be present. Notice any change in your feelings as you walk into the darkness in subsequent meditations. Journal your progress about this fear. As the fear goes away, the Light will be present.

My cathedral was more like a small living room. It wasn't very impressive. And there was wall to wall carpeting on the floor. So I didn't get to see much in the way of a mosaic. Everything was almost the same color.

Allow. The element of being in a large magnificent room is important. When you were a baby you had to adjust to seeing with physical eyes. You are like the baby in that you are gaining experience with seeing in a new way, so the size and color will change with every meditation until you have formed a clear vision of the Hall. These meditations are a process, the end is something else. The images I suggest pale in comparison to what is really there. The finished image will be more than you could possibly imagine. And words will fail when you try describing it to others. Go to a local church or temple to get a "real" experience of a large room.

Then aren't we just making it up? It's very frustrating to think that it can and will always change. I was hoping the Akashic Records would appear the same to everyone. That way I would know they were true.

At some point everyone sees the same image, the same room. And, yes, we make everything up from our expectations. Example: the route you take to work each day is made up of your expectations. Many an individual has suddenly become aware of a new building near its completion date. They have driven past the building site many times, and are only just now seeing the work of the last several months. And you're amazed when people say the building has been under construction for the past six months. You want to believe them, and how is it possible you could miss something so large? This happens every day. We have our expectations.

Our expectations are really what influence the changes in detail from meditation to meditation. If you are Catholic, you will expect perhaps a Gothic cathedral. If you are Jewish, a temple; Moslem, a mosque. If you are a Buddhist, Hindu, Sufi, Jainist, Baptist, etc., your expectations will project themselves into this meditation, creating variations suitable to your beliefs about Spiritual matters. During the process of remembering your way to the Akasha, the small details will change. This is because your beliefs about Creation will be changing. Eventually everyone does see the same room. At first their idea of what to expect is colored. Once in the Records you will see all religions as a process and the burden of your expectations will be lifted.

You are dealing with perceptions that are based here in this dimension. Allow your "real" world images to grow into the experience of the Great Hall of Records. With our conditioning it would be impossible to see the Great Hall immediately upon arriving there. The experience must grow on you. It is an acquired experience.

The rose colored Light didn't want to lift me. I imagined a rope in the center of the shaft of Light and pulled myself up to the ceiling.

Nice solution! Intention is what it's all about. If you intend to get into the Records, nothing will stop you. How did you get through the center of the star at the ceiling?

It was like a trap door. I had to push it open. The room was in a castle. The door in the floor was a secret passage.

Very nice images. Allow the solutions to any "problem" to be natural projections from your imagination. Our imaginations can find the solution to any block along our journey. Allow your imagination to be a dear friend, someone who is a wonderful helpmate. So many individuals have been convinced by society that their imaginations are of little value.

I was with every word you said until you suggested my head was pushing against the ceiling. As soon as I felt something pressing on the top of my head, I panicked, and jerked back into my body. Why was that my reaction? I'd like to know if any one else had a problem with the ceiling.

This response could be for many different reasons. A more common experience is, say, feeling the Light from below pushing you upward, then taking off like a rocket right through the ceiling and into a wonderful state of unconsciousness. This often happens. It has been my experience that when an individual has this type of occurrence it is nothing more than the part of you that thought perhaps this was just make believe, suddenly got how real it was and panicked. As soon as you realized the realness of what you were doing, you moved into performance anxiety, and your doubt brought you to its source – this dimensional world.

I couldn't visualize the upper chamber at all. I saw the mirror and had no problem moving to the other side. My problem was with the table that the book was on. It was liquid or something very unstable. I couldn't really tell what the book was resting on.

I have had individuals report that their book was simply floating in air. The image of the altar or table, is to give support to the Book of Life. Again, this is a process, allow whatever happens to happen. You are going to experience "Alice in Wonderland" types of images. We all do. Even after years of working with the Akashic Records and the Book of Life I still will occasionally experience something that seems totally out of place, or something that redefines my personal view of Creation. Rejoice in the diversity of the images. Allow your Book of Life to float upon a stream if it so desires.

When it came time to return to the other side of the mirror, to the upper chamber, I couldn't. I wasn't scared when I heard you counting down the steps. I just stood frozen on the other side. Then suddenly I was back here with my body. I thought I was making all the details up until I couldn't make up getting to the other side of the mirror. What a weird feeling to suddenly realize I wasn't just imagining it, it was really happening.

Yes, it is marvelous to move from imagination to experience. Remember, your intention will return you home. And just like the individual a moment ago – the fact that you suddenly realized this helped to create a form of performance anxiety. It was this fear that locked you behind the mirror. Just like Dorothy in the *Wizard of Oz*, you can always return home, when you so desire.

Explain why we must be on the other side of the mirror. I couldn't get there. I blanked out as soon as you mentioned placing my hands on the book.

The macro view is that Akashic information is formed <u>within</u> the upper chamber. The mirror is a portal, a non-reflective surface. If it were reflective, you could stand in front of it and see your answer reflected behind you. Then there would be the matter of reversing the images before you interpreted their meaning. In order to fully experience the answers to your questions you must become the witness, you must be on the outside looking in.

– Script Number Two –
Meditation: The Temple of Knowledge

Relax. Focus on your breath. Feel your body expand and contract as you breathe. Select only the finest quality of oxygen as you inhale. See those molecules of oxygen as tiny points of Light. Allow these points of Light to fill your lungs with a soothing wonderful healing glow. Exhale. Send the Light upward through your throat and into your brain. As the glow from the light touches your brain, it begins to soften. Your brain was like a tight fist, now it is becoming an open palm. Inhale, filling your lungs with brilliant sparkles of healing light. Your lungs are glowing. Send the light upwards, through your throat and into your brain. Your brain is bathing in a soft glowing light. Allow your brain to soften. Feel it softening, sagging against the back of the skull. Feel your brain relaxing, softening. Allow the softening to spread down into the brain stem, at the base of the brain, where the head and neck join. Feel the softness in the brain stem. Feel the back of the brain settling, softening, relaxing. Relax. Allow yourself to fully relax.

Allow the softness of your brain to spread down your spinal column. Feel the warm glow from your brain flowing through each and every nerve. Your muscles respond with joy as they soften.

– Pause –

Clear your throat. (Slight pause) Let out a deep sigh. And another. And another. Clear your throat again.

– Pause –

Relax. Whisper in your mind the sound, "LUM." (Slight pause) Whisper in your mind the sound, "VUM." (Slight pause) Whisper in your mind the sound, "RUM." (Slight pause) Whisper in your mind the sound, "YUM." (Slight pause) Whisper in your mind the sound, "HUM." (Slight pause) Whisper in your mind the sound, "AUM."

– Pause –

Mentally whisper, "LUM." (Slight pause) Mentally whisper, "VUM." (Slight pause) Mentally whisper, "RUM." (Slight pause) Mentally whisper, "YUM." (Slight pause) Mentally whisper, "HUM." (Slight pause) Mentally whisper, "AUM."

– Pause –

Mentally whisper, "LUM." (Slight pause) Mentally whisper, "VUM." (Slight pause) Mentally whisper, "RUM." (Slight pause) Mentally whisper, "YUM." (Slight pause) Mentally whisper, "HUM." (Slight pause) Mentally whisper, "AUM."

– Pause –

With your imagination begin to construct images of ancient Egypt. Great rising columns of stone. Rows of statuary. Giant pyramids. Now imagine yourself standing at the entrance to a secret garden. A polished stone obelisk stands at the very center of the garden. Three circles of plants surround the obelisk. The one closest touches the corners of the base. The next circle is eleven feet out from the first circle. The next circle is eleven feet out from the second circle. Each circle is interrupted by a single pathway that leads from where you are standing to the front side of the monument.

Walk toward the obelisk. There is a golden tablet recessed into its side just above head heighth. Notice how the Sun reflects off its golden surface. There is writing etched in this metal plate. Allow the Sun to reflect off the plaque and directly into your eyes. Read the message inscribed on the plaque through the sun's glare. Now close your eyes, see the message etched into your vision. Open your eyes. The message is gone.

Turn to your right and walk around the obelisk. The circles on the other side of the obelisk are again interrupted by a foot path. The path leads to a flight of stairs. On each step of the ascending stairs are two columns, one on either side of the step, rising some fifty feet into the air. Each column has the image of an animal carved at the very top. Each animal is different and is there to protect this place from those who would trespass. They are like stone because they have no senses. Their only Awareness is that of intention. Allow yourself to ascend the staircase.

There are thirty-three steps. Count each step as you ascend...1, 2, 3, 4, 5, 6, 7, 8, 9, 10, 11, 12, 13, 14, 15, 16, 17. Pause for a moment. There is an altar at the top of the stairs, the top of which is waist high. Behind the altar is a large rectangular window, with the vertical side being twenty-five feet high. Twenty-two feet above the window a pair of wings stretch across the temple from the tops of the last columns. The tips of the wings extend beyond the column tops by one foot. At the center of the wings is a circle filled with the image of a six pointed star; a triangle pointing up, overlaid at the exact center by a triangle pointing down. In the center of the star is a lapis blue circle. Engraved in the center of the circle is the unspoken name of the God/Goddess Creator.

Continue up the stairs...18, 19, 20, 21, 22, 23, 24, 25, 26, 27, 28, 29, 30, 31, 32, 33. The last step brings you directly in front of the altar and the window that looks out into forever. Feel your heart center expand to include all those who have come here before you and all those who will come here after you; include all those who have worked for the liberation of Human Consciousness from the illusion of this world; include all Light workers who have preserved the knowledge of this place, then softly within your mind say the name of the God/Goddess as it was written within the circle and the star.

Place both hands upon the altar. Ask that the answers to your questions be revealed within the frame of the window in a manner easily understood by your personality.

Ask your question. See a small faint image in the very center of the window. Watch as the image gets bigger and bigger. Now it begins to fill the darkness of the window. Allow your thoughts to interpret what has formed in the window. Hear yourself give the answer.

– Long Pause (1 minute) –

Ask another question. Watch as the answer rushes toward you from deep in the center of the window. Allow the answer to fill up the window. Allow your thoughts to interpret the visual symbols within the window. Allow the visual images to stimulate your other senses.

– Long Pause –

Ask another question. Allow the answer.

– Long Pause –

Ask another question. Allow the answer.

– Long Pause –

Remove your hands from the altar. Look up and repeat the name of God/Goddess softly within your mind. Turn and begin your descent...33, 32, 31, 30, 29, 28, 27, 26, 25, 24, 23, 22, 21, 20, 19, 18. Pause. Notice how the images at the top of the columns have changed. They are constantly changing to meet your expectations. Continue...17, 16, 15, 14, 13, 12, 11, 10, 9, 8, 7, 6, 5, 4, 3, 2, 1...Walk back into the garden. Move around to the front of the obelisk. Allow the Sun to reflect itself off the plaque, into your eyes. Read the message on the plaque through the sun's glare. Turn and walk the path that leads away from the garden, beyond the last circle.

– Pause –

Move your Awareness back into your physical body. Wiggle fingers and toes. Open your eyes.

– End –

Key Elements: (Those items in bold type are trigger elements.)

Secret garden • Stone obelisk rising out of a circle • Golden Light reflecting off the obelisk • **Thirty-three ascending steps** • Columns on each step • Altar • Window looking out into the void • Wings spread above the altar and window • **Circle within the wings • Star of David • Name of God/Goddess Creator** • Focused question

Explanation of the Key Elements:

Secret garden. The secret garden represents your inner self. The type, number and spacing of the plants, as well as their placement within the garden, allows you a glimpse at your inner nature. Objects of art, or structures within your garden, represent core beliefs. Objects such as image glyphs inscribed on rocks or trees represent moments of unification.

Stone obelisk rising out of a circle. The stone obelisk represents your Over-Soul. The gold plaque represents the personality of the Over-Soul – what we call our Higher-Self.

Golden Light reflecting off the obelisk. The gold Light reflecting off the plaque is the Light of Wisdom and Compassion. You are connecting the personality of your Over-Soul, your Higher-Self, with the personality of your Lower Self, your Ego, by allowing the Light to penetrate your vision. The message inscribed upon the plaque will change from time to time. Its meaning or relevance to your journey through Creation is only known by you.

Thirty-three ascending steps. The thirty-three steps are symbolic of the Etheric body's third eye. The third eye of the Etheric body is located in the eighth chakra of the center column of that body which corresponds with the crown chakra of the physical body.

Columns on each step. The columns on each step represent the dual nature of manifest reality. The animals at the top depict the opposing nature of the manifest reality that a given step represents.

Altar. The altar is the heart of the temple. The temple is your sanctuary.

Window looking out into the void. The rectangular window represents the holographic surface of the Akasha as seen from this temple.

Wings spread above the altar and window. A perfectly matched pair of wings stretch across the last columns to join the dual nature of the command to Be – Mastery and Mystery. Light and Dark. Doing and Being. Masculine and Feminine. The wings represent liberation from the struggle to balance duality.

Circle within the wings. The circle within the wings signifies completion.

Star of David. The triangle pointing downward overlaid at the center by a triangle pointing upward – the Star of David – represents the unification of Mastery and Mystery within the illusion of dual manifest reality – the Holy Matrimony within the Kingdom of God Creator.

Name of God/Goddess Creator. The unspoken name of Creator written at the center of the star represents the Alpha as the Omega – the Omega as the Alpha. The Everlasting unto Everlasting nature of Creation. Whispering this name deep within your mind connects you to Source.

Questions Concerning this Meditation

I really identified with the Egyptian motif. The problem I had was finding the golden plaque and seeing any words written upon it. Maybe I'm not ready to receive the message?

It is a question of willingness. Seeing a message is important, and you will still access the records without a message . This element of the meditation is of a highly personal nature. You with You. Sometimes, when we have been out of practice, it takes a few attempts to communicate directly with our Higher-Self. You are very worthy of the experience even if no message appears. You are just out of practice is all.

I am aware of people who have never received a message from the golden tablet placed in the obelisk, and they have wonderful experiences using this meditation to access the Records.

Then why put it as part of the meditation?

To allow even more experience into your meditation. As you might have already suspected, these techniques are about more than just the Akashic Records. This is about mysticism, about blending Mastery with Mystery. So even though this work is primarily about the Akasha, connecting with the highest aspect of Self is as important as getting into the Records.

I didn't even see the obelisk. As a matter of fact, I really didn't get any images until we started up the steps. Is the first part of the visualization important to accessing the Akasha?

As was just stated, this is not just about accessing the Akasha. This is about opening ourselves to greater understandings of Creation. Observing all the key elements of the meditation will give a fullness to your experience. I have observed that individuals who connect with all of the key elements in a meditation continue using the Akasha as a Source of guidance, both personally and for others. This willingness to experience more and more of yourself is important to the enlightenment process. I knew of one individual who was so insistent that he experience everything that he staged all the key elements of the meditation in the 'real' world and rehearsed each meditation over and over again until he could readily experience them in a meditative state. Actually, this was how early students were taught. They would be given everyday tasks that would then be incorporated into guided meditations. If you were to sit in on a vespers session at a monastery, you would soon get that the words they chant are about everyday activities. These practical elements help with the depth of their meditations because they are so well integrated within the body and mind experience. Something that is well known will have a soothing effect.

Eventually, you will only have to remember one key element to access the Records. You will relax, soften your mind, feel an upward flow of energy, remember the key element, ask your question and receive your information.

Is the golden Light reflecting into my eyes the same as when I look up into the sun before going into the cave in the Book of Life meditation?

One and the same. This is the moment when you shift your vision inward. This is critical to viewing images and symbols in the Records.

I blank out every time I begin counting the steps.

Counting is important to this meditation. We use Master's numbers of eleven, twenty-two and thirty-three because they represent specific levels of Consciousness that have corresponding points within the physical and Etheric bodies. Blanking out or loosing count is an indication of resistance within the personality self.

Practice this part of the meditation by finding a staircase that has at least thirty-three steps. Ascend the practice steps slowly. Count each step as you rest your foot upon it. This will help. And this goes with all the different aspects of a meditation. Find corresponding "real" world activities to enhance your visualization ability.

My columns were trees, and the wings were attached to a bird.

Nice imagery. The columns can be classic Greek or Roman, and I think your trees will do nicely.

The image of wings is important. They are symbolic of our liberation from the desires of the physical world, and our final Ascension. As far as your wings being attached to a bird, they usually are in the physical world. Individuals have reported the wings to be everything from a native American thunderbird design, to an inanimate blue neon art deco looking sign. Allow the wings to change from time to time.

I have a hard time with the Star of David.

The Star of David represents, at the subconscious level, the unification of the dual nature of Human Consciousness. This is where the illusion of duality is transformed into a singular expression of Creation. If you are having trouble with this symbol it is likely that you have many judgments concerning duality, such as, right and wrong, justice and injustice, Joe versus the Volcano, etc.

Ask the Records for insights about your difficulty with this symbol. Allow the answer.

My name of God was simply, "Mother." I was disappointed. I wanted the name of God to be exotic, unknown. I got, "Mother." Does this mean me as a mother? My mother? God as Mother? Goddess maybe?

In the beginning you will see many different names of God/Goddess. Does this mean we are making it up? We are simply peeling away the many different concepts we have of God/Goddess. One day you will realize that the name of God/Goddess within the star has become constant. This will be a wonderful day.

In all the meditations I forget my question. Then it takes me a while to think of something to ask. As soon as the answer begins to come, you ask us to return. It's very frustrating. Do you have any suggestions?

Much of this is about performance anxiety. If you decide to make your own tape give more time for the questions and answers. And, you should be able to get the answer to any question in a single moment. Time is not a constraint in the Records. In the minutes I allowed for this exercise all the information concerning several past lifetimes could have been transferred to you. The obvious answer is to be very focused before starting the exercise. If that does not work try a few sessions with questions that are very general and spontaneous.

– Script Number Three –

Meditation - Upper Chamber

Relax. Become aware of your breath. Select only the finest quality of oxygen as you inhale. See the molecules of oxygen as tiny points of light. Allow these points of light to fill your lungs with a soothing wonderful healing glow. Exhale. Send the light upward through your throat and into your brain. As the glow from the light touches your brain, it begins to soften. Your brain was like a tight fist, now it is becoming an open palm. Inhale, filling your lungs with brilliant sparkles of healing light. Your lungs are glowing. Exhale. Send the light upwards, through your throat and into your brain. Your brain is bathing in a soft glowing light. Allow your brain to soften. Feel your brain relaxing, softening. Sagging against the back of the skull. Allow the softening energy to spread down into the brain stem, the base of the brain, where the neck and the head join. Feel the softness in the brain stem. Feel the back of the brain settling, softening, relaxing.

– Pause –

With the power of your mind imagine yourself in a softly swinging hammock. Gently swinging back and forth...back and forth. The temperature is perfect. The canopies of the trees supporting the hammock are just the right colors. The smell in the air is a fragrance that reminds you of a time when you felt safe and secure. The gentle sounds of nature send waves of relaxation up and down your body. A wonderful, slightly sweet taste fills your mouth as your physical, emotional and mental bodies blend in profound relaxation.

Allow the hammock to continue its back and forth motion. Soften your vision. Images of a moment of past pleasure fills your mind. You in the moment. Your senses are again exposed to the ripeness of the world. You in one moment. Feel the moment of pleasure. Laughter. Joy. Open. Pleasure.

Allow the images to excite your senses. Taste the moment. Hear the sounds of your pleasure. See the color of your joy. Open. Feel the laughter in your body and mind. Allow your nostrils to awaken to the smell of your pleasure. Laughter. Joy. Open. Pleasure.

Relax. Allow the pleasure to move through your body, mind and Spirit. This is what we have come here for – to be pleased and pleasured with our Earth experience. To find ourselves in the midst of Creation's outpouring joy. To be ripe with the world.

Relax. Completely relax. Use your imagination. Imagine. Use your imagination to its fullest.

There, directly in front of you, is a standard door found in most all buildings and homes. This is a very common type of door. Look at the details of the door: the handle. The door frame. The width and height. The molding around the door. The finish on the door materials.

At the top of the door is a number. Above the number is a gentle light. Notice how the numbers are styled. Remember the numbers.

In just a moment you will open the door and walk into a very small room with an ascending spiral staircase. The staircase has thirty-three steps. As you ascend the staircase you must count each step. Before you open the door remember your intention for making this journey into the Records.

– Pause –

Gently open the door. A soft, pale blue glow fills the tiny room. In the center of this very small room is the upward spiral staircase. Look toward the top of the stairs. Notice how the light changes color with each step. The light begins as a summer sky blue and ends as a deep royal purple. Reach out and take the hand rail. Feel your hand tingle to the vibration of the hand rail. Step upward with your right foot leading. Allow feelings of excitement to move upward through your body. Relax. There is no hurry. Count each step as you ascend. 1, 2, 3, 4, 5, 6, 7, 8, 9, 10, 11, 12, 13, 14, 15, 16, 17...Pause for a moment. Notice the door at the top of the stairs. It's a wonderful, beautiful doorway. Continue upward, leading with your left foot...18, 19, 20, 21, 22, 23, 24, 25, 26, 27, 28, 29, 30, 31, 32, 33. The door magically begins to open as you place your foot upon the last step.

Light pours into the staircase from behind the door. Your first response is to reach up and shield your eyes. Allow the Light to burn away your vision. There is just the Light. Allow it to penetrate deep inside your eyes as you walk forward through the doorway. Trust, your feet know the way. Trust. Your ability to 'see' will return in just a moment.

– Pause (15 seconds) –

The room you are standing in is filled with artifacts from your many lives upon the earth, as well as the many other worlds in which you have played. Take a moment to look around. Notice any words or picture glyphs. Remember how they are placed in the room. Over on the far wall is a black mirror. Below the mirror is a long narrow table. In the exact center of the table is a book. This is your book. You wrote it and placed it here before your first incarnation. Approach the mirror and the book the way you would greet an old friend – open, trusting.

The book is open to a certain place. There is writing on the bottom half of each page. On the top half is an illustration. The text is complete and represents your life events for a given period of time. The illustrations are being finished. The illustrations are formed by your response to the events written at the bottom of each page. Allow yourself to browse through the pages. Turn the pages of the book forward. Notice that the pictures above the text are sketchy, with very little detail. Now, turn the pages backward. The farther back you go, the richer and more detailed the pictures become. Return the pages to where you began.

Hold your left hand several inches above the left page and ask the mirror to reveal the answers to your question of the past. Notice the pages of the book are flipping backward toward the answer. The images in the mirror are three-dimensional impressions of the pictures and text from the book. Allow the answer to be presented in the mirror.

– Long Pause (1 minute) –

Ask another question of the past about someone in this life who is genetically related to you. Notice the pages of the book are flipping backward toward the answer. Allow the answer to be presented in the mirror.

– Long Pause (1 minute) –

Ask another question of the past about someone you work with. Notice the pages of the book are flipping backward toward the answer. Allow the answer to be presented in the mirror.

– Long Pause (1 minute) –

Bring your left hand to your side. Ask that the pages of the book be brought back to the same place as when you first stood in front of the mirror.

– Pause –

Place your right hand above the right page of the book. Ask that the answers to your question of the future be displayed in the mirror. Notice the pages of the book flipping forward. Allow the answers to be presented in the mirror in images that are easily understood.

– Long Pause (1 minute) –

Ask another question of the future about someone who is genetically related to you. Notice the pages of the book flipping forward. Allow the answers to be presented in the mirror in images that are easily understood.

– Long Pause (1 minute) –

Ask another question of the future about someone you work with.. Notice the pages of the book flipping forward. Allow the answers to be presented in the mirror in images that are easily understood.

– Long Pause (1 minute) –

Place your right hand at your side. Ask that the pages of the book be brought back to the same place as when you first stood in front of the mirror.

– Pause –

Turn away from the book and mirror. Look around the room once again. Remember what you have just seen in the mirror. Remember the artifacts in this room. Move toward the doorway. Allow the Light to penetrate deep into your eyes. There is nothing now except the Light. Move through the doorway. Trust. Your feet know the way. The descending staircase appears as your ability to see returns. Step out with your right foot. Count each step as you make your way downward. 33, 32, 31, 30, 29, 28, 27, 26, 25, 24, 23, 22, 21, 20, 19, 18...Pause on the eighteenth step. Step out with your left foot and continue downward...17, 16, 15, 14, 13, 12, 11, 10, 9, 8, 7, 6, 5, 4, 3, 2, 1. As your right foot touches the last step move your Consciousness back into your physical body.

– End –

Key Elements: **(The elements in bold type are trigger elements.)**

Details of first door • Number at top of first door • Small room • Spiral staircase • Thirty-three steps • Changing color • Vibration in handrail • **Blinding light behind upper door** • **Upper chamber** • **Words or glyphs** • **Book** • Illustrations and text

Explanation of the Key Elements:

Details of first door. Focusing on the details of the door is the same activity as imagining an upward leading path through nature. This is the place of preparation. The more common the details, the deeper your concentration; the deeper your concentration, the more real your experience.

Number at top of first door. The numbers above the door can be a single digit number or a series of numerical symbols. It is impossible to understand the meaning of the numbers with the intellect, having a feeling of their meaning will be sufficient in the beginning. The numbers represent your Soul's pathway into this dimension. There are many interpretations of the Pythagorean theories concerning numerical expressions. The Akasha often speaks in numeric symbols, so it might be wise to become at least familiar with these ideas.

Small room. The image of the very small room represents the beginning place of your inner journey. It is through this chamber that you begin the journey away from the mundane concerns of your day-to-day existence and enter the dimensions associated with the mystical experience of Unified Mind.

Spiral staircase. Many seekers see the image of the spiral staircase as symbolic to the helix spirals of DNA. In this work the image represents the movement of Consciousness from the pineal to the pituitary. The pineal being the third eye and the pituitary being the crown chakra.

Thirty-three steps. The thirty-three steps are the numerical expression of the Inner Teacher, or the Higher Self.

Changing colors. Moving the quality of the Light from sky blue to deep royal purple allows you to clearly see the way from the third eye to the crown. This Light represents the changing levels of energy as you move your Consciousness to the Upper Chamber.

Vibration in handrail. The vibration of the handrail is your body's response to the sound current. Allow yourself to feel this throughout your body. The sound current is very healing in nature and brings balance to Human Consciousness.

Blinding light behind upper door. The blinding Light from behind the door of the Upper Chamber is the veil that separates the mundane sight of the third dimension from the cosmic sight of the fourth and fifth dimensions. Allowing the Light to blind you reveals your level of trust and the depth of your intention.

Upper chamber. The room within the Light is your upper chamber; your inner sanctuary; the inner temple; the joining of female and male; the moment when all duality is at rest; the resting place of the Holy Grail.

Words or glyphs. The writings from our past carry great importance when presented in the Upper Chamber. These writings are the themes of past lifetimes. You will be unable to read them with the intellect. Remember them through your ability to imagine them. Even if it seems at first that you are making them up, allow them to be there. At some moment you will experience them as real. They do exist in a real time/space dimension.

Book. There is only one Book of Life in the Akashic Records that represents you. From the macro: the Book was written by you prior to your first incarnation, and is a complete record of your travels in the third dimension. From the micro: this is truly a work in progress and would best be approached with the knowing that response determines outcome, outcomes determine circumstances, circumstances influence perceptions then expectation.

Illustrations and text. The illustrations and text represent the medium through which the Akashic Records impart Collective Mind data to your Book of Life. At times there will appear to be more text than illustration – the illustrations are created through your response to the events of your life. Therefore, the farther ahead you go in the Records, the more you will find text with less illustrations.

Questions Concerning this Meditation

I couldn't seem to create my door to be ordinary. It wanted to be elaborate. Why have a common door?

The symbol of a common door more closely represents a humbling of the intellect prior to moving into the staircase. Also, elaborate details are distracting to the intention of becoming the non-judgmental witness. Once you are in the Akasha you will be astounded by the amount of details. Concentrate upon the simplicity of the common, the ordinary, as a way to begin your journey.

I never get details, but this time they jumped out at me like I was using a magnifying glass or something. When it came time to read the numbers all I got was a blur. Then the rest of the meditation went like the first part – incredible details. Could you shed some light, please.

Many individuals have trouble catching the exact numbers at first and they will eventually be readable. These numbers may also appear as glyphs or ancient forms of cuneiform writing. Remember to ask for whatever appears above the door to be presented in a form that is meaningful to your present state of mind. Numbers are preferable.

Why not say in the meditation to see what's above the door. Why suggest numbers if there can be other things? I saw what looked like scribbling, but quickly turned it into numbers at your suggestion. I thought I was doing it wrong the first time.

We are looking for numbers. Whatever you are experiencing is far from wrong.

Imagining this information at the top of the door in numeric symbols will trigger a response deep in the subconscious mind. It is the point of this particular exercise to look as deeply as possible into the subconscious to that place that is connected to all Consciousness; that singular place within that is the window to the Collective Mind. In other words, the place within you that expresses itself as me. The place within me that expresses itself as you.

The numerical expression at the top of the door is a key.

Can the numbers be at the bottom of the door, say, woven in the fabric of the door mat?

These numbers represent your stream of Consciousness, your Soul's journey into this Kingdom of four dimensions. Following this stream to its source is an important step to Self-Realization and enlightenment. Once you have traced all of your Consciousness stringlets to their beginnings, you will be at the Alpha of your individuation from the Source of all manifest Creation.

The upward gaze is part of the preparation toward tracing your stringlets of Consciousness and energy in this dimensional reality. Move your numbers to the top of the door. It will improve your prospects greatly.

My room was so small I could barely move toward the steps. Should I try to make it bigger?

You must have done a lot of trailer camping as a child.

It is a question of function, more than size. This symbol is meaningful as it moves Conscious Awareness away from the physical into the Etheric body. This room represents the union of Doing with Being, Unified Mind, and will hopefully vary from meditation to meditation.

Were you able to get to the staircase without much trouble?

Yes. Interestingly, we, my four brothers and I, lived in a trailer until I was twelve.

I see. You must have felt very connected to life and wonderfully fulfilled at that time to recall the size of the trailer rooms as an image of the Unified Mind.

I didn't know that was what I was doing. (Pause) I remember that as the happiest time in my life. We were all so close.

There are a number of influencing factors present here, the main one is probably your ascent into womanhood. Out of curiosity, how was the course of your life after the age of twelve? Was there a sudden change in your relationships?

The trailer seems to be a dividing line in my life. We moved to a house when I started to go through puberty. Mother wanted me to have my own room. She had been forced to sleep in the same room with her older brother, and he sexually abused her. She didn't want that to happen to me. It was at about that time my father quit holding me while we watched TV. We did not start to hug again until just before he died. It was more me hugging him. He was very weak and couldn't really hug me back, you see.

Up until that time the five children had slept in two beds at the back of the trailer. After I started my period, I was put off by myself. The yearning to sleep with someone on either side has been getting stronger as I get older. That's why I've chosen to be in therapy. I think I'm looking for a time when I felt safe.

Or at the very least, a time when you felt included.

I didn't think learning how to look into the Akashic Records was going to mean having to deal with all the emotions.

We all have many layers of physical, emotional and mental energy that constantly influence our performance here in this worldly dimension. You will encounter yourself along this path to Self-Realization, or any other path for that matter. It takes an enormous amount of energy to contain the influences from our past. It is less draining to walk with an open hand, giving and receiving in the same moment, allowing the past and future to exist as creativity, instead of as lessons that must be learned. View the Records as you would a film; at once captivated, and removed.

Thanks. How do I do what you just said?

Give your sorrow and self pity over to God/Goddess Creator. When you feel the sorrow of having completely moved from the innocence of being non-sexually oriented, to being forced into the isolation of your womanhood, ask the God/Goddess to heal this wound. They will respond.

I don't really believe in prayer. I know too many people who have never found answers to their prayers. Why should I believe in something if there is no proof of its existence?

Fair enough. I have watched people in prayer. What they are doing is more like a crisis line conversation. Be in gratitude as you enter prayer. Gratitude is the key. Ask that your sorrow be lifted and KNOW that your prayer is heard and being responded to. This knowing that all your sorrow is lifted, is the Source of your gratitude. If you feel moved to have the same prayer an hour later, then by all means do so. And, as is with all things concerning God/Goddess, you need only ask once.

There is only one thing to know about the past, and that is it has no power, unless, of course, you are still trying to figure it out. If you are still trying to iron the wrinkles out of the past, then the past is really the current moment. If the past is the current moment, then what part of you is enjoying now? In this condition you are far from being fully present in the current moment. In this condition accidents of fate can, and will happen.

In short, give up your psychosis to a higher power. Pray. Interestingly, it has been proven that prayer works for individuals who are recovering from surgery, whether they know they are being prayed for or not. Their recovery time is greatly diminished.

Every time I try to envision stairs or steps, or even an upward pathway, I either blank out or go completely unconscious. What am I doing to create this frustration?

Are you able to get into the Records? Do you find yourself in the upper chambers or at the altar in front of the black mirror?

Kind of. When everybody is sharing their experience with the group, I suddenly re-

member mine. Yet, if you were to ask me to outline the meditation I would not be able to. I know I've been there and yet I can't really remember the details of what I saw or what you said until someone triggers me.

This you share with many, and you will fully experience the Records.

Go out and walk upward pathways and stairs. Burn the external experience of them into your cellular mind – feel your legs, watch how you are breathing, notice how your senses are at play while you are in these activities. Then take this external practice into the meditations.

The upward paths and stairs are symbolic of Consciousness moving through the mind. Fully experiencing the images of these suggestions will keep you out of exactly where it is that you find yourself now – doubt, frustration, self pity, etc. If you are moving your Consciousness along the lines of doubt, etc., you will remember your inner experiences as being vague, unless, of course, the remembrance is triggered by someone or something.

This is a process. Play with these techniques and give them their place in time. Let them happen and you will find yourself in the Records.

I had a straight staircase until the last four steps, then it curved slightly to the left. Could you comment?

When we use our imagination we draw upon stored data from the physical, emotional and mental bodies. In essence what we are doing when we imagine is calling upon these three bodies to work very closely together. As we, the witness, collect all the data needed to recreate an image of something in our mind, we excite corresponding areas within the three bodies. The thoughts, feelings and body sensations used to recreate the image of the spiral staircase are substantially different in dynamics than those used to create a straight staircase with a slight curve at the top. A spiral staircase is needed to stimulate the appropriate areas of the three bodies necessary to usher us into that part of the mind where we can view the Akasha.

Follow as closely as possible. If I suggest an upward path and you get the upward escalator, you are still okay, just a little lazy perhaps.

Everything was just as you suggested until I looked up to see the colors in the staircase. It was like there was an incredible rainbow in my room, the kind I used to see when we lived in Kansas City when I was a boy. That has never happened before in any of my meditations. It is the first time I have really spontaneously had something appear.

Congratulations! May you never recover.

A rainbow is just fine. Instead of imaging just the energy range between the throat chakra and the crown chakra, you have included the entire Human spectrum and then some.

The insides of my arches began to twitch as soon as I touched the handrail. There was no vibration in the rail itself, just in my feet. I almost laughed right out loud. Why in my feet and not in my hands?

There are twenty-one major chakras, energy centers in the cellular mind. We are most familiar with the seven core centers located in the center of the upper body. The first two centers of the twenty-one are in the arches of the feet; then in the calves; then at the inside and slightly to the back of the knees, etc. The image of the handrail and the vibration suggested is symbolic of the sound current and vertical Earth energies. When we direct our

Consciousness with certain thought forms, we excite the chakras and increase our Awareness of their presence.

You may also experience other energy centers "waking up." Enjoy the sensations. At some point in your journey you will realize you have not felt anything new in a long time. This is due to the fact that there is an openness to you and therefore no resistance. Moving Consciousness through or around our resistance is what causes the type of sensation you described.

I counted each step. Then the door opened. The light was so strong I almost lost my footing. I had to grab the handrail to keep from falling down the steps. Then I blanked out and don't remember anything else.

When did you regain Conscious Awareness?

When you started us back down the steps.

What are you feeling right now?

Cheated. Puzzled about my response. I love envisioning the light. Why this reaction?

You experienced the Light in a new and unfamiliar manner. This surprising presentation simply caught you off guard. Like most of us, you went to hide. And by the sounds of it you did a wonderful job. And there is no need for concern. After all, you are gaining experience. I guarantee you will never be surprised by that type of presentation again. Instead of being put off, learn from these moments. The inner worlds are full of surprises. Be at ease.

As far as being cheated. Expectations are at the root of those feelings. Expect the unexpected and you will fair well with such encounters. And just like our friend with his rainbow, this event tells me you are making fine headway.

I didn't want to walk forward until my sight returned, or until I could see where it was you were suggesting we go. I have a lot of trust issues. I don't mean that personally.

Thanks. I trust you as well.

Some teachers say that to be Human is to have an issue with trust.

These meditations will challenge existing emotional and mental blocks particularly the first few times they are tried. I have found that an individual's ability to get into the spirit of each meditation is vastly improved with each session. Trust is greater if an individual is familiar with the direction of each meditation.

Is the Light just always symbolic of our higher nature? I get very emotional each time I envision Light in my meditations. A reader once told me it was because my Twin Flame was not incarnate at this time and that I only know him as Light, so when I see Light I am reminded of my loss. It's funny but as soon as she told me that, I did cry less and felt generally better knowing my Twin was so close.

When disguised in Human form we Light Beings see little of our true nature. It is part of the rules of the game here in this dimensional reality. We are the Light in Creation. When you image Light in your meditations, you are remembering who and what you truly are.

The reason you were comforted by the words of this reader is, she told you the truth: your twin is Light. This explanation from the reader shed a new Light on the subject of your constant feelings of being alone. You, like many others, have chosen to incarnate alone, without the benefit of Soul group members, Soul Mates or Twin Flames. Alone in the wilderness, so to speak. A gloriously dreadful situation, and much is possible in this state. Enormous growth, and the aloneness is profound.

More than anything else, the Light is reminding you of who you are, and where it is you are from, and where it is you are going. You are going home after this incarnation is complete. You are finished here.

I'm sure you're going to say something like I don't want to see things, or something like that, but, the only way I could see anything in the room was out of the corners of my eyes. As soon as I would look directly at something it would disappear. What is that about?

If I look directly at a distant Light in the sky, it disappears. I want to look directly at the star to see it, and when I do it disappears. There are many reasons for this, the least of which is peculiar to the optics of the physical eye and has nothing to do with my desire. You are learning how to "see" in the Etheric realms. Be easy with yourself. If at first you are only able to see with your peripheral vision, so be it. Just as with the star, there are many reasons why this happens, the least of which is the fact that you are applying a new form of vision – singular. This takes a little getting used to. Again, accept the experience as it unfolds and be at ease.

I had a similar experience as hers with my Book of Life. It blinked in and out. Finally I just gave up trying to see it.

Were you able to image answers to your questions within the mirror?

Off and on.

Most individuals require a little time getting used to the notion that they are entitled to a direct answer from any source, let alone, a Source such as the Inner Teacher. We have suffered at the hands of individuals and religious organizations who attempt to block, then control the flow of knowledge from Creator to Creation. They have achieved this by placing themselves as the intermediary to this Omnipresent SOURCE. The last two thousand years have been very hard on Human Consciousness; there has been a great deal of misinformation offered about who and what we are, and our role to Source CREATOR.

Allow yourself direct and constant knowing from Source to your Conscious mind. If the images flicker, simply remind yourself that you are a Source for the Collective Mind and are entitled to see directly and clearly.

I must be working for Disney in a parallel life or something. I'm really tired of my very one-dimensional pictures when meditating. Is there anything I can do to get some depth into my inner life?

It is true that those who live in Toon Town are dimensionally challenged. You're not. Please be patient with the process. Your disappointment with past experiences is creating an expectation that is being fulfilled by the one-dimensional images. It is as though you fully expect the images to be flat. Command them to be multidimensional.

I was afraid to look into the mirror.

This response almost always indicates that you are afraid to see what might be in the Records.

One individual, a nationally known psychic, knew in her heart she'd find some awful immutable event in her future that she would be unable to influence. Once in the Akasha she found her fear was concerning the ability to perform. You see, she had an investment in being as good at reading from the Records, as she was at being psychic. She continues to be an excellent psychic. Now she has this as a tool as well.

The fact you were afraid to look into the mirror doesn't necessarily mean you will find something bad. It might simply mean you are worried about being able to interpret what is being revealed.

Nothing came up for the past, but a lot, too much, came up for the future. Could it mean I haven't had a lot of past lives? I feel pretty new at the Earth experience. I feel other worldly.

My guess would be that your interest in future events is simply much broader than your interest in the past.

Some say I'm a bit of a futurist. My first book was certainly about the wonderful possibilities of the future.

I read it some years ago.

I would also believe you to be deeply connected to the Atlatian and Lemurian projects. These both have a very futuristic feel to them. Many individuals who played major roles in those civilizations have taken less than the "normal" number of incarnations, that is to say, an incarnation every two hundred years or so, and therefore have the feeling of being other worldly. This is both the good news and the bad.

The good news – the individual gets to stay out of most of the day-to-day struggles of the masses. The bad news – the individual stays out of most of the day-to-day struggles of the masses.

†Σ†

Footnotes:

[1] Our waking states of Consciousness tend to push other dimensional realities away in favor of the sense oriented physical dimensions. This favoritism is the catalyst behind the fluctuation of Etheric energy surrounding physical human bodies. The Ether tide is at its greatest influence when the majority of Human Consciousness is in dream realms. That's why the time between 3am and 6am is the best time for meditation.

Animals, plants and minerals do not experience the Ether tides because they are multidimensional in their perception of this realm and include other greater possibilities within their waking moments.

Conclusion

Intention Drives the Process

To have a full and present experience of your Book of Life and the Akashic Records requires a strong intention to do so, <u>and</u> the knowing of where to begin your journey of discovery. Many individuals who have used this book's system of breathing and meditation have described their Spiritual journey into the Akashic Records as a direct path to their Inner Teacher. Direct paths are wonderfully exciting, and often times arduous. Exciting in that we are expanding our Consciousness to greater levels of knowing, and arduous in that, once we get the <u>scent</u>, we can become overly enthused, and obsessive in the desire to experience and know even more about the Source of the Eternal Fragrance.

In this work, as in all metaphysical undertakings, it is meaningful to move toward a balance in body, mind and Spirit. In the beginning of this undertaking you will find your journey into the Records very right brain oriented. You are, after all, using imagination to take you to the experience of the Records. Once in the Akasha you will experience a profound balance to your senses because you will be using your left brain to sort through and catalog the data for memory retention. This feeling of mental and emotional balance is due to the overwhelming Wholeness of the experience. When we are in balance we feel a deep inner awe. It is when we allow ourselves to experience the sensations of "awe" that we fully integrate body, mind and Spirit. The sheer vastness of the Records will thrill you in every way.

As we begin this journey, it is important to remember just who we are, to know our place within the scheme of things. Dr. Wayne Dyer put it very nicely when he said, *"We are Spiritual Beings having a Human experience, not human beings trying to have a Spiritual experience."*

This is so very important to know when undertaking this work: life is an issue of willingness, not an issue of ability. We have all come the distance to be here in this NOW. We have the knowledge of all 'things' within our cellular and non cellular minds. We are entitled to all that we allow ourselves to grasp. The master teacher, Jeshua Ben Joseph, promised in Matthew 7: 7 & 8 of the New Testament, *"Ask, and it will be given you; seek and you will find; knock, and it will be opened to you. For everyone who asks receives, and he who seeks finds, and to him who knocks it will be opened."*

Every proponent of the mystical experience has given similar comments. Without knowing this, little is possible. If you are unaware of your standing with Creation you will not allow yourself to progress beyond a certain point. You will yield to superstition rather than to Knowing; you will find yourself repeating present cycles of beliefs and their behaviors. This is a key to the study of any teaching: you are worthy of Knowing the Way. You are equal to the Truth.

The amount of information available in the Akashic Records and Book of Life is beyond our ability to comprehend, and even though the system of the Akasha works the same for each individual, it is more an art than a science. The intellect alone would find it difficult to sort out the details of how the Akasha works; the heart alone would be at a loss to effectively communicate what it is experiencing. When the head and heart join, Consciousness moves from the mundane concerns of the everyday world to the mystical experience of the Records. This Holy marriage of Male and Female is the Unified field of Human Consciousness so often alluded to in mystical writings. In this state, body, mind, and Spirit act as the Profound Urge. The Ultimate Desire of the Urge, as it expresses through Human Consciousness, is Enlightenment – Self-Realization. In this state we become both the question and the answer .

A few last minute points:

Always be gentle with yourself. Introspective endeavors that seem to take us longer than expected can cause us to be a little hard on ourselves. Allow your inner dialogue to be in the same tone and of the same quality as when you first speak to a dear friend whom you have only just seen after a long separation.

In the distant past, the type and amount of information offered on the preceding pages was usually given over a period of, say, some twenty years. The initiate would be introduced to a concept, then allowed whatever time was needed to incorporate the newer understanding into their response to life. This allowed the individual ample time to fully integrate what was being offered. If you feel overwhelmed by the content of this work, set it aside. Meditate on the different aspects of this study. Apply one concept at a time to your life. There is no hurry.

Again, and it bears repeating, the single most important thing to remember with this work is to be kind and nurturing to yourself. If you desire this experience, it will be yours. Take your time. Understanding the whole of the study is more important than just grabbing at the Book of Life or Akashic Record experience.

Once you have gained access to your Book of Life, or the Akashic Records, you will want to schedule regular visits. Create these visits to be purposeful. Time in the Records is truly a blessing and should be looked upon as sacred. Also, if you are scheduling your time correctly, you will not be overdoing it. There is nothing to be gained from spending large amounts of time in The Records.

Reading the Records for other individuals is very rewarding to you, the reader. The trust that happens between you and the client is most profound and is extremely uplifting to your Soul, and your contribution to his or her journey here on Earth will be remarkable. And it goes without saying, this trust is sacred. As has been stated before, you are in no way obligated to give information to a client unless he asks. However, if you are aware of information that could ease the physical, emotional, and/or mental burden of your client, find a way to get him or her to ask for the information.

When you get into the Records for historical data you will come across information that will have you thinking you are either making it up, or have, by some chance, ended up in the wrong place. This happens to everyone who reads from the Records. The historical truth of this physical world has been told by those in positions powerful enough to have a voice in history. These have almost always been the educated and elite. When you view historical accounts in the Records you will be amazed at just how much of our past has been slanted towards the victors and how little voice there has been for those who were not as loud or articulate.

Always be gentle with yourself.

Technique Review:

The technique for entering your Book of Life or for accessing the Akashic Records is basically the same, in that they both contain the same steps. When you create a meditation tape include the relaxation technique that best suits your personality. Give a brief pause between the relaxation sequence and the meditation.

Preparation:

- Do the breathing techniques. They help greatly.
- Clear your mental and emotional bodies by focusing intention toward Unity.
- List your questions.

Create a tape of the following:

Relaxation:

- Give recognition to the physical structure by creating a soothing environment.
- Give yourself permission to relax.

Scripting:

- A structured inward journey directs Consciousness to the appropriate areas of the Collective Mind.

Journal:

- Record the answers you receive to your list of questions. This will help you validate your Akashic experience.
- Record your general experience, including your feelings about the data being received.

Once you have found your perfect formula of breathing to relaxation to meditation, stick with it. The more you practice one particular sequence or technique, the more powerful it becomes.

Remember, the images in the black mirror are impressions of sensory data released back to you in forms that can first appear as simple flat glyphs, one-dimensional snapshots, or simple symbols. Do not be put off by these presentations. As you gain experience these symbols will engage all your senses and the images will appear holographic in structure. The reason for this is that the information contained within the Records enters as, and is stored as multi-dimensional geometric forms. These forms excite all your senses.

Remember to ask for information in a manner suitable and understandable to your current Conscious Mind and personality. Many individuals who "blank-out" once they get into the Records, are doing so because the information being given is integrating in areas of their mind that are unavailable to their waking Consciousness. This is the same phenomena as when you are unable to remember certain dreams or a sudden "Ah-Ha."

The Akashic Records will teach you how to use them. You do not have to spend a lifetime learning how to interpret each and every Akashic symbol. Remember to be clear about your questions. Many individuals ask the wrong questions. Ask yourself, "Is this the question that will give me the answer I am looking for?" If you are still uncertain, then ask any question to get the ball rolling. One question is undoubtedly going to lead to another. As strange as it may seem, at times the answer is the question. If the answer in the mirror seems to be mocking your question, look to the question for the answer. The Akasha is incapable of making fun of someone, so do not take this type of response personally.

I am always interested in hearing of the experiences of fellow travelers. They help form the body of research being compiled concerning the Records. If you have further questions or would like to share your discoveries, write me at the following address:

Gary Bonnell
c/o Richman Rose Publishing
Post Office Box 7766
Atlanta, GA 30357-0766

Thank you for your interest in this work and for sharing your knowledge with others. I would like to thank those who have been my teachers and students. It is with your help and inspiration that I have completed this work.

Journey well! And may you always find yourself in the best of circumstances.

Additional Reading

There are so many titles available to those seeking a greater Knowing of Creation. The following titles have helped clear the debris from my path on many occassions. Some had a direct influence on this work. Many of the authors listed have numerous titles.

A Course in Miracles. Tiburon, California: Foundation for Inner Peace, 1985

Abhishiktananda. *The Further Shore*. Delhi: ISPCK, 1975

Alexander, Thea. *2150 AD*. New York: Batam Books, 1979

Allen, Richard. *The Annals of China*.

Arraj, James. *St. John of the Cross and C.G. Jung*. Chiloquin, Oregon: Tools for Inner Growth, 1986

Bachofen, J. J. *Myth, Religion & Mother Right*. Princeton: Bollingen Series/ Princeton University Press, 1967

Bacon, Sir Francis. *The History of Winds*. London, 1671

Baker, M. E. Penny. *Meditation A step Beyond With Edgar Cayce*. New York: Pinnacle Books, 1973

Baigent, Michael & Richard Leigh. *The Dead Sea Scrolls Deception*. New York: Simon & Schuster, 1991

Bailey, Alice. *Esoteric Psychology*. Lucis Publishing Company

Bayley, Harold. *The Lost Language of Symbolism*. New York: Citadel Press, 1993

Becker, Robert and Selden, Gary. *The Body Electric*. New York: Quill - William Morrow, 1985

Besant, Mrs. Annie. *A Study in Consciounsess*. London, 1907

Bulfinch, Thomas. *Myths of Greece and Rome*. New York: Penguin Books, 1981

Calvin, William H. *The Cerebral Symphony*. New York: Bantam Books, 1990

Campbell, Joseph (with Bill Moyers). *The Power of Myth*. New York: Doubleday, 1988

——. *The Mythic Image*. Princeton, NJ: Princeton University Press, 1981

Castenada, Carlos. *The Teachings of Don Juan, A Yaqui Way of Knowledge*. New York: Simon & Schuster, 1990

Cayce, Edgar. *Edgar Cayce on Atlantis*. New York: Warner Books, 1988

Cooper, J. C. *An Illustrated Encyclopaedia of Traditional Symbols*. New York: Thames & Hudson, 1978

Cottrell, Leonard. *The Lost Pharaohs*. New York: Grosset & Dunlap, 1961

Crookall, Robert. *Psychic Breathing*. England: The Aquarian Press, 1979

Crossan, John Dominic. *The Historical Jesus*. New York: Harper-Collins, 1991

Drummond, Henry. *Natural Law in the Spiritual World*. New York, 1883

Dyer, Dr. Wayne. *Real Magic*. New York: Happer-Collins, 1993

Eddy, Mary Baker. *Science and Health with Keys to the Scriptures*. Santa Clarita, CA: Pasadena Press, 1992

Einstein, Albert. *The World as I See It.* New York: Citadel Press, 1995
Eisenman, Robert & Michael Wise. *Dead Sea Scrolls Uncovered.* New York: Penquin Books, 1992
Fix, Wm. R. *Pyramid Odyssey.* Urbanna, VI: Mercury Media Books, 1984
Fontana, David. *The Secret Language of Symbols.* San Francisco: Chronicle Books, 1993
Fortune, Dion. *The Mystical Qabalah.* York Beach, Maine: Samuel Weiser, 1984
Goldsmith, Joel. *The Mystical I.* San Francisco: Harper, 1993
Hall, Manly P. *The Secret Teachings of All Ages.* Los Angles: The Philosophical Research Society, Inc., 1989
Harvey, Andrew. *Hidden Journey*
Hogue, John. *Nostradamus & The Millennium.* New York: Double Day - Dolphin, 1987
Holy Bible. Revised Standard Version. New York: Thomas Nelson & Sons, 1953
Iyengar, B.K.S. *Light on Pranayama, The Yogic Art of Breathing.* New York: Crossroads, 1981
Jung, Carl Gustav. *Man and His Symbols.* New York: Doubleday, 1964
Kakar, Sudhir. *Shamans, Mystics & Doctors.* Delhi: Oxford University Press, 1986
Krishna, Gopi. *Kundalini – The Evolutionary Energy in Man.* Boulder & London: Shambhala, 1971
Lacarriere, Jacques. *The Gnostics.* San Francisco: City Lights Books, 1989
Llewellyn Sion of Glamorgan. *The Bardic Triads*
Monroe, Robert A. *Journeys Out of the Body.* Anchor Press, Doubleday, 1977
Moore, Thomas. *Care of The Soul.* New York: Harper Collins, 1992
Muktananda, Swami. *Kundalini The Secret of Life.* South Fallsburg, NY: SYDA Foundation, 1980
Nada-Yolanda. *Evolution of Man.* Miami: Mark Age Period & Programs, 1971
Newton, Michael. *Journey of Souls.* Saint Paul: Llewellyn Publications, 1994
On Mankind Their Origin and Destiny. London, 1872
Pagels, Elaine. *The Gnostic Gospels.* New York: Vintage Books, 1979
Rajneesh, Bhagwan Shree. *Beyond Psychology.* Cologne, West Germany: The Rebel Publishing House, 1986
Rennolds, Joyce. *The Energy Connection.* Atlanta: Rencor Publishing Company, 1987
Restak, Richard. *The Brain.* New York: Bantam Books, 1984
Roberts, Jane. *The Seth Materials.*
---. *Seth Speaks.*
---. *The True Nature of Reality.*
Robinson, James M. *The Nag Hammadi Library.* San Francisco: Harper Collins, 1990
Rogo, D. Scott. *Leaving the Body. A Complete Guide to Astral Projection.* New York: Prentice Hall Press, 1983
Rosenfield, Israel. *The Strange, Familiar and Forgotten.* New York: Alfred A. Knopf, 1992

Sheldrake, Rupert. *The New Science of Life: The Hypothesis of Morphic Resonance.* Rochester, Vermont: Park Street Press, 1995

Starhawk. *The Spiral Dance, a Rebirth of the Ancient Religion of the Great Goddess.* New York: Harper & Row, 1979

Steiner, Rudolph. *How to Know Higher Worlds.* Hudson, NY: Anthroposophic Press, 1994

Stewart, Mary. The Authurian trilogy: *Crystal Cave, Hollow Hills, and Last Enchantment.* Her last book in the series is, *The Wicked Day. New York:* Fawcett Press, 1984

Swedenborg, Emanual. *View From Within: A Compendium of Swendenborg's Theological Thought.*

Talbot, Michael. *The Holographic Universe.* New York: Harper Perennial, 1991

Taylor, Terry Lynn. *Creating with the Angels: An Angel Guided Journal.*

Walker, Barbara G. *The Woman's Dictionary of Symbols & Scared Objects.* NewYork: Harper & Row, 1988

Williamson, George Hunt. *Other Tongues – Other Flesh.* Albuquerque: Be Books,1954;

——. *Secret Places of the Lion.* Rochester, Vermont: Destiny Books, 1958

Wolf, Fred Alan. *Parallel Universes.* New York: Simon & Schuster, 1988

Yeats, W.B. *Fairy & Folk Tales of Ireland.* New York: Macmillan, 1983

Yogananda, Paramahansa. *Autobiography of a Yogi.* Los Angles: Self-Realization Fellowship, Twelfth Edition, 1981

Yogi Ramacharaka. *Science of Breath.* Chicago: Yogi Publication Society, 1904

Index

Some listings appear throughout the book. In those cases, only the first page reference is listed.

P

Q

R

S

T

U

V

W

Y

Z

Symbols

Order Form

Fax Orders: 404 874-5892

Telephone Orders: 800 871-4996

Postal Orders: Richman Rose Publishing
Post Office Box 7766
Atlanta, Georgia 30357-0766

e-Mail: RRose8@mindspring.com

Please send the following books or products:
I understand that all tapes are guaranteed and will be replaced if defective.

☐ YOUR BOOK of LIFE Accessing the Akashic Records
192 pages paperback., Bibliography, index. **$15.95 x ___ + $4.00 ea. S&H* = $ ______**

☐ Accessing the Akashic Records **$15 x ___ + $3.50 ea. S&H* = $ ______**
2 tape set. Introduction on side A, guided meditations on sides B, C & D

☐ Accessing Your Book of Life **$15 x ___ + $3.50 ea. S&H* = $ ______**
2 tape set. Introduction on side A, guided meditations on sides B, C & D

☐ The Twelve Days of Light – The Photon Field **$25 x ___ + $3.50 ea. S&H* = $ ______**
3 tapes, six hours of information from the Akashic Records concerning the coming photon field that is causing a great shift in Consciousness.

☐ Please send me the quarterly *Akasha Journal* newsletter. There is a one time fee of $10 to enter you in our mailing program. $______

Sub Total: **$ ______**

Sales tax: Georgia residents add applicable sales tax. **$______**

Shipping: *If ordering more than one item, add .75 S&H for each additional item. **$ ______**
Call for next day or second day air delivery cost.

Total. **$ ________**

Payment: ☐ Credit Card ☐ Check payable to Richman Rose Publishing
Name on card: ______________________________
Card number: ______________________________ Exp. Date: ____/____

Signature: ______________________________

Send to: Name ______________________________
Address ______________________________
City/State ______________________ Zip ____________